Tara
McPherson

▼ ▼ ▼ ▼ ▼ ▼ ▼ ▼ ▼ ▼ ▼

Feminist in a
Software Lab
Difference
+
Design

metaLABprojects
- - - - - - - - - - -
Harvard University Press
Cambridge, Massachusetts, and London, England
2018

*Library of Congress Cataloging-in Publication Data*

McPherson, Tara, author.
Feminist in a software lab : difference + design / Tara McPherson.
MetaLABprojects.
Cambridge, Massachusetts : Harvard University Press, 2018. |
Series: Metalabprojects | Includes bibliographical references.
LCCN 2016010548 | ISBN 9780674728943 (alk. paper)
LCSH: Humanities—Data processing. | Computer
software—Development. | Scholarly electronic publishing. | Software
engineering—Social aspects. | Computers and women.
LCC AZ195 .M35 2017 | DDC 001.30285—dc23
LC record available at https://lccn.loc.gov/2016010548

Graphic Design:
xycomm (Milan)
Daniele Ledda
with
Fabrizio Cantoni
Filippo Ferrari
Alessandro Tonelli

# Table of Contents

# A Visual Introduction

The work of the Vectors Lab began in dialogue with several earlier projects that engaged the visual and aesthetic dimensions of the humanities and the digital. These multimodal experiments across the humanities, the arts, and computation offer a different set of antecedents for the digital humanities from those typically narrated in histories of the field.

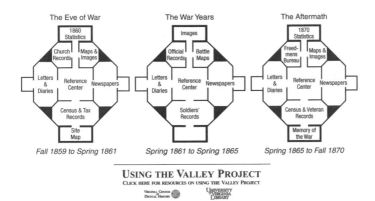

I.1 "The Valley of the Shadow," by Ed Ayers, 1993–2007.

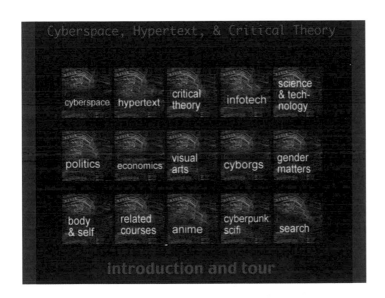

I.2 HTML version of George Landow's "Cyberspace, Hypertext, & Critical Theory" project, begun as an Intermedia web and transferred in 1992 to Eastgate System's Storyspace and to HTML in 1995.

I.3  *Electronic Book Review,* issue on image and narrative
(winter 1997–1998).

I.4  The Interactive Frictions Exhibition (1999).

I.5 The Labyrinth Project, a still from
"Tracing *The Decay of Fiction*" with Pat O'Neill (2002).

I.6 From Erik Loyer, *Chroma* (2001), an award-winning interactive serial.

I.7a  *Writing Machines* by N. Katherine Hayles (2002).

I.7b  Erik Loyer's "Hollowbound Book," an "interactive webtake"
on the print book, part of the Mediaworks Pamphlet Series (2002).

I.8 The *HorizonZero* project was a creative collaboration between the Banff New Media Institute (BNMI) and the Culture.ca Gateway. Begun in early 2002, the project concluded its live production cycle in December 2004.

I.9 *e-misférica*, the online journal of the Hemispheric Institute, which was launched shortly before *Vectors*. It explores multimedia expression in performance studies.

# Opening Vectors

This book tells in words and images the story of the Vectors Lab in Los Angeles while also locating that story within a number of other histories. For over a dozen years the lab has been experimenting with digital scholarship both through the online publication *Vectors* and through the development of Scalar, a multimedia, digital authoring platform.

This story runs alongside and sometimes intersects with a much longer tale about computation in the humanities, a narrative now often told as the story of the digital humanities. Wikipedia offers this version:

> Digital humanities descends from the field of humanities computing… whose origins reach back to the late 1940s in the pioneering work of Roberto Busa.
>
> The Text Encoding Initiative, born from the desire to create a standard encoding scheme for humanities electronic texts, is the outstanding achievement of early humanities computing. The project was launched in 1987 and published the first full version of the *TEI Guidelines* in May 1994. In the nineties, major digital text and image archives emerged at centers of humanities computing in the U.S. (e.g., the *Women Writers Project,* the *Rossetti Archive,* and the *William Blake Archive*), which demonstrated the sophistication and robustness of text-encoding for literature.

Though the origin of the term *digital humanities* is the subject of some debate, most agree that the term came into widespread use following the publication in 2004 of the substantial *Companion to Digital Humanities,* edited by Susan Schreibman, Ray Siemens, and John Unsworth. That book begins with a preface by Father Busa and, while it includes sections on film, music, and the performing arts, the volume's central emphasis is on a "half century of textually focused computing." That is an important tale to tell, but it is not our story. Our story turns its attention at least partially away from a focus on massive data sets, on text mining, and on the connection of the digital humanities to the sciences in order to mine the relations between the digital, the arts, and more theoretically inflected humanities traditions. (Fig. I.10)

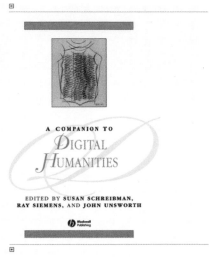

A COMPANION TO

*Digital Humanities*

EDITED BY **SUSAN SCHREIBMAN,**
**RAY SIEMENS,** AND **JOHN UNSWORTH**

Blackwell
Publishing

I.10
*A Companion to Digital Humanities,* edited by Susan Schreibman, Ray Siemens, and John Unsworth.

An alternative origin story for the digital humanities might begin not with experiments in text markup but instead with various engagements with the expressive audiovisual capacities of electronic screen culture. During the same period that Father Busa was working with IBM to produce the *Index Thomisticus,* the collaborative arts group E.A.T. brought together a heady mix of artists and Bell Labs engineers to test the sensory capacities of new technologies. From the landmark 1966 performance *9 Evenings: Theatre and Engineering* to their work for the Pepsi Pavilion at Expo '70 in Osaka, Japan, E.A.T. experimented with collaborative work processes and, as Frances Dyson relates, explored themes of "fluidity, spontaneity, liveliness, transparency, immersion and intimacy between artist and audience." Rather than plumb the possibilities of text, these collaborations investigated how artists might contribute to technological development while also producing new technologically rich aesthetic experiences. (Figs. I.11 / I.12)

The mid-twentieth century witnessed several such en-

14

I.11 / I.12
E.A.T. at the Pepsi
Pavilion in Osaka,
Japan, 1970.
Daniel Langlois
Foundation,
*Collection of*
*Documents*
*Published by*
*E.A.T.*

deavors, including the launch of SIGGRAPH, a computer graphics society, in the early 1970s. In Los Angeles the Eames Office also explored the expressive capacities of visual information. From their innovative 1959 multiscreen exhibition Glimpses of the U.S.A. (which premiered in Moscow and was

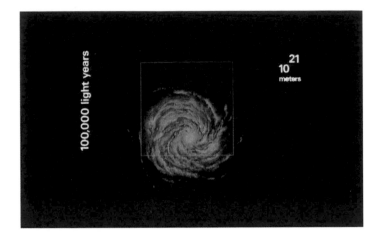

seen by millions) to their museum displays for corporate
clients like IBM, Charles and Ray Eames and their staff developed complex methods for visualizing abstract information
and for relating image, text, sound, and even smell. They were
also deeply engaged with computer culture from an early date,
producing books and exhibits designed to illustrate the importance of the computer. Further, their interest in computation
extended far beyond works that directly address the machines
as subject matter. Rather, the very *form* of their investigations
into media design predicted the intermedial constructs that so
characterize today's digital technologies, including the prototype zoom function of their classic short film *Powers of Ten*
and the remix aesthetic through which they navigated and reused their massive slide collection. The Eameses were deeply
interested in how the presentation of visual and audio material
affected its ability to impart meaning, and their work engages
with issues of speed, scale, relation, juxtaposition, and variation
in compelling ways. Their designs also attempted to deploy media in the service of an enhanced public sphere by illustrating
new civic uses of information and imagination. (Fig. I.13)

I.13 A film
still from
*Powers of Ten,*
an imaginative
exploration
of scale by
the Eames
Office (1977).

16

From E.A.T. to the Eames Office, we can see that computation has long been deeply intertwined with visuality, aesthetics, and the sensory. The origin stories for the digital humanities have often privileged text and its processing, but these stories do not tell the full tale of computation's intersections with the humanities and the human. They also unnecessarily cleave the humanities from aesthetic questions, frequently edging the humanities toward the sciences rather than the arts. In her insightful book, *Beautiful Data,* Orit Halpern maps a radical shift in cultural attitudes about the display of information from the 1960s forward, a midcentury exploration of visualization that has everything to do with cybernetics and emerging forms of governmentality. While her work reminds us that the arts are often complicit in new forms of rationality and management (and certainly the work of Eames Office illustrates this as well), our understanding of the messy histories of the digital humanities (DH) must also encompass questions of aesthetics and design. We should also resist the tendency to narrate the history of the digital humanities as a series of progressive stages.

We see this tendency again and again. For instance, the Digital Humanities Manifesto proclaims, "The first wave [of DH] was quantitative, mobilizing the vertiginous search and retrieval powers of the database. The second wave is qualitative, interpretive, experiential, even emotive." *A Companion to Digital Humanities* locates the emergence of multimedia in DH "especially" in the 1990s, following decades of text-centric computation. I am also guilty of such teleologies. In a 2009 essay in *Cinema Journal,* I narrated the history of the digital humanities as moving from the computational humanist through the blogging humanist toward the multimodal humanist. (Julie Klein notes many more instances of this tendency in her comprehensive *Interdisciplining Digital Humanities.*)

Such mappings obscure as much as they clarify, erasing the untidy, overlapping conjunctures of text, media, and database in computational history. Feminist scholars have recently challenged the dominant model of periodizing feminism's history as a series of waves, from the suffragettes of the first wave to the activists of the 1970s second wave on to the "sex-positive" third wave of the 1990s. For instance, Kathleen Laughlin has observed that the wave metaphor tends to privilege a "'singular" feminism in which "gender is the predominate category of analysis" (77) rather than recognizing the often contested and multiple forms of feminist activity that existed at any one moment. A similar logic is at work when we frame the digitization and archival projects of the 1980s as Digital Humanities 1.0. This move erases the differences between projects that were motivated by sometimes competing ideas, while also eclipsing a whole range of computational undertakings that were focused less on the archive or text and more on sound, image, and aesthetic experimentation. It also suggests that such work is relegated to the past, when digitization remains a pressing need today. Finally, such a strategy also recapitulates Silicon Valley's own techno-utoptian logic that gleefully frames the web as inevitably moving from 1.0 to 2.0 to the cloud and beyond, making it harder to see what we have lost as the web is increasingly dominated by the likes of Amazon and Google and by the walled enclosures of the app and the template.

I recount these tales at the outset to suggest that the work of the Vectors Lab, while always multimodal, intertwines the "retrieval powers of the database" with the experiential and the emotive. Our lab was developed as a space for experimentation in screen languages, interactive argumentation, open access publishing, and collaborative design and authorship. At the outset in the early 2000s, when the term *digital humanities* was still taking form, I would say we were working in parallel to many existing "humanities and technology" centers, focused more on questions of the expressive capacities of media and interface than on large-scale digitization, text markup, or geographic information systems (GIS). We aimed to publish work that couldn't exist in print, pushing beyond the "text with pictures" or PDF model that categorized most of online journal publishing at the time, and to query increasingly standardized paradigms of "transparent" web design. We were also exploring ways in which interface design might mitigate the database's relentless logic, refusing the tyranny of the template, even as we obviously were still working under the sign of computation. In exploring relations of form to content, we privileged particular kinds of content, choosing to work on projects that engaged issues such as gender, race, affect, memory, sexuality, perception, temporality, nationhood, emergence, and social justice. These concerns were and are at the core of our research, and they profoundly shaped (and continue to shape) how we use and design technological systems. We began the journal motivated by a series of research questions. We were interested in how multimodal expression might allow for different relationships of form to content and wanted to explore the specificities of digital media for scholarly communication. We asked how scholarship might more directly engage the emotions and multiple senses. We investigated how we might play an argument as we play video games or immerse ourselves in scholarship as we do in films. Such questions led us to create projects that mine the intersection of design and the humanities much more than the science-humanities nexus that drives much digital humanities work. Thus, our work harked back more to the work of E.A.T. or the Eames Office than to Father Busa.

The lab's work is possible because of the complex and multiple entanglements of the humanities, the arts, and computation over decades. These entanglements include a

deep commitment to the role of theory within the humanities, particularly to feminism and critical race theory and to the tensions between older and newer forms of materialism. The lab emerged as a place to bring theory into productive tension with practice—not surprising, given our location within a cinema school and the long tradition of theory-loving filmmakers from Sergei Eisenstein to Maya Deren to Laura Mulvey. Our goal is not "less yack, more hack." We are not aiming to "sunset ideology" (as if one could), but we do take seriously the notion that theory is but one way of grappling with the world. Our approach draws from histories of activism that have creatively merged theory and other modes of doing and being. It also embraces the turn to critical making that has been explicated by numerous scholars and artists over the past several years, including Matt Ratto, Garnet Hertz, Jentery Sayers, Roger Whitson, and Carl DiSalvo. We draw particular inspiration from feminists walking the theory-practice line: Marsha Kinder, Anne Balsamo, Johanna Drucker, Alex Juhasz, Joanna Zylinska, Dene Grigar, Sarah Kember, Miriam Posner, Jessica

I.14 The *Vectors* piece "Killer Entertainments," by Jennifer Terry and designed by Raegan Kelly.

Pressman, Liz Losh, Jacqueline Wernimont, and many others.[1]

While we do not believe, as does Bruno Latour, that critique has entirely run out of steam, we do value Sarah Kember and Joanna Zylinska's insight that "creative practice can alter reality by intervening in it at the material level" (72). Jane Bennett writes of the craftsperson's desire to see what a material can *do* (as opposed to the scientist's desire to learn what a material *is*). This curiosity about the material, this desire to understand what things can do, operates in a different register from critique. The theorist might resist such a framing, arguing that she works with words as her "material," seeing what they might reveal when stretched beyond the vernacular of common sense. She is right, but there are other materials we might engage, other agencies to explore, that exist beyond the discursive realm, agencies that might move us toward new alliances and new practices. (Fig I.14)

Within the realms of critical making and computation, these practices of creation can open us up to what else words might do when brought into conjunction with the agency of the database or of video. For instance, in the *Vectors* project "Killer Entertainments," the scholar Jenny Terry and the designer Raegan Kelly bring together a collection of amateur videos produced by soldiers in Iraq and Afghanistan. The videos are not simply analyzed and described. They are an integral part of the project, forming three spines through which to engage, experience, and reflect on the ways that "visual codes pertaining to [recent] wars are in the grain of other popular entertainments that... serve to make the violence of war something that we have already incorporated into daily life and bodily practice, but of whose many effects we remain disturbingly unaware" (Terry, Author's Statement). The videos *matter* here, as records of the embodied visuality of warfare but also in their recontextualization through Terry and Kelly's own creative input. *Killer Entertainments* points toward the agency of video within the world, to the work that it does that exceeds our careful explications and critique. As we move from composing to practices perhaps better understood as compositing, we defamiliarize the work of critique, aligning it productively with other ways of seeing, knowing, and becoming. Hermeneutics is at work here, certainly, but it is not the only game in town.

It is not surprising that the denizens of the Humanities and Technology Camps (THATCamps) and other DH workshops can seem a bit giddy about making things. Whether they are wielding a soldering iron or hacking circuits, they have encountered the agency and energies of the materials they work with in the process of creation. I still recall the heady rush of learning to work with HTML in the mid-1990s, my gateway drug into a twenty-year fascination with what computers can do. There's an optimism born of making that can be hard to reconcile with the often negative force of critique. But the emphasis on tools, on coding, on building, and on making that has been foregrounded in some recent digital humanities rhetoric can frame theory and practice in an unproductive binary relation. Natalia Cecire, Bethany Nowviskie, and Miriam Posner have all commented on various aspects of this tendency, highlighting as well the gendered dimensions of calls for coding. This severing of theory from practice is sometimes framed as a move toward methodology (and, hence, away from theory), but scholars from Paulo Friere to Chela Sandoval to Diana Taylor teach us that the theoretical and the methodological are not easily separated. Nor should they be. In fact, performance studies offer a useful way to think about the relation between theory and method while also retaining a sense of political urgency, from Friere's theories of dialogic action to the embodied practices of the repertoire theorized by Diana Taylor to micha cárdenas's recent figuring of the stitch and the shift as political and theoretical forms of practice.

This linking of performance and making points toward some interesting questions that motivate the work of the Vectors Lab and that map the terrain for this volume. Does it matter if a feminist or critical race scholar is doing the making? What would the difference be? What formulations of feminism or critical race theory might be relevant to such an inquiry? Can software or tools *be* feminist or are tools simply wielded with feminist intent? Can design foreground the modes of critical inquiry that matter to fields invested in social change? How do histories of computation shape what is possible to do? How does culture shape computation?

The ideas and projects examined in this book emerged from creating a space—both physical and virtual—for sustained practice. For almost fifteen years, we have explored the iterative loops that exist between ideas and experiments. We did not build projects or tools to test the theories as much as we labored to create work that brought theory into a productive tension with tool design and project creation. That is, our goal was not to build a platform that illustrated the assemblage, a theoretical formation that will surface again in this book. Rather, our platform is like an assemblage because the scholars with whom we have collaborated already inhabited such modes of thinking.

Feminist software or critical race platforms might most realistically be a utopian project, an aspiration, a dream to intervene in technological legacy systems that often route our machines away from our feminist desires. Nonetheless, this book describes a series of projects and experiments that are real and that do exist and locates them within longer histories of computation and theory. These projects are often imperfect. They may confuse or fall short. They draw from speculative traditions but are not simply speculative. They are meant to be and to work even if they will not work forever. They point the way toward aesthetic, technological, and collaborative practices that figure computation and its histories differently. I believe that these differences do matter.

## Who Is This "We"?

Humanities scholarship often bears the name of a single author, but we know that our work is always at some level collaborative. Research unfolds through practices of citation and reference that bring together a chorus of voices and ideas even if we are tapping away on a single keyboard alone in an office. We are never really writing or even thinking alone, even if the university as an institution still holds on to (and rewards) the idea of the scholar as solitary genius. This book is collaborative in that more traditional way, but the collaborations it draws from extend far beyond the chains of reference embedded in footnotes or bibliographies that form one mode of typically asynchronous scholarly collaboration.

The collaborations that have unfolded among the core *Vectors* team are the richest intellectual (and often personal) experiences of my academic career. They represent a vibrant model of alliance across difference that has been generative, fraught, utopian, messy, chaotic, difficult, and easy over the years. They continually restore my faith in intellectual and creative work at a time when the university often registers as intensely corporate and managerial. I feel enormously lucky to have worked alongside members of the *Vectors* team, to have learned from them, and to count them among my friends. This "original" core group was small. It consisted of Co-Creative Directors Raegan Kelly and Erik Loyer, Information Design Director Craig Dietrich, and Co-Editors Steve Anderson and me. But this small core operated rather like a starter in making sourdough bread, continually growing and fermenting through the integration of countless like-minded travelers from the fellows in our many summer institutes to wonderful student research assistants to additional designers, programmers, administrators, and project assistants who have collaborated with us over the years. Raegan has since moved on to new endeavors, but Erik, Craig, Steve, and I continue to ferment as much as we can. I have tried in this volume to include their voices and the voices of many others through extensive quotations of design and editorial statements and of various documents of our design process. The Acknowledgments at the end of this book name a large number of our collaborators over the years. I doubt I have managed to capture all the vectors of *Vectors* and apologize for the elisions.

If this book is an imperfect register of the richness of our lab's collaborative processes, it may also seem ironic that the book is a print document, albeit a beautifully designed one. One of the core mandates of the journal *Vectors* was that it publish only work that could not exist in print. Our investigations into the relation of form and content, of interactivity, of shifting screen languages, and of emergent genres for scholarly publishing are necessarily flattened in a bookish format. The tactility of this book is richly analogue, and it is lovingly visual, but the images do not always capture every detail of the screen's real estate and certainly do not capture movement and change. Nonetheless, there is a value to this stability. The print instantiations of this volume will probably outlast all the projects described within it. For all the lures of digital scholarship, durability is not highest on the list. Still, I encourage you to engage many of these projects in their born-digital form, exploring their expressive and interactive capacity and feeling their movements.

# How to Read This Book

This book comprises several sections, including two long essays and several image-driven "windows." The windows are interspersed throughout the book. They aim to capture something of the multi-modal scope of *Vectors* and Scalar and give precedence to the visual dimensions of our work. They also acknowledge the collaborative nature of our process, drawing as they do from author's statements, design documents, and more. The book does not privilege a sequential reading, despite its linear form. The two essays and the windows may be read in any order, even as they refer to one another. The first essay, "Designing for Difference," explicitly argues that we need a more pronounced connection between histories of computing and theories and histories of difference. It draws widely (and perhaps eclectically) from moments in the development of digital computation and from theories of difference, feminism, and new materialism. It suggests that the tendency toward encapsulation and modularity that we see in digital computing aligns (and is complicit) with broader cultural shifts toward segmentation in a host of cultural practices from city planning to management theory to identity politics to highly specialized academic fields, as well as more contemporary theories of object-oriented ontologies. The second essay, "Assembling Scholarship: From *Vectors* to Scalar," unpacks the history of the Vectors Lab, detailing our work on *Vectors* and on Scalar. This chapter is more thickly descriptive, although it also traces the ways in which our practice is deeply informed by theoretical concerns. Those interested in the practical work of the lab may prefer to start with this section, whereas those invested in debates about feminist theory, social justice, computational history, or new materialisms might want to begin with the first essay. This recombinatory structure risks giving in to the very modularity that this book critiques, but the various sections are meant to speak to each other even as they can also stand alone. The book's form in many ways hints at the flexibility and pathed possibilities of the Scalar platform, one of its key objects of study, even as it is delivered in a more conventional form. (Fig. I.15)

**VECTORS**

Journal of Culture and Technology in a Dynamic Vernacular     I.15

# CHAPTER 1

# Designing for Difference

----------------------------------------

In his purposefully provocative essay "Where Is Cultural Criticism in the Digital Humanities?" Alan Liu argues that "the digital humanities are noticeably missing in action on the cultural-critical scene. While digital humanists develop tools, data, and metadata critically,… rarely do they extend their critique to the full register of society, economics, politics, or culture" (491).

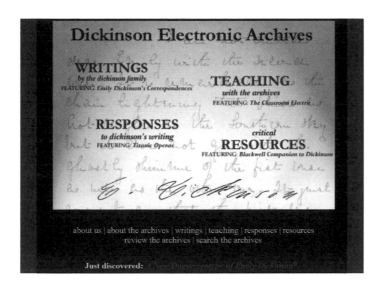

Liu usefully insists that our current political moment demands that the digital humanities engage both theory and politics, but such debates are not entirely new. Martha Nell Smith, among others, has for many years narrated a particular history of humanities computing (and, later, the digital humanities) as a kind of reaction formation to the "concerns that had taken over so much academic work in literature—[those] of gender, race, class, sexuality" (4). Smith writes partly as polemic. Her own earlier work, as well as that of scholars such as Susan Brown, Melissa Terras, Laura Mandell, Amy Earhart, and Julia Flanders, illustrates the degree to which the computational humanities did sometimes take issues of gender or race as a central concern. John Unsworth was certainly no stranger to "high theory." Steve Ramsay and Geoff Rockwell have further argued that tool building is inherently theoretical. Nonetheless, Smith's experiences also attest to the difficulty of centering theory and politics in the longer arc of the computational humanities, and certainly Liu's critique rang true for many. (Fig 1.1)

1.1 An early version of the Dickinson Electronic Archive, initially conceived by Martha Nell Smith.

I here attend to some recent variations on this debate about the role of cultural theory within the digital humanities and its close analogs in order to argue for a theoretically explicit form of digital praxis within the digital humanities. I take seriously Gary Hall's recent claim that the very goals of critical theory and of quantitative or computational analysis may in fact be incommensurable or, at the very least, that their productive combination will require "far more time and care... than has been devoted to it thus far." From a very different disciplinary space, Stephen Nichols echoes Hall's concerns when he observes that the processes of abstraction on which so much of computation depends knock roughly against the accretive research practices favored within the humanities. Nichols writes that rather than abstraction "that strips out extraneous details, literary study promotes recursive reading aimed at accumulating meaningful data to create a thick description" (12). While there are many ways to privilege context and accretion within digital scholarship, the hesitancies of Hall and Nichols are worth engaging.

I feel as though I have lived the textures of the incommensurability that Hall describes across my professional life as I've attempted to hold together my theoretical allegiances with my commitments to praxis. An example will help illustrate this disjuncture. In mid-October 2008 the American Studies Association (ASA) hosted its annual conference in Albuquerque, New Mexico. According to its website, the ASA "is the nation's oldest and largest association devoted to the interdisciplinary study of American culture and history." Over the past two decades the ASA conference has emerged as a leading venue for vibrant discussions about race, ethnicity, indigeneity, transnationalism, gender, and sexuality. Though the ASA represents scholars with a diverse array of methodological approaches and from a variety of disciplines, the society is a welcome home to academics whose work is interpretative, theoretical, and explicitly political. During the meeting, I attended a variety of panels engaging such issues and approaches and came away feeling energized and re-freshed, my intellectual imagination stoked by the many ways in which race and ethnicity were wielded as central terms of analysis throughout the long weekend.

The following week I was off to Baltimore, where I at-tended "Tools for Data-Driven Scholarship," a workshop fund-ed by the National Science Foundation (NSF), the National Endowment for the Humanities (NEH), and the Institute of Museum and Library Services. This invitation-only event was co-hosted by George Mason University's Center for History and New Media (CHNM) and the Maryland Institute for Technology in the Humanities (MITH), two pioneering cen-ters in the computational (and, more recently, digital) human-ities. This workshop built on several years' conversation (par-ticularly following the 2003 NSF Atkins report on cyberinfra-structure) about the need for a digital infrastructure for hu-manities computing. The goal of the workshop was defined in the e-mail invitation as a report "that discusses the needs of tools developers and users; sets forth objectives for addressing those needs; proposes infrastructure for accomplishing these objectives; and makes suggestions for a possible RFP [Request for Proposals]." This meeting was also lively, full of thoughtful discussions about the possibilities for (and obstacles in the way of) a robust infrastructure for scholars engaged in computa-tion and the humanities. The conversation certainly fired up my technological imagination and subsequently led to useful discussions with my collaborators in technological design.[1]

As I flew home following this second event, I found my-self reflecting on how far my thoughts had ranged in the course a mere week: from diaspora to database, from oppression to ontology, from visual studies to visualizations. And, once again, I found myself wondering why it seemed so hard to hold together my long-standing academic interests in race, gender, and certain modes of theoretical inquiry with my more recent (if over a decade-old) immersion in the world of digital production and design.

Though the workshop I participated in at ASA was titled "American Studies at the Digital Crossroads" and drew a nice crowd, the conference as a whole included remarkably little discussion of digital technologies (although there were some analyses of digital texts such as websites and video games).[2] It is largely accurate, if also a generalization, to say that many in the membership of the ASA treat computation within the humanities with some level of suspicion, perceiving it to be complicit with the corporatization of higher education or primarily technological rather than scholarly.[3] (Indeed, this attitude is shared by a large number of "traditional" humanities scholars across any number of fields or professional societies who do not work with digital media as "practice.") In a hallway chat following our workshop, one scholar framed his unease as a question: "Why are the digital humanities, well, so white?" And, while my memory is far from perfect, I think it is safe to say that the Baltimore workshop included no discussion of many topics much in evidence at ASA, topics including immigration, race, and incarceration. To be fair, this was a workshop focused on the notion of tools and infrastructure, so one might not expect such discussions. Nonetheless, this essay will argue that we desperately need to close the gap between these two modes of inquiry. Further, I will argue that the difficulties we encounter in knitting together our discussions of race (or other modes of difference) with our technological productions within the digital humanities (or in our studies of code and platforms) share structural similarities with the very designs of our technological systems, designs that emerged in post–World War II computational culture. These origins of the digital continue to haunt our scholarly engagements with computers, underwriting the ease with which we partition off considerations of race in our work in the digital humanities and digital media studies.

Following a route that will move us from contemporary debates about the roles of theory and politics in the digital humanities (DH) to a more historical examination of computation and modularity to a brief investigation of object-oriented ontologies and the new materialisms, I ask what it might mean to design—from their very conception—digital tools and applications that emerge from the more contextual concerns of cultural theory and, in particular, from a feminist concern for difference. In doing so, I ask how various practices of modularity and separation (in code and in theory) might be seen to be at odds with the accretive and contextual practices many value in the interpretative humanities. These practices of modularity also shape our disciplines, making it hard to bring together, say, scholarship on the case of blackness with an examination of the structure of relational databases. This is an expansive and often difficult road to travel. I am interested in tracking a series of correspondences across time, and I hence join sets of objects and theories not typically held together in order to explore their possible connections. Certain relations will be mined less in the name of causality or depth and more in the tenor of provocation, assembling a set of objects and ideas that might point one way toward a productive joining of the concerns of DH and ASA. And, after some time, this path will lead us back to the Vectors Lab and its ongoing efforts at the intersection of theory and praxis, matter and relation, platform and politics, database and difference. (Fig. 1.2)

TRANSFORMDH TUMBLR    2015 CONFERENCE & THATCAMP ▾    2015 VIDEO SHOWCASE ▾    ABOUT #TRANSFORMDH

## Into the Fray

The need to attend with more time and care to the potential intersections of theory and the digital humanities has been the subject of recent and often heated online discussions, conference panels, and various publications, which suggests that many scholars have also sought to move beyond a feeling of incommensurability. Groups of emerging scholars have organized under such rubrics as #TransformDH, #DHPoco, and GO::DH (Global Outlook::Digital Humanities) to catalyze just such exchanges, as has the collaborative FemTechNet organization. (Figs. 1.3 / 1.4)

1.2 The #transformDH hashtag emerged from the American Studies Conference in 2011. It marks the work of a collective aiming to tilt the work of DH toward issues of social justice, accessibility, and inclusion.

One open thread initiated by Adeline Koh and Roopika Risam on the "Postcolonial Digital Humanities" blog in May 2013 fostered a lively and sometimes heated debate in response to the question "Is DH a refuge from race/class/gender/sexuality?" I will not attempt to summarize that conversation here (Koh and Risam have undertaken a summary on their blog, prompting even more conversation and a shared Google doc), but I do want to zero in on a few points in the exchange to stage the beginnings of a claim for a particular mode of enacting the digital humanities (or, following Katie King, one might say "reenacting" the digital and the humanities). Entering the forum's fray by "tapping" on his phone, Ian Bogost wrote: "On the one hand, anyone who believes computational platforms are transparent doesn't really understand those platforms. But on the

other hand, a blind focus on identity politics above all other concerns has partly prevented humanists from deeply exploring the technical nature of computer systems in order to grasp those very understandings." Bogost's insistence that we must explore the technical nature of the computer resonates with various formulations of the digital humanities, even if Bogost himself might not claim membership in that group. It aligns as well with a good deal of digital media studies, including hardware and software studies, where Bogost's research has been quite prolific and important.[4] For instance, his insightful analysis of the mechanisms of perceived freedom in the video game *Grand Theft Auto* links technical analysis and cultural critique in lively registers. My own work has frequently called for scholars to push beyond the surface of our screens and questions of representation to better understand the functions of code and networks. In the conversation that unspools throughout the thread, Bogost goes on to observe that "doing hardware and software studies sometimes requires one to bracket identity—even if just for a moment, in order to learn something in the latter's service. But those of us who do that work are frequently chide[d] for failing to focus all energy and all attention at all times on the accuser's notion of what comprises the entire discourse on social justice." Certainly, it is hard to sustain a focus "at all times" on the "entire discourse of social justice" while undertaking technical (or any other) investigations, but I find two things especially curious in this formulation. First, it is in-

1.3 / 1.4 Global Outlook::Digital Humanities (GO::DH) and FemTechNet work in different ways to broaden the reach of the digital within the humanities, focusing on global and feminist goals, respectively.

teresting that a forum originally framed quite broadly as being about the "intermingling of race, class, gender, sexuality and disability in the digital humanities" quickly moves to a discussion of "identity politics" as the natural or likely terrain for such concerns. Later in the forum, Anne Balsamo observes that there are certainly many ways to address questions of feminism and of difference that do not narrowly default to identity politics, and she points the forum toward the work of the feminist philosopher Karen Barad. In her book *Designing Culture: The Technological Imagination at Work,* Balsamo builds on Barad's theory of "intra-actions" to develop a complex model of design practice that understands the relationship between materiality and discursivity, between objects and subjects, and between nature and culture to be fluid, open-ended, and contingent. In such a model, design (of technologies, of software, of code) proceeds from an acknowledgment of our messy entanglements with matter and with each other. For Barad, "To be entangled is not simply to be intertwined with another, as in the joining of separate entities, but to lack an independent, self-contained existence" (*Meeting the Universe* ix).

Given this formulation, a second element of the forum exchange cited above stands out: the notion of the "bracketing" of identity or other signs of culture that might prevent one from accessing the technical nature of the computer. Similar ideas surface in a number of moments across the discussion. For instance, Andrew Smart observes that "digital technology, at its lowest level, relies on the physical laws of how information is represented in voltage. The way computers and networks work is determined (or maybe very constrained) by the laws of physics." The tendency to describe computation as a series of levels increasingly abstracted from culture surfaces in other online venues as well. A further interesting example is found at "Lambda the Ultimate," a site that "deals with issues directly related to programming languages" and is populated largely by programmers. On May 5, 2010, Travis Brown created a forum there under the heading "Critical Code Studies," asking the Lambda community to reflect on the idea of critical code studies as articulated by the new media scholar Mark Marino, linking to a Call for Papers and an essay by Marino as well as to essays by the scholars N. Katherine Hayles and Rita Raley. The ensuing discussion lasted several days. Though a few contributors were intrigued by the possibility that cultural theory might be useful in the study of code, many were skeptical or rejected the idea out of hand.[5] Typical comments included:

> To begin with: "code" can be a byproduct of a software
> design. "Code" can be automagically generated
> from a formal model, for instance, so there're no "socio-
> historical context" to study there. (vieiro, May 15, 2010)

> What I mean is that the "sociological" aspects
> of "code" are not in the code itself, they're elsewhere.
> (vieiro, May 18, 2010)

> You have the code and the math and the reasoning behind
> the code, and you have the history. Both are interesting but
> should be treated separately. (Jules Jacobs, May 14, 2010)

In these examples, code functions much as Smart imagines it does, in a realm determined by math, physics, or reason, apart from the messy realms of culture.

This tendency to frame computational technologies in levels is also reflected in the description of the book series Platform Studies, edited by Ian Bogost and Nick Monfort for the Massachusetts Institute of Technology (MIT) Press. On the website describing the series, Bogost and Monfort offer a chart delineating five "stacked" levels of analysis for new media stud-

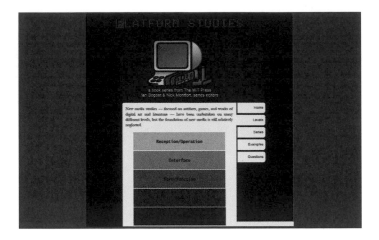

ies; from top to bottom, these are reception/operation, interface, form/function, code, and platform. The platform is framed as the "foundation" layer, "an abstraction layer beneath code" and obviously given primacy within the series itself. A later revision of this chart in their book *Racing the Beam* encloses the five levels in a box labeled "culture and context," and the authors stress that "we see all of these levels—not just the top level of reception and operation—as being situated in culture, society, economy, and history" (147). (Fig. 1.5)

Yet the very model of discrete boxed layers neatly enclosed in the larger box of history puts into place a conceptual framework that undervalues entanglements and intra-actions, encouraging a focus on individual layers rather than a focus on the complex ways in which the layers themselves come into being, delineate particular possibilities and boundaries, and foreclose potential futures and becomings. A 2006 article by Nick Monfort offers a similar figure, in which context forms a border around the five levels. Here the platform receives primacy in the literal numbering of the levels and is seen as providing an authorizing function that will "enable and constrain

**1.5** A visual representation of the Platform Studies book series.

what happens in higher levels." A more recent illustration published by David Berry on his Stunlaw blog borrows the computer science technique of a software stack to show "the range of activities, practices, skills, technologies, and structures that could be said to make up the digital humanities as an ideal type." The diagram includes, from top to bottom, the following layers: interface, systems, shared structures, code/data, institutions, and encoding and education. Each layer is made of various components; for instance, the code/data layer contains digital methods, digital archives, and metadata. Curiously, one of four components of the interface layer is "critical/cultural critique." While Berry notes on the blog that he "would have preferred for the critical and cultural critique to run through more of the layers," in the end he chose the simplicity of the stacked diagram. The image does offer an interesting mapping of various elements we might think of as relevant to the digital humanities, but it also visually and conceptually sidelines the role of critique within DH, locating critique at the level of interface rather than, for instance, with the creation of metadata. The choice to work with a diagrammatic method from computer science—the software stack—privileges a modular approach to representing the complexity of the digital humanities. Like the Monfort-Bogost chart, this modularity makes it hard to think of culture and critique as processes that cut through every layer and component of the stack. (Fig. 1.6)

Obviously, we need to focus our scholarly attentions somewhere, on particular things, processes, or ideas, but the models we work from are important. To follow Barad, if matter matters, *how* we focus on matter also matters. One might compare these charts representing particular takes on platform studies and DH to Anne Balsamo's investigation of the intersections of culture, technology, and design. Her interests are still in the object itself, mapping as she does elements of

| c | | c |
|---|---|---|
| o | [5] reception & operation | o |
| n | [4] interface | n |
| t | [3] game form | t |
| e | [2] game code | e |
| x | [1] platform | x |
| t | | t |

design, technology, raw materials, engineering conventions, built form, and more. Yet she also strives to capture a relational understanding of the design, manufacture, and use of a digital device (a subsequent version of the graph diagrams this type of investigation for the iPod). The object here flows in many directions, from its technological affordances to various forms of congealed labor to the waste created at different stages of production and use. The object matters, but not in a decontextualized or abstracted manner. Here context, history, and culture are not imagined as a vague wrapper surrounding a technological fetish object but as vital elements in technological design and production. Temporality is also accounted for in the diagram in interesting ways, suggesting a recursive relationship that privileges accretion and context. The thing is attended to but not as a series of black-boxed or modular levels. Her methodology is materialist, but it is more relational than object oriented, a point we will return to as we move across computational histories, design decisions, and feminist praxis. Relationality matters. Matter is relational. There is more to learn from feminist interventions such as Balsamo's, as we shall explore in this essay's close. (Fig. 1.7)

Despite this critique, I value and learn from the work of code and platform studies, including the careful examinations of specific platforms in Bogost and Monfort's series, some of which pay careful attention to the cultural contexts of technology. I, too, have written about how hard it is to entangle exam-

1.6 Nick Monfort's Platform Studies diagram (2006).

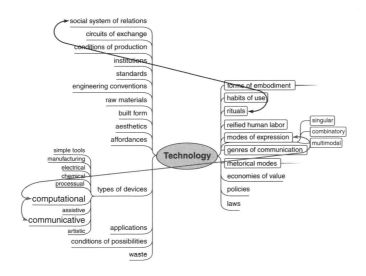

inations of code with cultural critique, how easy it is to give in to the lure of the bracket. I have called for humanities scholars to take code seriously and to make things. But I also worry that the digital humanities, software studies, and platform studies all too often center computation and technology in a way that makes intra-action hard to discern and context hard to trace. I am not worried that this iteration of platform studies doesn't privilege the human above all else. I worry that it does not sufficiently attend to the objects it claims to adore because its very model abstracts and encapsulates. Bogost writes about the critiques of platform studies in various places, from his blog to his book *Alien Phenomenology.* He tends to reduce these critiques to a desire on the part of his critics always to center the human or to insist on identity politics and analyses of representation, but we might instead see a diagram like Balsamo's as more respectful of the object than the neat layers of platform studies. She is not calling for a return to identity politics or for a proliferation of representational analy-

1.7 Anne Balsamo's contextual mapping of technology and culture.

ses. Rather, she aims to pursue the object across many actants and through many agencies. The conceptual bracketing of Platform Studies, this singling out of code or platform from culture, replicates the organization of knowledge production that computation has disseminated around the world for well over fifty years. The difficulties we encounter in knitting together our discussions of race and other modes of difference with our technological productions within the digital humanities (or in our studies of code) actually correspond with the very designs of our technological systems, designs that emerged in post–World War II computational culture. These origins of the digital continue to haunt our scholarly engagements with computers, underwriting the ease with which we partition off considerations of difference in our work in the digital humanities and digital media studies.

## Modularity at Midcentury: Thinking Race + UNIX

Let us turn to two fragments from history, around the 1960s.

### Fragment One

The first fragment concerns the early 1960s when computer scientists at MIT were working on Project MAC (Mathematics and Computation), an early set of experiments in Compatible Timesharing Systems for computing. By 1965 Multiplexed Information and Computing Service (MULTICS), a mainframe timesharing operating system, was in use, jointly developed by MIT, General Electric, and Bell Labs, a subsidiary of AT&T. The project was funded by the Advanced Research Projects Agency (ARPA) of the Defense Department at $2 million a

year for eight years. MULTICS introduced early ideas about modularity in hardware structure and software architecture. In 1969 Bell Labs stopped working on MULTICS, and that summer one of their engineers, Ken Thompson, developed the beginning of UNIX. Though there are clearly influences of MULTICS on UNIX, the later system moved away from the earlier one, pushing for increased modularity and for a simpler design that was able to run on cheaper computers. (Fig. 1.8)

In the simplest terms, UNIX is an early operating system for digital computers, one that has spawned many offshoots and clones. These include both Mac OS X and LINUX, which indicates the reach of UNIX over the past forty years. The system also influenced non-UNIX operating systems such as

1.8 Ken Thompson (sitting) and Dennis Ritchie working at a PDP-11.

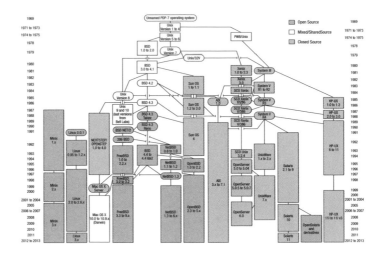

Windows NT and remains in use by many corporate IT divisions. UNIX was originally written in assembly language, but after Thompson's colleague Dennis Ritchie developed the C programming language in 1972, Thompson rewrote UNIX in that language. Basic text-formatting and editing features were added (i.e., early word processors). In 1974 Ritchie and Thompson published their work in the journal of the Association for Computing Machinery, and UNIX began to pick up a good deal of steam.[6] (Fig. 1.9)

UNIX can also be thought of as more than an operating system, as it also includes a number of utilities such as command line editors, application program interfaces (APIs) (which, it is worth noting, existed long before our iPhones made them sexy), code libraries, and so on. Furthermore, UNIX is widely understood to embody particular philosophies and cultures of computation, "operating systems" of a larger order that we will return to.

1.9 A diagram showing the key Unix and Unix-like operating systems.

**Fragment Two**

Of course, for scholars of culture, of gender, and of race, dates
like 1965 and 1968 have other resonances. For many of us,
1965 might not recall MULTICS but instead the assassination
of Malcolm X, the founding of the United Farm Workers, the
burning of Watts, or the passage of the Voting Rights Act. The
mid-1960s also saw the origins of the American Indian Movement (AIM) and the launch of the National Organization for
Women (NOW). The years1968 and 1969 mark the citywide
walkouts of Latino youth in Los Angeles, the assassinations of
Martin Luther King Jr. and Robert F. Kennedy, the Chicago
Democratic convention, and the Stonewall Riots. The founding of the Black Panthers and the Young Lords also occurred
in that decade. Beyond the United States, we might also remember the Prague Spring, Tommie Smith and John Carlos
at the Summer Olympics in Mexico City, the Tlatelolco Mas-
sacre, the execution of Che Guevara, the Chinese Cultural
Revolution, the Six-Day War, and the student uprising in Paris, all occurring from 1966 through 1968. On the African
continent, thirty-two countries gained independence from
colonial rulers. In the United States broad cultural shifts
emerged across the decade, as identity politics took root and
countercultural forces challenged traditional values. Resistance to the Vietnam War mounted as the decade wore on.
Abroad, movements against colonialism and oppression were
notably strong. (Figs. 1.10 / 1.11)

The history just glossed as "fragment one" is well
known to code junkies and computer geeks. Numerous
websites archive oral histories, programming manuals, and
technical specifications for MULTICS, UNIX, and various
mainframe and other hardware systems. Key players in the
history, including Ken Thompson, Donald Ritchie, and
Doug McIlroy, have a kind of geek-chic celebrity status, and

1.10 California's 40th Armored Division in an area of South Central Los Angeles that was burning during the Watts riots, 1965.

differing versions of the histories of software and hardware development are hotly debated, including nitty-gritty details of what really counts as "a UNIX." In media studies, emerging work in "code studies" often resurrects and takes up these histories.

Within American cultural and ethnic studies, the temporal touchstones of struggles over racial justice, antiwar activism, and legal history are also widely recognized and analyzed. The perils and possibilities of identity politics have been scrutinized and elaborated. Not surprisingly, these two fragments typically stand apart in parallel tracks, attracting the interest and attention of very different audiences located in the deeply siloed departments that categorize our universities. As the opening of this chapter suggests, many would position mainstream work in the digital humanities within the computational camp.

But why?

In short, I suggest that these two moments are deeply interdependent and entangled. In fact, they correspond strongly with one another, comprising not independent slices of history but, instead, related and useful lenses into the shifting epistemological registers driving US and global culture in the 1960s and after. Both exist as operating systems of a sort, and we might understand them to be mutually reinforcing.

This history of intertwining and mutual dependence is hard to tell. As one delves into the intricacies of UNIX (or of Extensible Markup Language [XML] or the affordances of Python), race in America recedes far from our line of vision and inquiry.[7] Likewise, detailed examinations into the shifting registers of race and racial visibility post-1950 do not easily lend themselves to observations about the emergence of object-

1.11 Cesar Chavez speaks at a rally in 1974.

oriented programming or the affordances of databases. Very few audiences who care about one lens have much patience or tolerance for the other. We should work harder to hold these seemingly disparate areas of study together and mine the contextual relationships between certain developments in computation and wider cultural shifts occurring as those developments took shape.

Early forays in new media theory in the late 1990s and much concurrent work in the computational humanities rarely worked to bridge such divides. Theorists of new media often retreated into forms of analysis that Marsha Kinder has critiqued as "cyberstructuralist," intent on parsing media specificity and on theorizing the forms of new media, while disavowing twenty-plus years of critical race theory, feminism, and other modes of overtly politicized inquiry. As Smith recounts, some work in the digital humanities also proceeded as if technologies from XML to databases were neutral tools.[8] Many who had worked hard to instill race (and gender and other vectors of difference) as a central mode of analysis in film, literary, and media studies throughout the late twentieth century were disheartened and outraged (if not that surprised) to find both new media theory and emerging digital tools seemingly indifferent to those hard-won gains.

Early research on race and the digital was happening in this period, and it often took one of three forms. First, scholars produced critiques of representations *in* new media, noting the ways in which digital media did (or did not) perpetuate racist or sexist imagery (as in Lisa Nakamura's important efforts in *Cybertypes*), serve to facilitate hate speech (as in the work of Jessie Daniels), or allow for alternative or oppositional modes of expression (as in Tu et al.'s *Technicolor* or in Anna Everett's research). This work was aimed largely at the surface of our screens rather than at code or computation. A second

mode focused on the building of digital archives about race, including a variety of recovery projects that shared many impulses with the computational humanities. Amy Earhart has documented many of these endeavors, while also noting that such efforts often lacked robust institutional support. Many of these projects are no longer accessible. A third trajectory, often rooted more in the social sciences and communication studies, raised concerns about access to media, that is, the digital divide, and the social effects of media. Such work rarely tied race to the analyses of form, phenomenology, and computation that were so compelling in the work of Lev Manovich, Mark Hansen, and Jay Bolter and Richard Grusin. Important scholarship emerged from all these areas, but the research focused on race and that which centered on form or code rarely intersected. A few events attempted to force a collision between these areas, but the going was not easy. For instance, at the two Race in Digital Space conferences colleagues and I organized in 2001 and 2002, the vast majority of participants and speakers were working in the first three modes mentioned above.[9] The cyberstructuralists were not in attendance. (Fig. 1.12)

1.12  A poster from the second Race in Digital Space event, at the University of Southern California and the Museum of Contemporary Art in Los Angeles in fall 2002, organized by Anna Everett, Henry Jenkins, Tara McPherson, Erika Muhammed, and Chris Robbins. Design by Chris Robbins.

But what if this very incompatibility is itself part and parcel of the organization of knowledge production that operating systems like UNIX helped disseminate around the world? Might we ask if there is not something *particular to the very forms* of electronic culture that seems to parallel just such a movement, a movement that partitions race off from the specificity of media forms? Put differently, might we argue that the very structures of digital computation correspond to larger cultural shifts that seek to cordon off race and to contain it? Further, might we come to understand that our own critical methodologies are heirs of this epistemological shift?

From early writings by Sherry Turkle and George Landow to more recent works by Alex Galloway and others, scholarship in digital media has noted the parallels between the ways of knowing modeled in computer culture and traditions in structuralism and poststructuralism. Critical race theorists and postcolonial scholars like Chela Sandoval and Gayatri Spivak have illustrated the structuring (if unacknowledged) role that race plays in the work of poststructuralists such as Roland Barthes and Michel Foucault. We might bring these two arguments together, triangulating race, electronic culture, and poststructuralism, and, further, argue that race, particularly in the United States, is central to this undertaking, fundamentally shaping how we see and know as well as the technologies that underwrite or cement both vision and knowledge. Scholars of earlier technologies have also underscored the coupling of race and media. For instance, Brian Winston and Richard Dyer both write about the complex interlocking of ideology and technology, race and visuality, in the naturalization of whiteness in film stock. Winston argues that "ideologically charged cultural assumptions about the nature of [skin] colour condition and affect the work of the people involved in the development of colour film and lie behind and beneath what they accomplished," producing film that poorly capture dark skin while also whitening Caucasian skin (45). He concludes that his careful archival research "points up the existence of choices in the development of these processes and suggests that in situations of choice, consciously or unconsciously, cultural determinants will operate—as much in the scientific environment of a research laboratory as anywhere" (57). Like Balsamo's chart, his book *Technologies of Seeing* is interested in situating the materiality of film stock within a web of relations.

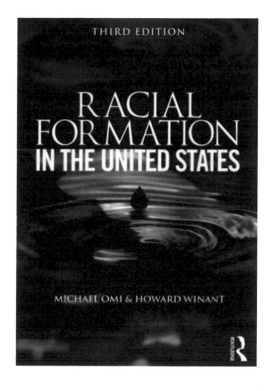

Certain modes of racial visibility and knowing coincide or dovetail with specific ways of organizing data: if digital computing underwrites today's information economy and is the central technology of post–World War II America, these technologized ways of seeing and knowing took shape in a world also struggling with shifting knowledges about and representations of race. Michael Omi and Howard Winant argue that racial formations serve as fundamental organizing principles of social relations in the United States, on both the macro and micro levels (55). How might we understand the infusion of racial organizing principles into the technological organization of knowledge after World War II? (Fig. 1.13)

1.13 Michael Omi and Howard Winant's groundbreaking book *Racial Formation in the United States: From the 1960s to the 1980s* introduced racial formation theory in 1986.

Omi and Winant and other scholars have tracked the emergence of a "race-blind" rhetoric at midcentury, a discourse that moves from overt to more covert modes of racism and racial representation (for example, from the era of Jim Crow to liberal color blindness.) Drawing from those 3-D postcards that bring two or more images together even while suppressing their connections, I have earlier termed the racial paradigms of the postwar era lenticular logics. The ridged coating on 3-D postcards is actually a lenticular lens, a structural device that makes simultaneously viewing the various images contained on one card nearly impossible. The viewer can rotate the card to see any single image, but the lens itself makes seeing the images *together* very difficult, even as it conjoins them at a structural level (i.e., within the same card). In the post–Civil Rights United States, the lenticular is a way of organizing the world. It structures representations as well as epistemologies. It also serves to secure our understandings of race in very narrow registers, fixating on sameness or difference while forestalling connection and interrelation. As I have argued elsewhere, we might think of the lenticular as a covert mode of the pretense of "separate but equal," remixed for midcentury America (*Reconstructing Dixie* 250).

A lenticular logic is a covert racial logic, a logic for the post–Civil Rights era. We might contrast the lenticular postcard to that wildly popular artifact of the industrial era, the stereoscope card. The stereoscope melds two separate images into an imagined unity, privileging the whole; the lenticular image partitions and divides, privileging fragmentation. A lenticular logic is a logic of the fragment or the chunk, a way of seeing the world as discrete modules or levels, a mode that suppresses relation and context. As such, the lenticular also manages and controls complexity.

And what in the world does this have to do with those engineers laboring away at Bell Labs, the heroes of the first fragment of history this section began with? What's race got to do with that? The popularity of lenticular lenses, particularly in the form of postcards, coincides historically not just with the rise of an articulated movement for civil rights but also with the growth of electronic culture and the birth of digital computing (both—digital computing and the Civil Rights movement—being products in quite real ways of World War II). We might see in UNIX one way in which the emerging logics of the lenticular and of the covert racism of color blindness are echoed in our computational systems, both in terms of the specific functions of UNIX as an operating system and in the broader philosophy it embraces.

## Situating UNIX

In moving toward UNIX from MULTICS, programmers conceptualized UNIX as a kind of tool kit of "synergistic parts" that allowed "flexibility in depth" (Raymond 9). Programmers could "choose among multiple shells. . . . [And] programs normally provide[d] many behavior options" (6). One of the design philosophies driving UNIX was the notion that a program should do one thing and do it well (not unlike our deep disciplinary drive in many parts of the university), and this privileging of the discrete, the local, and the specific emerges again and again in discussions of UNIX's origins and design philosophies.

Books for programmers that explain the UNIX philosophy turn on a common set of rules. Though slight variations on this rule set exist across programming books and online sites, Eric Raymond sets out the first nine rules:

1. Rule of Modularity: Write simple parts connected by clean interfaces.
2. Rule of Clarity: Clarity is better than cleverness.
3. Rule of Composition: Design programs to be connected to other programs.
4. Rule of Separation: Separate policy from mechanism; separate interfaces from engines.
5. Rule of Simplicity: Design for simplicity; add complexity only where you must.
6. Rule of Parsimony: Write a big program only when it is clear by demonstration that nothing else will do.
7. Rule of Transparency: Design for visibility to make inspection and debugging easier.
8. Rule of Robustness: Robustness is the child of transparency and simplicity.
9. Rule of Representation: Fold knowledge into data so program logic can be stupid and robust. (13)

Other rules include the Rules of Least Surprise, Silence, Repair, Economy, Generation, Optimization, Diversity, and Extensibility.

These rules implicitly translate into computational terms the chunked logics of the lenticular. For instance, Brian Kernighan wrote in a 1976 handbook on software programming that "controlling complexity is the essence of computer programming" (quoted in Raymond 14). Complexity in UNIX is controlled in part by the Rule of Modularity, which insists that code be constructed of discrete and interchangeable parts that can be plugged together by means of clean interfaces. In *Design Rules*, volume 1, *The Power of Modularity*, Carliss Baldwin and Kim Clark argue that computers from 1940 to 1960 had "complex, interdependent designs," and they label this era the "premodular" phase of computing (149). Though individuals within the industry, including John von Neumann, were beginning to imagine benefits to modularity in computing, Baldwin and Clark note that von Neumann's groundbreaking designs for computers in that period "fell short of true modularity" because "in no sense was the detailed design of one component going to be hidden from the others: all pieces of the system would be produced 'in full view' of the others" (157). Thus, one might say that these early visions of digital computers were neither modular nor lenticular. Baldwin and Clark track the increasing modularity of hardware design from the early 1950s forward and also observe that UNIX was the first operating system to embrace modularity and adhere "to the principles of information hiding" in its design (324).

There are clearly practical advantages of such structures for coding, but they also underscore a worldview in which a troublesome part might be discarded without disrupting the whole. Tools are meant to be "encapsulated" to avoid "a tendency to involve programs with each others' internals" (Raymond 15). Modules "don't promiscuously share global data," and problems can stay "local" (84–85). In writing about the Rule of Composition, Eric Raymond advises programmers to "make [programs] independent." He writes, "It should be easy to replace one end with a completely different implementation without disturbing the other" (15). Detachment is valued because it allows a cleaving from "the particular... conditions under which a design problem was posed. Abstract. Simplify. Generalize" (95). Though "generalization" in UNIX has specific meanings, we also see here the basic contours of a lenticular approach to the world, an approach that separates object from context, cause from effect, level from level.

In a 1976 article, "Software Tools," Bell Lab's programmers Brian Kernighan and P. J. Plauger urged programmers "to view specific jobs as special cases of general, frequently performed operations, so they can make and use general-purpose tools to solve them. We also hope to show how to design programs to look like tools and to interconnect conveniently" (1). The language here is one of generality (as in "general-purpose" tools), but, in fact, the tool library that is being envisioned is a series of very discrete and specific tools or programs that can operate independently of one another. They continue, "Ideally, a program should not know where its input comes from nor where its output goes. The UNIX time-sharing system provides a particularly elegant way to handle input and output redirection" (2).

> Programs can profitably be described as filters, even
> though they do quite complicated transformations on their
> input. One should be able to say
> program-1... | sort | program-2 . . .
> and have the output of program-1 sorted before being
> passed to program-2. This has the major advantage that
> neither program-1 nor program-2 need know how to sort,
> but can concentrate on its main task (4).

In effect, the tools chunk computational programs into isolated bits, where the programs' operations are meant to be "invisible to the user" and to the other programs in a sequence:

"The point is that this operation is invisible to the user (or should be). . . . Instead he sees simply a program with one input and one output. Unsorted data go in one end; somewhat later, sorted data come out the other. It must be *convenient* to use a tool, not just possible" (5). Kernighan and Plauger saw the "filter concept" as a useful way to get programmers to think in discrete bits and to simplify, reducing the potential complexity of programs. They note that "when a job is viewed as a series of filters, the implementation simplifies, for it is broken down into a sequence of relatively independent pieces, each small and easily tested. This is a form of high-level modularization" (5). In a video history, Kernighan talks about UNIX file systems stripping away complexity and context: "You basically don't have to think of any of those complexities that you have in other systems." Ken Thompson observes that, in UNIX, "a file is simply a sequence of bytes. Its main attribution is its size. By contrast, in more conventional systems, a file has a dozen or so attributes. To specify or create a file, it takes endless amounts of chit chat. If you want a UNIX system file, you simply ask for a file and you can use it interchangeably wherever you want a file." In their own way, these file systems function as a kind of lenticular frame or lens, allowing only certain portions of complex data sets to be visible at a particular time (to both the user and the machine).

Here is Doug McIlroy on creating the pipe concept for UNIX:

> At the same time that Thompson and Ritchie were on their blackboard, sketching out a file system, I was sketching out how to do data processing on this blackboard by connecting together cascades of processes and looking for a kind of prefix notation language for connecting processes together, and failing because it's very easy to say "*cat* into *grep* into . . . ," or "*who* into *cat* into *grep*," and so on; it's very easy to say that, and it was clear from the start that that was something you'd like to say. But there are all these side parameters that these commands have; they don't just have input and output arguments, but they have the options, and syntactically it was not clear how to stick the options into this chain of things written in prefix notation, *cat* of *grep* of *who* [i.e. *cat*(*grep*(*who* . . .))]. Syntactic blinders: didn't see how to do it. So I had these very pretty programs written on

the blackboard in a language that wasn't strong enough to
cope with reality. So we didn't actually do it."[10]

The technical feature that allowed UNIX to achieve much of
its modularity was the development by Ken Thompson (based
on a suggestion by Doug McIlroy) of the pipe, that is, a vertical
bar (the | symbol) that replaced the "greater than" sign (>) in
the operating system's code. As Doug Ritchie and Ken Thompson described it in a paper for the Association of Computing
Machinery in 1974 (reprinted by Bell Labs in 1978), "A *read*
using a pipe file descriptor waits until another process writes
using the file descriptor for the same pipe. At this point, data
are passed between the images of the two processes. Neither
process need know that a pipe, rather than an ordinary file, is
involved." In this way, the ability to construct a pipeline from a
series of small programs evolved, while the "hiding of internals" was also supported. The contents of a module were not
central to the functioning of the pipeline; rather, the input or
output (a text stream) was key. Brian Kernighan noted, "While
input/output direction predates pipes, the development of
pipes led to the concept of tools—software programs that
would be in a 'tool box,' available when you need them" and
interchangeable.[11] Pipes reduced complexity and were also linear. In "Software Tools," Kernighan and Plauger extend their
discussion of pipes, noting that "a pipe provides a hidden buff-
ering between the output of one program and the input of another program so information may pass between them without ever entering the file system" (2). They also signal the importance of pipes for issues of data security:

> And consider the sequence
> decrypt key <file | prog | encrypt key > newfile
> Here a decryption program decodes an encrypted file, passing

the decoded characters to a program having no special
security features. The output of the program is re-encrypted at
the other end. If a true pipe mechanism is used, no clear-text
version of the data will ever appear in a file. To simulate this
sequence with temporary files risks breaching security (3).

While the affordances of filters, pipes, and hidden data are often talked about as a matter of simple standardization and efficiency (as when Kernighan and Plauger argue, "Our emphasis
here has been on getting jobs done with an efficient use of
people" [6]), they also clearly work in the service of new regimes of security, not an insignificant detail in the context of
the Cold War era. Ironically, the MULTICS system that pre-
dated UNIX was undoubtedly more secure, but security was
very much a part of the conversation about computational systems at the moment of UNIX's emergence. In their retrospective assessment of MULTICS vis-à-vis security issues, Paul
Karger and Roger Schell note that MULTICS was probably
more secure than most of our current operating systems, both
because it was designed for multiple users who "might well
have conflicting interests and therefore a need to be protected
from each other" and because it was developed with military
and government uses in mind (119). Access controls were
built into the system itself, integrating security in the very conception of the system. In 1974 the US Air Force evaluated
MULTICS for security purposes, and these national anxieties
about security clearly form one backdrop to the development
of UNIX. Though the security of the UNIX system may have
been more imagined than real, the language of hidden data is
part and parcel of this conversation, shaping the development
of UNIX even while the mantra of simplicity decreased the
system's security with long-standing implications for computation, as Karger and Schell discuss. (Fig. 1.14)

Programming manuals and UNIX guides again and again stress clarity and simplicity ("don't write fancy code"; "say what you mean as clearly and directly as you can"), but the structures of operating systems like UNIX function by hiding internal operations, skewing "clarity" in very particular directions. These manuals privilege a programmer's equivalent of "common sense" in the Gramscian understanding. For Antonio Gramsci, common sense is a historically situated process, the way in which a particular group responds to "certain problems posed by reality which are quite specific" at a particular time (324). I am arguing that, as programmers constituted themselves as a particular class of workers in the 1970s, they were necessarily lodged in their moment, deploying common sense and notions about simplicity to justify and explain their innovations in code. Importantly, their moment was overdetermined not only by Cold War security concerns but also by the ways in which the United States was widely coming to process race and other forms of difference in more covert registers, as I noted above, even if the programmers themselves did not explicitly understand their work to be tied to such racial paradigms.[12] Issues of security in the United States in the 1960s and early 1970s responded not only to Cold War threats but also to the reality of domestic unrest that was playing out in racial terms, a point to which we will return.

1.14 A UNIX T-shirt foregrounds pipes as a key feature of the platform.

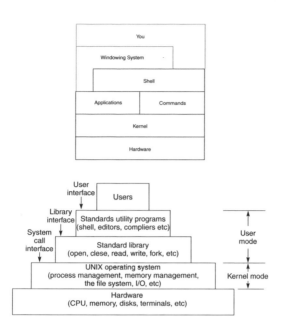

Another rule of UNIX is the Rule of Diversity, which insists on a mistrust of the "one true way." Thus, UNIX, in the words of one account, "embraces multiple languages, open extensible systems and customization hooks everywhere," which reads much like a description of the tenets of neoliberal multiculturalism (Raymond 24). In the ample literature on UNIX, certain words emerge again and again: modularity, compactness, simplicity, orthogonality. UNIX is meant to allow multitasking, portability, time sharing, and compartmentalizing. It is not much of a stretch to layer these traits over the core elements of post-Fordism, a mode of production that began to remake industrial-era notions of standardization in the 1960s: time-space compression, transformability, customization, a public-private blur, and so on. UNIX's intense modularity and information-hiding capacity were reinforced by its design, that is, in the ways in which it segregated the kernel from the shell.

1.15 / 1.16
Diagrams
illustrating
the structure
of UNIX.

The kernel loads into the computer's memory at startup and is "the heart" of UNIX (managing "hardware memory, job execution and time sharing"), although it remains hidden from the user (Baldwin and Clark 332). The shells (or programs that interpret commands) are intermediaries between the user and the computer's inner workings. They hide the details of the operating system from the user behind "the shell," extending modularity from a rule for programming in UNIX to the very design of UNIX itself.[13] (Figs. 1.15 / 1.16)

Diagrams similar to these are used in computer science classes to teach the structure of UNIX. They illustrate the ways in which UNIX "hides" its core operations from the user and seeks to separate core functions into discrete levels. They also bear a strong resemblance to the diagrams discussed earlier in relation to platform studies and the digital humanities stack as conceived by David Berry. As scholars and makers of digital media, it is important that we grapple with such encapsulated and modular ways of knowing, seeking to understand their wider effect in the world.

## Modularity in the Social Field + the Database

This push toward modularity and the covert in digital computation also reflects other changes in the organization of social life in the United States by the 1960s. If the first half of the twentieth century laid bare its racial logics, from "Whites Only" signage to the brutalities of lynching, the second half increasingly hid its racial "kernel," burying it below a shell of neoliberal pluralism. These covert or lenticular racial logics took hold at the tail end of the Civil Rights movement at least partially to cut off and contain the more radical logics implicit

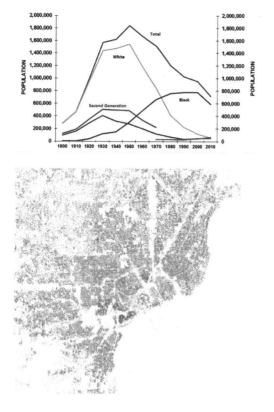

in the urban uprisings that shook Detroit, Watts, Chicago, and Newark. In fact, the urban center of Detroit was more segregated by the 1980s than in previous decades, which reflects a different inflection of the programmer's vision of the "easy removal" or containment of a troubling part. Whole areas of the city might be rendered orthogonal and disposable (also think post-Katrina New Orleans), and the urban black poor were increasingly isolated in "deteriorating city centers" (Sugrue 198). The historian Thomas Sugrue traces the rising unemployment rates for black men in Detroit, rates that rose dramatically from the 1950s to the 1980s, and maps a "deproletar-

1.17 Changing demographics in Detroit produced an increasingly homogeneous city after midcentury.

1.18 Segregation in Detroit, circa 2000. The blue zones are African American; the red zones, white.

ianization" that "shaped a pattern of poverty in the postwar city that was surprisingly new" (262). (Figs. 1.17 / 1.18)

The convergence between computation models and urban planning is not simply metaphorical. In her excellent *From Warfare to Welfare: Defense Intellectuals and Urban Problems in Cold War America,* Jennifer Light carefully tracks the diffusion of Cold War computation models, including databases and simulations, and their relation to urban planning methods. City managers and mayors understood military technologies to be important new "weapons" in efforts to control urban uprisings. She notes how cities such as Los Angeles increasingly deployed military computational technology "to help planners to predict urban system performance and to promote rationality in planning" (77). The city created the computationally driven Community Analysis Bureau (CAB) in 1966 to explore the "potential urban application of military innovations" and as "a direct response to urban unrest" (78–79). She underscores the reality that "urban blight" was identified as a problem requiring military-based computational solutions and reproduces in her book a chart from a 1970 city report, *Design Requirements for the Data and System Support Essential to an Urban Blight Systems Analysis.* (Fig. 1.19)

The chart models ideas for urban planning directly on military weapons systems. Both schematics turn on a model of information that flows through a series of discrete boxes—not unlike the schematics for the UNIX pipe. Even as the systems being proposed in cities such as Los Angeles were meant to manage urban complexity and introduce systems thinking, they also simultaneously deployed models of data that privileged modularity and discrete zones of information. The city was conceptualized in similar ways, as a map of derelict zones and urban blight that computation could isolate and contain.

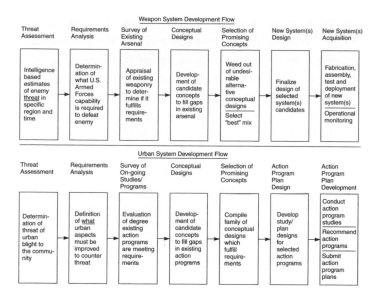

As Orit Halpern has argued, urban planning projects in the 1960s and 1970s displaced overt engagements with "discourses of structure, class and race" with a vision of the city as a data space "both radically isolated and always networked" into cybernetic systems (85). The city could be managed rationally and computationally, and technological design was harnessed for this process. Anxieties about race and its shifting contours within the United States were a crucial element motivating this change, particularly as computational systems are recruited into the management of cityscapes in a way that conceals overt language about race (or class) within a seemingly neutral language of data and information management. Urban management adopts the color-blind rhetoric unpacked by Omi and Winant even as it tries to build cities that can contain racial protest and unrest. Such city planning systems also become a way of toggling between the relationship of part and system, node and network, difference and universality. Though sys-

1.19 Chart from a 1970 city report, *Design Requirements for the Data and System Support Essential to an Urban Blight Systems Analysis.*

tems thinking and cybernetics are important at this moment, strategies of isolation and containment are also key, a fact we often overlook as we focus relentlessly on networks.

Across several registers, the emerging neoliberal state begins to adopt the Rule of Modularity. For instance, we might draw an example from across the Atlantic. In her careful analysis of the effects the Paris student uprising of May 1968 and its afterlives, Kristin Ross argues that the French government contained the radical force of the uprising by quickly moving to separate the students' rebellion from the concerns of labor, deploying a strategy of separation and containment in which both sides (students and labor) would ultimately lose (69).

Modularity in software design was meant to decrease "global complexity" and cleanly separate one "neighbor" from another (Raymond 85). These strategies also played out in ongoing reorganizations of the political field throughout the 1960s and 1970s in both the Right and the Left. The widespread divestiture in the infrastructure of inner cities can be seen as one more insidious effect of the logic of modularity and computational analysis in the postwar era. But we might also understand the emergence of identity politics in the 1960s as a kind of social and political embrace of modularity and encapsulation, a mode of partitioning that turned away from the broader forms of alliance-based and globally inflected political practice that characterized both labor politics and antiracist organizing in the 1930s and 1940s.[14] Identity politics produced concrete gains in the world, particularly in terms of civil rights, but we are also now coming to understand the degree to which these movements curtailed and short-circuited more radical forms of political praxis, reducing struggle to fairly discrete parameters.

Let me be clear. By drawing analogies between shifting racial and political formations and the emerging structures of digital computing in the late 1960s and early 1970s, I am not arguing that the programmers creating UNIX at Bell Labs and in Berkeley were *consciously* encoding new modes of racism and racial understanding into digital systems. (Indeed, many of these programmers were themselves left-leaning hippies, and the overlaps between the counterculture and early computing culture run deep, as Fred Turner has illustrated.) I also recognize that their innovations made possible the word processing program I am using to write this book, a powerful tool that shapes cognition and scholarship in precise ways. Nor am I arguing for some exact causal relation between the ways in which encapsulation or modularity work in computation and how they function in the emerging regimes of neoliberalism, governmentality, and post-Fordism. Rather, I am highlighting the ways in which the organization of information and capital in the 1960s and 1970s powerfully responded—across many registers—to the struggles for racial justice and democracy that so categorized the United States and the globe at the time. Many of these shifts were enacted in the name of liberalism, aimed at distancing the overt racism of the past even as they contained and cordoned off progressive radicalism. The emergence of covert racism and its rhetoric of color blindness are not so much intentional as systemic. The structures of digital computation developed side by side with the movement from overt to covert racial paradigms. There is a synergy between the two, not least because these computational systems are being used to manage the eruptions of race within the social field in areas like urban planning. It seems at best naive to imagine that cultural and computational operating systems don't mutually influence one another. Digital computation emerged as a part of a larger system of cultural control that tilts toward covert racism. Still, the argument here is not a *causal* one that somehow the midcentury move to covert forms of racism di-

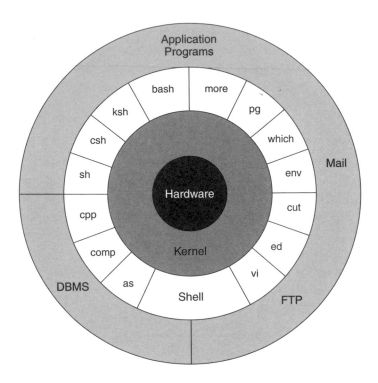

rectly led to the structure of the pipe or the shell in UNIX. Rather, I want to get at a complex set of interrelations that emerged at a particular moment in time.

An earlier version of my work on UNIX was the object of a heated series of exchanges on the SIGCIS listserv, under the subject heading "Is Unix racist?" The conversation was fascinating, even if the subject heading was misleading and illustrated well the perils of interdisciplinary scholarship. I am not arguing that UNIX is inherently racist but am instead claiming that, as Nabeel Siddiqui summarized on the listserv, "Certain programming practices reflect broader cultural ideas about modularity and standardization. These ideas also manifest in ideas about race during the Civil Rights movement and beyond.... Compu-

**1.20 Another popular textbook image of UNIX's modular structure.**

tation is not simply about the technology itself but has broad implications for how we conceive of and think about the world around us.… The sort of thinking that manifests itself in 'color-blind' policies and civil rights backlash have parallels with the sort of rhetoric expressed in Unix programming manuals."[15] This thinking also resonates with structures *within* UNIX, including its turn to modularity and the pipe. (Fig. 1.20)

Thus, we see modularity take hold not only in computation but also in the increasingly niched and regimented production of knowledge in the university after the Second World War. For instance, Christopher Newfield comments on the rise of New Criticism in literature departments in the Cold War era, noting its relentless formalism, a "logical corollary" to "depoliticization" (145) that "replaced agency with technique" (155). He attributes this particular tendency in literary criticism at least in part to the triumph of a managerial impulse, a turn that we might also align (even if Newfield doesn't) with the workings of modular code (itself studied as an exemplary approach to "dynamic modeling systems" for business management in the work of Baldwin and Clark, cited above).[16] He observes as well that this managerial obsession within literary criticism exhibited a surprising continuity across the 1960s and beyond. Gerald Graff has also examined the "patterned isolation" that emerged in the university after World War II, at the moment when New Criticism's methods took hold in a manner that deprivileged context and focused on "explication for explication's sake." Graff then analyzes the routinization of literary criticism in the period, a mechanistic exercise with input and output streams of its own (227). He recognizes that university departments (his example is English) began to operate by a field-based and modular strategy of "coverage," in which subfields proliferated and existed in their own separate chunks of knowledge, rarely contaminated by one another's "internals" (250). (He also comments that this modular strategy included the token hiring of scholars of color who were then cordoned off within the department.) Graff locates the beginning of this patterned isolation in the run-up to the period that also brought us digital computing; he writes that it continues to play out today in disciplinary structures that have become increasingly narrow and specialized. Patterned isolation began with the bureaucratic standardization of the university from 1890 until 1930 (61–62), but this "cut out and separate" mentality reached a new crescendo after World War II as the organizational structure of the university pushed from simply bureaucratic and Taylorist to managerial, a shift noted as well by Christopher Newfield.

Many now lament the overspecialization of the university; in effect, this tendency is a result of the additive logic of the lenticular or of the pipeline, where "content areas" or "fields" are tacked together without any sense of intersection, context, or relation. Today we risk "adding on" the digital humanities to our proliferating disciplinary menus without any meaningful and substantial engagement with fields such as gender studies, critical race theory, and the like. Many of the archival recovery efforts in the early years of DH deployed a similar additive logic, despite their good intentions. When these efforts focused on adding race or gender to digital archives and data sets, there was an implication that simply adding new data as content is all that is needed to get at some truth about race or gender. While it is hard to argue against, for example, including women authors in a database of nineteenth-century writers, such an approach is more additive than integrative or relational. It might add gender or race as categories but will not allow us to see how gender and race also operate within systems, helping to produce regimes of sorting, classification, and knowledge from the outset. As Zahid Chaudhary has argued, "Hegemonic structures tend... easily to produce difference through the very

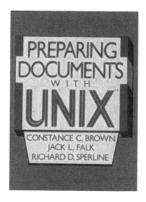  

mechanisms that guarantee equivalence. Laundry lists of unique differences, therefore, are indexes of an interpretive and political desire, a desire that often requires recapitulation to the familiar binarisms of subordination/subversion, homogeneity/ heterogeneity, and increasingly, immoral/moral" (153). In the "Postcolonial Digital Humanities" forum discussed earlier, Ted Underwood observes in a comment that "we don't have good metadata for most of these categories" (such as race, class, and gender) and proposes that scholars create these metadata as a key intervention of the digital humanities. This is helpful but also fixates on the creation of more data as the solution to conceptual problems, including the disciplining power of the archive and the limits of the index. There is not an easy fix here. Refusing metadata or archive expansion hardly seems a good solution. But as we participate in debates over metadata (like the efforts of trans activists to shift Text Encoding Initiative [TEI] vocabularies) and various archiving practices, we would also do well to remember, alongside Chaudhary, that "enumerating differences, gaps, caesurae, and so on, cannot in itself be the object(ive) of history writing if capital produces and relies upon difference *because* of its logic of equivalence" (175; emphasis in original).[17] (Figs. 1.21 / 1.22 / 1.23)

1.21 / 1.22 / 1.23 Many "how-to" books document UNIX's close relation to text processing and preparation.

It is interesting to note that much of the early work performed in UNIX environments was focused on document processing and communication tools and that UNIX is a computational system that very much privileges text. (It centers on the text-based command line instead of on the Graphical User Interface, and its inputs and outputs are simple text lines.) In a perhaps apocryphal tale, Rudd Canaday, a computer programmer involved with MULTICS, UNIX, early relational databases, and much more, wrote that Dennis Ritchie and Ken Thompson convinced Bell Labs' patent lawyers to buy them a PDP-11 computer by agreeing to "provide them with a system to do their paperwork. This is why the early UNIX contained so many text-processing tools (e.g. NROFF, TROFF, GREP, etc.). UNIX was built, the Patent department used it, and UNIX took off." UNIX was developed from an imaginary tied to particular goals, especially the managerial goals of document processing. Many of the methodologies of the humanities from the Cold War through the 1980s also privileged text while devaluing context and operated in their own chunked systems, which suggests telling parallels between the humanities' operating systems and privileged objects and those of the computers being developed on several university campuses in the same period.

Lev Manovich has noted the modularity of the digital era and also backtracked to early twentieth-century examples of modularity from the factory line to the creative productions of avant-garde artists, both in *The Language of New Media* and elsewhere. In a posting to the Nettime listserv in 2005, he framed modularity as a uniquely twentieth-century phenomenon, from Henry Ford's assembly lines to the 1932 furniture designs of the Belgian designer Louis Herman De Kornick. In his account, the twentieth century is characterized by an accelerating process of industrial modularization, but I think it is useful to examine the digital computer's privileged role in the process, particularly given that competing modes of computation were still quite viable until the 1960s, modes that might have pushed more toward the continuous flows of analog computing rather than the discrete tics of the digital computer. Is the modularity of the 1920s really the same as the modularity modeled in UNIX? Do these differences matter, and what might we miss if we assume a smooth and teleological triumph of modularity? How has computation pushed modularity in new directions, directions in dialogue with other cultural shifts and ruptures? Why does modularity emerge in so many of our systems with such a vengeance across the 1960s? Computation does not alone inaugurate such segmentation, but it is a powerful driver in the larger shift to heightened modularity. As the historian Andrew Russell has argued, "Modularity became a way of seeing, knowing, and ordering" (259) in the second half of the twentieth century across a diverse array of fields following the rise of modular electronics and computers. This modularity masked "technical, organizational, cultural, and political conflicts" (258). Russell focuses on Cold War military operations as a key driver in the spread of modular computation, but other historians, including Mary Dudziak, have illustrated the complex interrelation of Cold War politics and U.S. civil rights struggles. The rise of covert racism in America is partially a response to the government's recognition that overt racism was undermining Cold War goals. Digital computation emerges from a cultural context in which race is very much an issue of concern for the military. (Fig. 1.24)

I have here suggested that our technological formations are deeply bound up with our racial formations, and that each underwent profound changes at midcentury, changes also reflected in urban planning, managerial discourse, university specialization, and the rise of identity politics. Again, I am ar-

1.24 Moshe
Safdie's Habitat
67 signals
the spread of
modularity in
the social field at
the moment of
UNIX's origin.

guing not that one mode is causally related to the other but, rather, that they both represent a move toward modular knowledges, knowledges increasingly prevalent in the second half of the twentieth century. These knowledges supported and enabled the shift from the overt standardized bureaucracies of the 1920s and 1930s to the more dynamically modular and covert managerial systems that were increasingly prevalent as the century wore on, ways of knowing that Orit Halpern has called communicative objectivity. These latter modes of knowledge production and organization are powerful racial and technological operating systems that coincide with (and reinforce) structuralist and poststructuralist approaches to the world within the academy. Both the computer and the lenticular lens mediate images and objects, changing their relationship but frequently suppressing that process of relation, much like the divided departments of the contemporary university. The fragmentary knowledges encouraged by many forms and experiences of the digital neatly parallel the lenticular logics that underwrite the covert racism endemic to our times, operating in potential feedback loops, supporting each other. If

## Proctor Houston parked cars to earn his B.A.

### Now he's managing 9 salesmen at IBM.

Pick it up. Park it. Run back for another. Fifty cars a night. Six nights a week. That's what Proctor Houston did while he was in college.

But it wasn't enough to finance four years of college. So he also worked as a tobacco-wrapper and as a laborer on construction jobs. Hard work. And it all paid off when he got his B.A. in Social Science from St. Paul's College in 1959.

After working a few years, he came to IBM for an interview. "I was a little apprehensive about selling," he recalls. "But after making the rounds with an IBM salesman, I knew I could do it."

**A manager in 4 years.**

He did. As an office products sales representative, he exceeded his quotas two out of three years. And recently Proctor was promoted to field sales manager in a branch office.

"This may sound trite," he said recently, "but marketing really is challenging and exciting. You never get stale."

**People with ideas make IBM go.**

In less than two decades, the computer business has become the world's fastest growing major industry. And IBM is a leader in the field. What success we've enjoyed has come because of the people who work here.

People with ideas. People like Proctor Houston.

**An Equal Opportunity Employer**

# IBM.

scholars of race have highlighted how certain tendencies within poststructuralist theory simultaneously respond to and marginalize race, this maneuver is at least partially possible because of a parallel and increasing dispersion of electronic forms across culture, forms that simultaneously enact and shape these new modes of thinking. (Fig. 1.25)

Though the examples here have focused on UNIX, it is important to recognize that the core principles of modularity that it helped bring into practice continue to influence a wide range of digital computation, especially the C programming

1.25 An IBM ad from 1970 suggests the degree to which the corporation had acclimated to shifting racial formations after the Civil Rights era, as it adopts a rhetoric of multicultural diversity.

language, itself developed for UNIX by Ritchie and based on Thompson's earlier B language. While UNIX and C devotees bemoan the non-orthogonality and leakiness of Windows or rant about the complexity of C++, the basic argument offered above—that UNIX helped inaugurate modular and lenticular systems broadly across computation and culture—holds true for the black boxes of contemporary coding and numerous other instances of our digital praxis. In an intriguing look at the performativity of code, Adrian Mackenzie tracks the development of Linux from UNIX as a move from "academic-industrial computer science" toward a mind-set of a system built "by hackers for hackers," as computation increasingly took the form of personal computing and consumer electronics. In insisting on the performativity of code, Mackenzie also highlights the ways in which "the authorizing context for Linux includes gendered and classed practices which usually remain unremarked" (82), particularly to the extent that Linux emerged from the celebration of a particularly classed and masculine style of late-night programming. Near the end of his essay, he asks, "How does computer code become cultural?" (87). This is a crucially important question, but the example of UNIX offered above suggests that code does not become cultural after the fact. Rather, code emerges from culture in all its complexity even as it exerts its own agential force on the social realm. To the extent that the modularity of UNIX as well as its pipe structure were homologous with shifting racial paradigms in US culture in the 1960s and 1970s, these elements might be seen, to borrow Mackenzie's language, to "completely pervade Linux" as well (83). (Fig. 1.26)

The modularity we have been tracking also shaped the development and design of relational databases. Developed in roughly the same time period as UNIX and replacing the

IBM General Products Division in San Jose, California . . . Voted "One of America's 10 most beautiful plants."

"THINK" 1985!

hierarchical databases that were then more common, relational databases are the predominant form of database in use today and are behind a good deal of the data we interact with on the web, as well as in programs like Access and Oracle. First described by Edgar Cobb at IBM in 1970, they organize data in a set of formally described tables. This allows a user to quickly sort a large amount of data through different queries but also requires an atomistic view of data. If UNIX was bound up in its cultural moment, the same might be argued of the relational database. That is, its highly atomistic structure was perhaps part and parcel of broader cultural changes under way at that time, including the turn to modularity mapped by Russell. Many scholars have commented on the centrality of the database in digital media. Whereas Manovich has argued that the database has ousted narrative, Marsha Kinder, N. Katherine Hayles, and Alex Galloway, among others, have challenged this reading. Hayles has offered as well a nuanced and lucid description of the relational

1.26 A postcard of IBM's San Jose plant in 1962 imagined a modular future; it was here that Edgar Codd developed the relational database.

database. For our purposes, she notes "a well-constructed [relational] database's self-containment," which can be queried with operations because it is "a formally closed logical system" (177). These databases cannot handle indeterminacy (178). She contrasts the self-describing nature of the databases and their dependence on enumeration with the embrace of ambiguity by narrative.

---

E. F. Codd writes on the objectives of normalization beyond 1NF (First Normal Form):

1. To free the collection of relations from undesirable insertion, update and deletion dependencies;
2. To reduce the need for restructuring the collection of relations, as new types of data are introduced, and thus increase the life span of application programs;
3. To make the relational model more informative to users;
4. To make the collection of relations neutral to the query statistics, where these statistics are liable to change as time goes by. (34)

---

The database depends on the loss of the thing itself. At one level, this loss is literal, as the "thing"—say a photo or film—is digitized and transformed into data. At another level, this loss is also a key aspect of the functioning of the technology. The new media theorist Matthew Fuller has argued that in the development of the relational database, categories come to trump things. Databases work by "normalizing" data, a process that in effect privileges abstract relations among data while also stripping "things" of context. Elements in a database get sorted by a set of structuring relations that depend on abstraction. If the card catalog and the filing cabinet of the late nineteenth-century archive also defined relations, they still bore a connection to the object that was archived. The relationality of the database takes this abstraction to a very different level. (Here it might be noted that while we might as humanities scholars think of relationality as a good thing, perhaps related to concepts such as sociability, a relational database, as is often the case in computer jargon, is less about sketching rich and detailed relations between objects than it is about rigid categorizations and formal logic.)

In a position reminiscent of Alan Liu's linking of post-Fordist "metamanagement" to the mediations of the database (*Local Transcendence* 227), Paul Dourish maintains that "the specific kinds of relationality that are expressed in database forms are historically and materially contingent" (4). He discusses the alternatives that existed to relational databases in the 1970s and goes on to note that "one key feature of the relational model... is the separation it creates between the structure and content of a database." Furthermore, "defining or constructing a database is the process of setting up the database schema. Subsequently using the database is the process of adding, removing, updating, and searching the data records that make up its content. The separation is both temporal and spatial. It is spatial because the database schema is represented separately from the data; it is temporal because the schema must be set up before any data can be entered (and because, in many cases, the schema is difficult or impossible to change once data entry has begun)" (10). As we will see in Chapter 2, this rigidity of the relational database has consequences for how humanities scholars might engage computation, particularly those scholars doing interpretative research. Dourish's

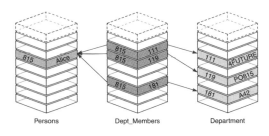

Persons      Dept_Members      Department

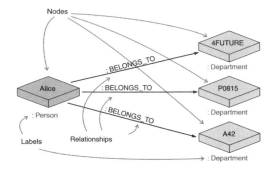

work also underscores the fact that the materiality of the relational database, its thingness and structures, is deeply contextual. For instance, Dourish explains how the conception of the relational data model, the design of the hardware on which it ran, and its privileging of transactions had everything to do with its development at IBM at a particular moment. In the ascendancy of the relational database, he writes, "we find at work highly entwined sociomaterial configurations" (13), "allowing us to trace a bidirectional relationship between, on the one hand, computer system structure and, on the other, the organizations that employ them" (14). (Figs. 1.27 / 1.28)

1.27 / 1.28
These images from the website of Neo4j illustrate the differences between relational databases and newer graph databases.
The relational database stores highly structured data, whereas the graph databases aim for flexible connections and relations.

To loop back to my earlier discussion of UNIX, both the relational database and the operating system work through separation, decontextualization, and abstraction. As Michael Castelle maintains, "The crucial difference between the network model and the relational model [of databases] should be clear. Where the network model enforces referential (i.e., pointing) links between entities at the logical level, the relational model enforces the *absence* of such reference" (12; emphasis in original). Like Dourish and Liu, he argues that the relational database "can be seen as the ideal medium" for commercial manufacturing interests and a hyper-managerial state (20). Neither Dourish nor Castelle really pushes beyond the corporate contexts of the relational database's development to larger systems of social relations, but the relational database platforms they describe were deployed in the offices of the urban planners addressing civil unrest just as surely as they were used to manage goods and money. Extending Dourish's and Castelle's insights, we can explicitly connect their material investigations to larger ideological contexts, the very kinds of context that encapsulation and abstraction work so hard to strip away. As Halpern and Light both detail, computation develops in symbiosis with larger efforts to manage the urban sphere. Light notes that this development was a direct response to the urban unrest that marked cities such as Detroit and Los Angeles from the 1940s through the 1960s. Military-based computational systems were deployed and adapted as city management tools, and this process then influenced computation. To be clear, what is being managed by these systems is race as much as the documents of the metamanagerial class, intertwining new methods of containing racial unrest with the very origins and processes of computation.

It is perhaps easier to see the connections between banking and software and to track how those industries developed together than to see that the abstractions that got built into computation at midcentury also mirror an increasing set of abstractions about race in the cultural field, abstractions that supported the turn to covert racism. It is hard to produce a neat example of a racist consequence that occurred because UNIX deploys modularity and encapsulation in a mode that echoes US society's move toward covert racism. This is in part because covert racism works by disavowing racism, by separating the overtly racist from the systemically racist. My inability to produce such a concrete example certainly annoyed the historians on the CIGSIC listserv. Earlier I mentioned the work of Brian Winston documenting the ways in which film stock encoded into its material structures cultural ideologies regarding race. In a related vein, feminists such as Laura Mulvey and Constance Penley have illustrated the ways in which gender overdetermines cinematic technologies and representational systems. In these cases, the consequences of the intertwining of culture and technology are a bit easier to see, for film is a technology of vision; we can see the male gaze of the camera or the limited hues of film stock (at least once someone calls them to our attention). But operating systems and databases are not visual systems in the same way. They emerge at a different cultural moment and work by abstraction; thus, the correspondences between covert racism in the social field and modularity in computation can't be easily tracked to a neatly delineated and subsequent racist effect. Instead, both code and covert racism work by sleight of hand, by hiding their particulars. Both covert racism and computation perform (as Rodney Coates has argued of the former) in service of expediency through regimes of obfuscation. In the epilogue to her magnificent book *Programmed Visions,* Wendy Chun briefly takes up race and software, arguing that both are "nebulous entities… yet solid everyday experiences. We are expected to be as blind to software as we are to race; but race and software both act" (178). Importantly, they also act *together* even if that connection is hard to trace among the black boxes and kernels of our culture. From UNIX to databases, from urban planning to post-Fordism, we can see at work here the basic contours of an approach to the world that separates object from subject, cause from effect, context from code.

## Moving beyond Our Boxes
## + Mapping Materialisms

We need conceptual models for the digital humanities and for digital media studies that can help us attend to software, code, databases, and more in ways that push beyond modularity and that help us understand that these digital objects and systems exert their own agencies even as they also emerge from culture. Given our ongoing and increased immersion among any number of interacting and interactive devices since the rise of personal computing, it is perhaps no coincidence that the last few decades have seen a proliferation of theoretical investigations of mediation, new materialisms, speculative realisms, and object-oriented ontologies. In short, things, stuff, and objects abound in contemporary theory and philosophy, unspooling through ample, diverse, and contested approaches. Mel Chen frames this proliferation of object studies as "a combination of intuitive phenomenologically acquired abstractions and socially acquired histories of knowledge about what constitutes proper 'thingness'" (5), suggesting with that very description the tensions that might unfold in this terrain. Although these emerging intellectual formations take many twists and vectors, and the debates between different camps (and from the "outside") can be quite fierce, most of the approaches share a desire to decenter the human and to move beyond an anthropocentrism that makes less and less sense the more we learn about the world and our effect on it. Though much of this quite far-ranging scholarship looks back toward long-standing philosophical traditions ranging from Spinoza to Kant to Descartes, it is hard to account for the way in which it has taken root and spread in the academy today without acknowledging the simultaneous proliferation of computation as the dominant context for contemporary existence in global capitalism. Certainly, everything from rocks to recycling bins must seem more animate, more ready to speak, to those who are endlessly engaging networked devices—from iPads to talking wall thermostats—while surrounded by endless chatter about ubiquitous computing, clouds, and big data.

The watch
reimagined.

It delivers important information when
and where you need it. Helps you
easily perform everyday tasks in
seconds. Instantly connects you to the
people and things you care about
most. All while keeping precise time.
Yes, it's a watch. But unlike any you've
ever imagined.

Watch the "Welcome to Apple Watch"
Guided Tour ⓟ

I here begin to parse a few strands of these various theoretical engagements with matter and objects to return us to the opening frame of this essay and to suggest lines of thought that might join histories of computation and DH practice with theories of feminism and difference. I have come to favor particular inflections of the new materialisms that tilt toward relation and away from modularity while also taking up questions of race and how it matters today. Along the way, I bring together several unusual suspects in order to surface connections among kinds of work that are not often thought of together. If, as I noted earlier, it is hard to hold together work in DH and that of the fields converging at ASA, it is also hard to join some variants of object studies with theoretical investigations of race and difference. The turn to objects might even seem to occupy a different register from those of concepts like race. Nonetheless, it is possible to plot pathways through this potential impasse through wily assemblage and intersection. I move quickly here, by means of association, attempting to push back against the modularity of our disciplines. (Fig. 1.29)

1.29 Devices like the Apple Watch heighten our awareness of diverse object agencies.

For every scholar enlivened by the conceptual turn toward objects and matter, there are others who have reacted quite ada-

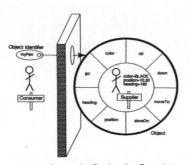

**Figure 4.1.** Consumer/supplier viewpoints. Encapsulation means that a consumer sees only the services that are available from an object, but not how those services are implemented. Only the supplier has visibility into the object's procedures and its data.

mantly against it. Such objections often note that the correspondence between these theories and forms of computation is undertheorized and rarely acknowledged. To take one example, Alex Galloway asks, "Why, within the current renaissance of research" among the object-oriented ontologists and speculative realists, "is there a coincidence between the structure of the ontological systems and the structure of the most highly evolved technologies of post-Fordist capitalism?" He refers to computer networks and especially object-oriented computer languages "such as C++ or Java" ("Poverty of Philosophy" 347). He goes on to articulate in great detail a marked correspondence between Alain Badiou's work and "the design of certain computer languages," focusing in particular on Badiou's borrowing of the notions of belonging and inclusion from set theory and relating these to the concepts of membership and inheritance in Java (349–352). If, as we have seen, Brian Winston illustrates that the seemingly neutral technology of film stock is shot through with a series of choices that also reflect larger cultural systems, the imaginary that gives rise to object-oriented computer programming languages is heavily shaped by the production and movement of objects at a post-Fordist global scale. (Fig. 1.30)

1.30 A computer textbook illustration of encapsulation. The "consumer" is the user of a piece of code, usually a programmer, and the "supplier" is the programmer who created the code. The programmer creating the code separates *how* the computation is performed from *what* the computation does.

85

While I do not entirely agree with all of Galloway's conclusions about speculative realism and object-oriented ontology (OOO), I do concur that we witness in object-oriented ontologies an overlap between OOO's foundational concepts and methods of computation. To offer another example and to return us to a theorist cited in this essay's opening, take Ian Bogost's very feisty *Alien Phenomenology; or, What It's Like to Be a Thing*. There is much to enjoy there. The book is lovingly rendered, beautifully written, and thoroughly imaginative. Bogost has deftly blended theory and praxis in his career. I love his brief examination of the computer: "Anyone who has ever had to construct, repair, program, or otherwise operate on a computational apparatus knows that a strange and unique world does stir within such a device" (9). Plus, the book is fun to read. And yet it troubles me and not entirely in a good way. Its focus relentlessly returns to the thing, pushing aside the thing's relations and even the fissures of "vicarious causation" that Bogost's fellow traveler Graham Harman might pursue. For Bogost, the first question, the real question, is "What is a thing?" (11). He rejects the dominant two totalizing "systems operations" of our times, that is, scientific naturalism and social relativism, for their beliefs, respectively, in true knowledge and "finger wagging" (13). He concludes that, of course, these two positions are "cut from the same cloth" (14). Bogost goes on to articulate his own interesting contributions to OOO, in particular his concept of a tiny ontology. He draws from his earlier work on computation here and proposes as his focus of analysis the unit (rather than the object or the thing). He maintains that this concept of the unit is lifted from chemical engineering, but it seems more properly located within the realms of object-oriented computation. The unit is "isolated, unitary, and specific" (25); a unit may become part of a configurable system, but, even as it conjoins, it retains its fierce indi-

viduality, "still keeping something secret" (27). "Units are isolated entities trapped together inside other units, rubbing shoulders with one another uncomfortably while never overlapping" (28). Later, he argues that "the inherent partition between things is a premise of OOO" (40) as he discusses the philosophical work of a Latourian litany, those lovely long lists of objects that percolate throughout the writings of Latour and of OOO.[18] (Fig. 1.31)

Here we are back in the terrain of the pipe and the legacies of UNIX, operating through the processes of encapsulation and abstraction that drive object-oriented programming languages. These segmented formulations mime computational systems. David Golumbia has cogently framed object-oriented programming languages as obsessed with both hierarchy and classification, an obsession that weds computation to particular ideological paradigms (210). A 1990s programming textbook by David Watt notes, "Abstraction is a mode of thought by which we concentrate on general ideas rather than on specific manifestations of these ideas. Abstraction is the whole basis of philosophy and mathematics, and is also fruitful in many other disciplines, including all branches of computer science" (89). While we might puzzle over this second sentence just a bit, consider the correspondence between the first line, and these sentences drawn from Bogost: "Speculative realisms remain philosophies of first principles. They have not yet concerned themselves with particular implementations." This is a curious kind of universalism, stripped clean of con-

1.31 Ian Bogost's Latour Litanizer with an exploded view in the header.

text. There is an interest in things—but oddly abstracted ones that can stand in for whole categories. We witness a formalism here that imagines that the things, the first principles, can be articulated from the outset and that differences and the particulars can be tacked on later, an additive form of the lenticular that emerged to manage or suppress differences.[19] Bogost later writes that "being is unconcerned with issues of gender, performance, and its associated human politics" (99), suggesting that such particularities impede our pursuit of the unit or the thing. He tends here and elsewhere to equate human politics with a narrow version of identity politics, obscuring decades of feminist or queer-of-color theory that think gender, race, and other vectors of difference far beyond the terrain of essentialism.

Watt's programming textbook goes on to observe that "abstractions support... separation . . . : only the programmer who implements an abstraction is concerned with *how* the embodied computation is performed; the programmers who subsequently use the abstraction by calling it need be concerned only with *what* the computation does" (89; emphasis in original). As is true of object-oriented ontologies, the unit of code pretends to autonomy, wrapped up tightly in its module, but the programmer is in there. He has left his mark. The fantasy of modularity, of the unit, object, or thing cut free, is a fantasy under the control of the programmer—or the philosopher—an abstraction. A tampon, a toaster, a nuclear reactor, a Snapchat post, a function abstraction: all indeed are objects, things, units. Can we attend to them with care without a pretense of their radical separateness? Doesn't our writing about them already violate this fantasy? In a lively discussion on the Empyre listserv, Bogost wrote (among many other things), "But, the truth is, microprocessors and integrated circuits are as extant as the social factors that drive their design." They are extant and often lovely. But they cannot be extracted from the relations within which they exist and from which they emerged. Relations exist, even in the hidden secrets that these things keep mutely from us. Relations are *in there* already.[20]

As the title might suggest, aliens haunt Bogost's book, appearing through the invocation of Roswell, New Mexico, and through tales of the Atari *E. T.* video game cartridge. But they also wrap around a curious passage that kicks off with reflections on blackness. The passage begins with a quote from Graham Harman about the background noise of peripheral objects, the "black noise of muffled objects hovering at the fringes of our attention" (33). Blackness then erupts into Bogost's text, italicized as *"black"* and *"blackbody radiation,"* then black bodies, then black holes. A litany of black, there, then gone again. Might we see in such an odd moment in the book a disorder of some kind, the ghost in the machine of object-oriented programing and object-oriented ontology rattling the cage of the unit, escaping from encapsulation and the pipelines of UNIX? Race destabilizes the neat separation of the units, but we will need to venture beyond the objects of OOO to tell that story.

Bogost's repeated use of *black* is not intended to signal race, which, for him would probably inhabit the realms of human politics that are not of interest to his take on OOO. Nonetheless, recent theorists of blackness have plumbed its ontological status, querying its ability to toggle between thing and context in ways that are pertinent to the study of units and objects. Their work also helps explain why blackness may erupt in unexpected places. One such scholar is Fred Moten. In his stunningly original engagement of the thing (and the object) within but also through the writing of Frantz Fanon and by way of Heidegger, contra Kant, Moten has investigated the case of blackness. While he is not speaking directly about computation, his insights are deeply relevant here.[21] He is speaking of the figure of the oppressed, especially in Fanon, and writes, "So I am interested in how the ones who inhabit the nearness and distance between *Dasein* and things (which is off to the side of what lies between subjects and objects)... are perhaps best understood as the extra-ontological... [as] a destructive, healing agent. . . . At the same time, this dangerous supplement, as the fact out of which everything else emerges, is constitutive" (186–187). He continues, "Blackness needs to be understood as operating at the nexus of the social and the ontological, the historical and the essential." Here we might begin to see the work of blackness within the encapsulated logics of object-oriented programming (and even OOO itself). Blackness is operating as a switch within the system, a relay point between particularity and the general, between the social and the computational, between difference and sameness, between thing and context. Though Moten does not directly take up the digital in his essay, his language is evocative, speaking as he does of set theory and calculation. He observes that blackness operates as an "ontology of disorder... as a general critique of calculation even as it gathers diaspora as an open set—or as an openness disruptive of the very idea of set—of accumulative and unaccumulable differences, differings, departures without origin." The "stolen life" of "the colonized, the enslaved, and the enclosed" "disorders" the system (187). Units cannot stay pure, self-contained, neatly apart from the social. Blackness is already in there. This work, along with various feminist investigations of materialism, points us beyond modularity and the decontextualized objects of OOO.

Several scholars have commented on speculative realism and object-oriented philosophy's tendency to isolate object from context and to avoid the political. For instance, Galloway argues, "One risks switching from a subjective essentialism (patriarchy, logocentrism, ideological apparatuses) to a system of 'objective' essentialism (an unmediated real, infinity, being as mathematics, the absolute, the bubbling of chaos). Is it time to trot out the old antiessentialist arguments from our Marxist, feminist, and postcolonial forebears?" ("Poverty of Philosophy" 357). Yes and no. His focus on the tendency for Quentin Meillassoux, Graham Harman, and others to divorce metaphysics from politics (or to attend to politics as something of an afterthought) is convincing enough, and I will not here rehearse the parrying that has ensued since his essay's publication. In a similar vein, David Berry has identified "an unexamined formalism" in OOO that points "towards a potential political conservatism." He notes, in relation to Bogost's work, that it aims to save us "from the 'crushing' problem of repetitive accounts of marginal inequality and suffering. This is achieved by a new 'humanism' that rejects the human as having any special case," including "the marginal problems of women, LGBT, immigrants, asylum seekers, and the poor."[22] Presumably this new humanism no longer requires cranky feminists either. Suffice it to say that much more work will need to be done to satisfy OOO's critics in this regard, although Tim Morton, Michael O'Rourke, and others have begun this work, as have several scholars I would locate outside OOO entirely, such as Jane Bennett and Steve Shaviro.[23] Other of Galloway's conclusions are less satisfying to me. He goes on to write that, in OOO's overturning of correlationism, one must discard "much of second- and third-wave feminism, certain kinds of critical race theory, the project of identity politics in general, theories of postmodernity, and much of cultural studies" (358). Here I am not so sure, particularly if we do not turn our attentions to Badiou, Meillassoux, and Harman but instead follow various new vectors of materialist thought from feminists and scholars of color, work that, while sometimes

1.32
The feminist media scholar Amelie Hastie edited "Objects of Media Studies" for *Vectors,* a project that attended carefully to objects' contexts and histories through a relational structure. Design by Raegan Kelly.

still resisting correlationism, moves in directions quite different from that of much of OOO. If Galloway asks us to choose sides between the new realists and the historical materialists, certain endeavors refuse the starkness of that binary, mapping a different way that does not jettison the insights of feminism, queer-of-color critique, and other earlier theoretical formations. These feminist scholars (and I count myself among them) also recognize that the field we occupy is not clearly drawn and that any effective tactic—in metaphysics or in politics or, more likely, in their messy entangling—is unlikely to somehow magically extricate itself from the conditions of production and the cultural logics of computation that we inhabit. Though we might aim for theories and practices that don't simply recapitulate the structures of code, we are never entirely free of the master's tools. Like Bogost, such feminists are not averse to certain practices of carpentry and making. We might not want our units fully encapsulated, but there's still much to be done with code, a tactic we'll return to when our story (at long last) returns the work of the Vectors Lab after a quick routing through various alternative materialisms that shift our focus from the isolated object to the object in relation. (Fig 1.32)

To be wildly reductive and yet suggestive, why do scholars of gender, race, and other markers of difference not seem particularly drawn to OOO in large numbers? Perhaps because we have a different and long history of thinking about the status of the object as well as of imagining the object in relation. While the response of many in the OOO camp is that, sure, there is room for feminism here if you want to join us and we're all about the openness (or, in the words of Graham Harman, "Girls Welcome!!!"), one might argue that feminist, queer, indigenous, and other engagements with materiality, relationality, and the status of objects predate the emergence of OOO by quite some time. In many ways, OOO feels like an enclosure, an encapsulation, as it were, of trajectories within feminist and other materialist thinking at least from the early work of Donna Haraway, Rosi Braidotti, Chela Sandoval, and others, even as it moves away from certain registers of that important scholarship (often without acknowledging any debt to these thinkers, skipping conveniently back across time to Spinoza instead). Feminist, indigenous, and critical race scholars do attend to materialisms in wonderful and weird ways, but, not surprisingly, much of their work extends great care to understanding relationality as well. For instance, scholarship like Jane Bennett's turns resolutely to things and yet still privileges relation, not demanding that the object withdraw from other vital pulses. Kim Tallbear's work on the rock called pipestone frames it as sentient within indigenous ontologies and yet as deeply connected to the human. Thus the unit, the thing, or the object is not privileged (nor are first principles) among these scholars.

unfolding

enfolding

image

information

experience

1 2 3 4 5 6 7 8
Foliated Kufic, Al-Azhar mosque, Cairo (972)

1.33
Laura Marks's *Vectors* project, "Enfolding and Unfolding," examines the ways in which artworks and other objects facilitate (or perhaps inhibit) the movement among experience, information, and image.

Another set of operations and modalities emerges instead: the cut, intersectionality, the assemblage, alliance, and other modes of mediating between subject and object, particular and universal, and node and network are explored in their work. The difference is subtle but more than semantic, and it is a difference born of studies of race, gender, and sexuality and their varied, conflicting legacies as well as of activism beyond the academy. My goal here is not to engage at great length with feminist materialist thought or to map its plentiful pathways in all their scope. That work has been undertaken elsewhere. Rather, I want to signal a few suggestive configurations that emerge from this work, operations that move us beyond the bracket, the fragment, or the unit toward different possibilities, possibilities much at play in the work of the Vectors Lab. I turn here to various models we might group under a porous notion of newer materialisms to bring into productive tension writers who foreground mediation and the relational and those who foreground differences (race, gender, sexuality, and so on). Some do both. My framing here is itself a political act, a choice of where and how to focus my (and your) attention and a movement beyond the modularity that shapes much of the academy. It is also signals a history of the notion of alliance and intersection that emerges out of feminist and women-of-color critique. This very summary risks a modularity of its own, reducing complex arguments sometimes made over long careers into a series of swatches cut from whole cloth. Certainly, it brings together thinkers who would not always (or happily) see themselves as aligned as it joins theories of the posthumanism, the assemblage, intersectionality, and the cut. (Fig. 1.33)

If OOO displaces the human in its pursuit of pure objects, feminist theory has also queried the status of the human in a number of far-ranging contexts. A recent example is Rosi Braidotti's *The Posthuman,* which takes up many themes we've circled around thus far, including questions of postanthropocentric thought, life under digitality, and the possibilities for humanities scholarship that extend beyond critique toward the affirmative and the creative. While her work would probably prove too wedded to a theory of the subject for many OOO scholars, her figuration of the posthuman subject still decenters the human, striving to blur the distinction between the human and nonhuman and figuring the human as one among "the flow of relations with multiple others" (50). She takes Latourian-style science and technology studies to task for their "analytical posthumanism" and for lacking a theory of the subject (42), a critique she would almost certainly wage toward OOO. Her subject is embodied and embedded, materialist and vitalist, not postmodern or antifoundationalist, and yet she remains invested in understanding difference (51). If a focus on the unit privileges isolated and unique objects, Braidotti might see this as a dangerous "neutralization of difference" (88) that undermines our capacity for understanding or theorizing relationality. Her work also moves to articulate

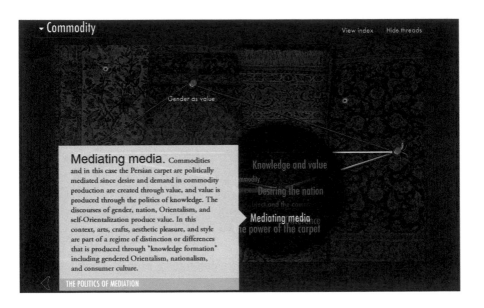

1.34 Working with Erik Loyer, the postcolonial feminist scholar Minoo Moallem created "Nation on the Move" to explore the generative function of the Persian carpet in the U.S. national imaginary, mapping complex intersections of object, politics, and aesthetics. Published in *Vectors*.

political possibility with some clarity, as she does not shy away from engaging posthuman ethics. This political stance necessitates embodiment and location, as she articulates in a recent interview: "To me, however important it is that we concern ourselves with a-subjective or non-human matter, the politics of location of the subject is something we cannot let go."[24] Her subject is "a more complex and relational subject framed by embodiment, sexuality, affectivity, empathy and desire as core qualities," (26), interested in difference but not as in the "dialectical scheme of thought" where difference produced the other to a universal subject (27). Here, difference—of race, gender, sexuality—is ontological yet connected to the social, where difference can still hurt (101). Difference *matters.* (Fig. 1.34)

Feminist and queer-of-color critiques have often turned to theories of intersectionality to frame the complex interplay of vectors of difference. Such a model can have drawbacks, sometimes defaulting into an additive lenticular logic of its own, tracking toward a kind of positivist accounting or tabulation of separate forms of identity (the kind of identity politics that Bogost collapses all of feminism into). At the end of a book that has sometimes deployed intersectional strategies, Jasbir Puar clearly queries the limits of intersectionality, noting the ways in which it can encase difference "within a structural container that simply wishes the messiness of identity into a formulaic grid" (212). She moves toward a theory of the assemblage but also notes that "intersectional identities and assemblages must remain as interlocutors in tension," for intersectional identities emerge out of attempts to still the "perpetual motion of assemblages" (213). Yet, as Puar notes, "Many feminists, new social movement theorists, critical race theorists, and queer studies scholars have argued that social change can occur only" from a precise position or location (212). Puar's eloquent conclusion comes down on the side of the assemblage's perpetual motion as she writes: "Assemblages allow us to attune to movements, intensities, emotions, energies, affectivities, and textures as they inhabit events, spatiality, and corporealities. Intersectionality privileges naming, visuality, epistemology, representation, and meaning, while assemblage underscores feeling, tactility, ontology, affect and information" (215). While there is much to learn from Puar's work, there is also perhaps too much movement in this model, where "there are no sides... the sides are forever shifting, crumpling, and multiplying" (218). One wants to think both fixity and movement, node and network, the break and the flow, the thing and the social.

Other recent investigations of intersectionality spin Puar's take to different possibilities, holding on to this framework as an important model for investigations of difference. Rod Ferguson argues that both the dominant embrace of intersectionality and the dominant critique seem to presume that the destination for the concept is "predetermined" (93). On the one hand, "the dominant affirmation... posits the category as the means to a positive and authentic knowledge" of oppressed peoples while the "dominant critique... falls along two axes," faulting the category for an "idealist outlook" or for falling prey to "an ideology of discreteness" (92). Both the affirmative and negative position see it as a "theory that is ideologically suited for positivist errands" (94), producing the "structural container," the modularity, of Puar's critique. Ferguson instead works through a number of recent theorizations of intersectionality to pull it away from its fixity, positivism, and discreteness, pushing it toward vitality, citing Fatima El-Tayeb's notion of "fuzzy edges" (97) and stressing the need for mutable arrangements and flexibility, especially in terms of social movement. These fuzzy edges push intersectionality in a new direction but also suggest the possibility for sides, if always fuzzy and temporary ones. A fuzzy edge might help us see, following Patricia Clough, that "race, class, sexuality, ethnicity, and gender are not simply matters of subject identity and surely not of authentic subject identity"; rather, they are "elements of a machinic assemblage" that "points to the direct links between microintensities and various territories—human bodies, cities, institutions, ideologies, and technologies." She argues that they might be "rethought in terms of... the interlacing of given materialities of the human body and cultural inscriptions" (135). To recall Moten, they are "operating at the nexus of the social and the ontological." Despite its overloaded signification and its tendency to tilt toward positivism, I find it valuable to reclaim the intersectional in an affective and materialist register, as both fuzzy edge and point, a break in the flow, a form of relay within a messy assemblage that might include many agencies, human and otherwise.[25] An intersection can offer a place and context to locate, if momentarily, Braidotti's posthuman subject. To retain and repurpose the intersectional also builds "direct links" to the history of social movement and activism and to feminist and queer-of-color critique, generative practices of creation and doing that exceed the theoretical even while in dialogue with it.

We might even imagine the intersectional along the lines of the cut, purposefully connecting the cut's potentiality to race, gender, sexuality, class, and nation. These markers of difference are not hallmarks of an authentic identity but interlacing forces within assemblages. Gender, race, sexuality, class, and disability might then be understood not as things that can simply be added on to our analyses (or to our metadata) after the fact, after the first principles, but instead as operating principles of a different order, always already coursing through discourse and matter. And, if we cannot study all discourse and all matter at once, Karen Barad offers up not the bracket or the unit but the agential cut as a method through which, "in the absence of a classical ontological condition of exteriority between observer and observed," we might enact "a local causal structure among 'components' of a phenomenon" ("Posthuman Performativity" 815). If bracketing tends to recapitulate the modularity of code, treating difference at the level either of content (i.e., as something on the screen or something that narrative is about) or of background (i.e., as part of the box that wraps around technology), the cut is fluid and mobile even as it recognizes the constitutive work of difference. As Barad notes, cuts are "part of the phenomena they help produce" (*Meeting the Universe* 145). Sarah Kember and Joanna Zylinska have highlighted the dual ontological and ethical dimensions of Barad's agential cut, observing that the cut is a "causal procedure that performs the division of the world into entities, but it is also an act of decision" (82). That is, where and how we focus matters. The cut also produces intersections, if temporary ones. By thinking of the cut in relation to intersectionality, we move it more forcefully toward ways of theorizing difference. This concept of an intersectional cut resonates (if unevenly and imprecisely) with a number of other feminist conceptual paradigms, including Katie King's reenactments, Chantal Mouffe's articulations, Chela Sandoval's differential consciousness, micha cárdenas's shift and stitch, even Jane Bennett's vital materiality. While the various theoretical models catalogued here are as different as they are alike, they all offer ways to understand relations between and beyond object and subject, discourse and matter, and identity and difference. Their joining here is meant to be generative and productive even if the theorists themselves might not appreciate this mingling. The notion of the intersectional cut also links directly to the work in our lab and to the technological design and implementation of the digital platform Scalar, as I explore further in this book's second essay. (Fig. 1.35)

In this mapping, I am less interested in producing a "master" theory (preferring instead the "modest theory" of Nigel Thrift) and more interested in how one models (in many senses of the word) forms of practice that embrace yet exceed theory. Interestingly, many of the authors referred to in this whirlwind survey express a similar interest. For example, Bennett writes, "We need not only to invent or re-invoke concepts like... actant, assemblage... and the like but also to devise new procedures, technologies, and regimes of perception that enable us to consult non-humans more closely" (108). King's reenactments seek to move scholars toward transdisciplinary practices and transmedia knowledge production, exploring expression and being across multiple types of media, while Puar calls for tactile knowledge. Braidotti asks, "How does the posthuman affect the practice of the humanities today?" (3).

Her answer is largely abstract, but it need not be. She wants
theory to be generative and not only negative (5), reclaiming
the potential for theory after Latour and an antitheoretical
turn within the humanities. She seeks "a strong critical and an
equally strong creative function" (190), returning the "active"
to "activism" (11). She hopes to "empower the pursuit of alternative schemes" (12) and calls for "combining critique with
creative figurations" (163) and praxis (92). Her book vibrates
with such calls, as does the writing of Bennett and others, yet
the work stays quite conceptual, tilting toward its own abstractions even while explicating other ways of being and knowing
that might entangle the scholar more thoroughly with matter.
All these scholars understand that we are profoundly shaped
by technology, caught up in assemblages that destabilize an
easy belief in human exceptionalism. One senses that they also
recognize that, as feminists and scholars of difference, we
might also shape technology in weird and wonderful ways.
The work often stops short of articulating *how* we might do so,

1.35 micha
cárdenas's
concept of the
stitch emerged
from her work
with electronic
garments but
has expanded to
become a possible
operation for the
trans movement.
Image from
"Autonets."

calling for practice and creativity, but never quite inhabiting terrains of making. Might an engagement with technological practice help enact this dual commitment to politics and to matter in ways that complement or even exceed the force of critical theory? Ian Bogost offers us not only a *concept* of carpentry or an enthusiasm for it, but also an account of his own practices of making. He speaks to the ways in which making might inform theory, working in recursive loops, and also notes that making is both hard and undervalued within the academy (92–100). On these points, we agree. (Fig. 1.36)

Here, of course, we are drawn back into an interesting relation to the digital humanities. If I opened this essay by citing numerous calls for DH to explicitly embrace theory and criticality, now we have feminists calling for theory to turn to practice, from creativity to activism and other modes of praxis. This is an intersectional cut of real interest. What might emerge in this joining? While they do not operate directly under the banner of DH, we see glimpses of feminist making in the work of Sarah Kember and Joanna Zylinska, who turn to both fiction and the photograph as vital forms of feminist endeavor, creative matterings that might make feminism differently. Anne Balsamo's *Designing Culture* traces over two decades of creative practice that merges feminist insight with the technological imaginary. Her recent work with Alexandra Ju-

1.36 Bogost undertakes a variety of work that might be understood as carpentry, including the project *A Slow Year*.

# signal/noise
collected student works from a feminist docc

hasz and many, many others on the FemTechNet coalition likewise models feminist making, building a massive and shifting assemblage that might challenge the instrumental force of the Massive Open Online Courses (MOOC) within the corporate university. These are vital models for digital media studies, DH, and feminism, as they operate at the pressure point between theory and practice in lively and generative ways. Other feminist scholars offer models of how such practice-based work might unfold. At the risk of inserting even more names into this already dense survey, I offer here a feminist litany rather than a Latourian one: Susan Brown, micha cárdenas, Kim Christen, Anne Cong-Huyen, Sharon Daniel, Cathy Davidson, Joanna Drucker, Amy Earhart, Kathleen Fitzpatrick, Mary Flanagan, Julia Flanders, Marsha Kinder, Lauren Klein, Virginia Kuhn, Elizabeth Losh, Bethany Nowviskie, Veronica Paredes, Amanda Phillips, Miriam Posner, Margaret Rhee, Susana Ruiz, Laila Shereen Sakr, Martha Nell Smith, Jacqueline Wernimont, and Laura Wexler.[26] (Fig. 1.37)

Participants in both the #DHPoco and the Lambda forums, and in the digital humanities more generally, call on humanities scholars to learn to code or, at the very least, to acquire advanced technological literacies. I agree, but I would also issue a reciprocal call for coding humanists (and perhaps

1.37 The FemTechNet collective has offered the Distributed Open Collaborative Course (DOCC) as a grassroots alternative to the model of the Massive Open Online Course (MOOC). The DOCC is a robust assemblage for feminist research and praxis. The group is publishing student work produced for the DOCC in *Signal/Noise*, an online publication.

engineering students everywhere) to engage feminist material-ism as well as critical race theory, queer-of-color critique, and related theorizations of difference. What implications does this have for the digital humanities? Alan Liu maintains that "the appropriate, unique contribution that the digital humanities can make to cultural criticism at the present time is to use the tools, paradigms, and concepts of digital technologies to help rethink the idea of instrumentality" (501). If a core activity of the digital humanities has been the building of tools, we should design our tools differently, in a mode that explicitly engages power and difference from the get-go, laying bare our theoretical allegiances and exploring the intra-actions of cul-ture and matter.

We will need to continue to examine with rigor and de-tail the degree to which dominant forms of computation—what David Golumbia has aptly called "the cultural logic of computation" in his update of Frankfurt School pessimism for the twenty-first century—continue to respond to shifting ra-cial and cultural formations. Might emerging modes of com-putation like cloud computing or NoSQL databases be read as symptoms and drivers of our "postracial" moment, refracting in some way national anxieties (or hopes?) about a decreasing-ly "white" America and a diffusion of difference? We should also remain alert to how contemporary techno-racial forma-tions infect privileged ways of knowing in the academy. Though both the tales of C. P. Snow circa 1959 and the Sokal science wars of the 1990s sustain the myth that science and the humanities operate in distinct realms of knowing, powerful operating systems have surged beneath the surface of what and how we know in the academy for well over half a decade. It would be foolish of us to believe that these operating sys-tems—in the above examples, best categorized by UNIX and its many close siblings as well as by the relational database—do not at least partially overdetermine the very critiques we imagine that we are performing today.

We must better understand the machines and networks that continue to powerfully shape our lives in ways that we are often ill-equipped to deal with as media and humanities scholars. This necessarily involves more than simply studying our screens and the images that dance across them, moving beyond studies of screen representations and the rhetorics of visuality. We might read representations seeking symptoms of information capital's fault lines and successes, but we cannot read the logics of these systems and networks solely at the level of our screens. Capital is now fully organized under the sign of modularity. It operates by means of the algorithm and the database, simulation and processing. Our screens are often cover stories, disguising deeply divided forms of both machine and human labor. We focus exclusively on them increasingly to our peril.

Scholars in the digital humanities and in the emerging fields of software or platform studies are taking up the challenge of understanding how computational systems developed and operate. We must insist, however, that these fields not replay the formalist and structuralist tendencies of new media theory circa 1998. The digital humanities and code studies should also take up the questions of culture, power, and meaning that animate so many scholars of race in fields such as the "new" American Studies. Likewise, scholars of race should analyze, use, and produce digital forms and not assume that to engage the digital directly is simply to be complicit with the forces of capitalism. The lack of intellectual generosity across our fields and departments only reinforces the "divide and conquer" mentality that the most dangerous aspects of modularity underwrite. We must develop common languages that link the study of code and culture. We must historicize and politicize code studies. And, because digital media were born as much of the Civil Rights era as of the Cold War era (and of course these eras are one and the same), our investigations must incorporate race from the outset, understanding and theorizing its function as a "ghost in the digital machine."

This does not mean that we should simply "add" race to our analysis in a modular way, neatly tacking it on or building digital archives of "racial" material, but that we must understand and theorize the deep imbrications of race and digital technology even when our objects of analysis (say, UNIX or search engines) seem not to "be about" race at all. This will not be easy. In the writing of this essay, the logic of modularity continually threatened to take hold, leading me into detailed explorations of pipe structures in UNIX, departmental structures in the university, and theories of new materialisms, taking me far from the contours of race at midcentury or in the present. It is hard work to hold race and computation together *in a systemic or relational manner,* just as it is difficult to join theory to practice, but feminism offers rich models to engage and expand in this vital endeavor.

# Introducing *Vectors*

The Editorial Statement for *Vectors* is itself multimodal, designed in collaboration with Raegan Kelly. As Steve Anderson and I worked with Raegan on the piece, we talked a great deal about our goals for it. We knew we wanted it to be a digital project. We also had other ideas about what it might achieve. In an e-mail to Raegan, we noted some of what we envisioned, including such remarks as "We'd like some kind of sense of progression, accumulation, or transformation to emerge from the user's experience rather than just (obviously) the clicking on 40 different words," and "The Editorial Statement is an opportunity to introduce the site and begin teaching visitors how to explore it." Raegan suggested that the piece might reveal its operations in its use, an idea we embraced. The process of creating the piece began with conversations about goals and potential structures and then moved to Steve and my mapping out the various terms included in the piece using stacks of notecards on my sunroom floor. We continued in iterative conversations with Raegan. The whole undertaking was especially valuable for our insights into the *Vectors* workflow, as it afforded Steve and me a chance to experience the collaborative design process from the point of view of authors rather than editors. (Fig. W1.1)

W1.1

In introducing the piece, Steve and I wrote:

It seems fitting that the editorial statement for a multimedia journal should itself be enacted in a dynamic form. Yet text continues in many ways to provide us with the means for our clearest form of expression. Thus, we commend this editorial statement to you as a hybrid introduction and metaphor for beginning to experience some of the ideas and pathways that weave their way throughout *Vectors*. This editorial "statement" attempts in part to represent the multiple collaborations and conflicts that take place in interactive and computational media, highlighting not only the virtual dialogue between creator and producer, but also the tenuous alliance of human and machine intelligence. To launch the statement, simply click the image above.

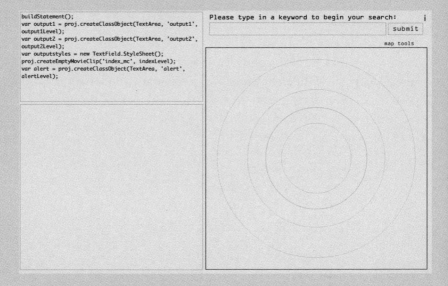

```
buildStatement();
var output1 = proj.createClassObject(TextArea, 'output1',
output1Level);
var output2 = proj.createClassObject(TextArea, 'output2',
output2Level);
var outputstyles = new TextField.StyleSheet();
proj.createEmptyMovieClip('index_mc', indexLevel);
var alert = proj.createClassObject(TextArea, 'alert',
alertLevel);
```

Please type in a keyword to begin your search:

submit

map tools

**W1.2 The Editorial Statement when first opened. The reader is not given many clues about what type of keyword to enter in the search box.**

One of the primary and ongoing tensions in an academic multimedia journal is the question of how to deal with text. This is not a new question nor is it one that is peculiar to electronic publishing. One of the ways of dealing with text in a screen-based vernacular is to think of it as an instance of images. Usually this is marked by the shift from plain text to typography, which broadens the expressive palette to include fonts, layout, color, composition, contrast, opacity, dynamism, etc. Instead of treating text as images, we decided to explore—through our collaboration with *Vectors* Creative Director Raegan Kelly— what happens when we treat written text as an instance of code— more rather than less like the way the computer understands it.

The statement thus became a three-way conversation between us, Raegan, and the computer, seeking to create an environment where the words that we wrote

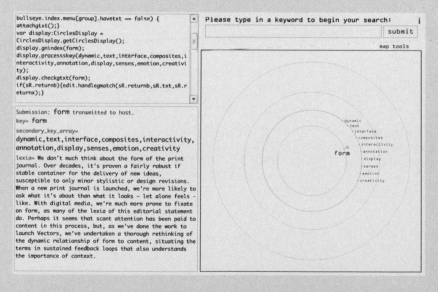

```
bullseye.index.menu[group].havetxt == false) {
attachgtxt();}
var display:CirclesDisplay =
CirclesDisplay.getCirclesDisplay();
display.gnindex(form);
display.processskey(dynamic,text,interface,composites,i
nteractivity,annotation,display,senses,emotion,creativi
ty);
display.checkgtxt(form);
if(sR.returnb){edit.handlegmatch(sR.returnb,sR.txt,sR.r
eturnx);}}
```

```
Submission: form transmitted to host.
key= form
secondary_key_array=
dynamic,text,interface,composites,interactivity,
annotation,display,senses,emotion,creativity
lexia= We don't much think about the form of the print
journal. Over decades, it's proven a fairly robust if
stable container for the delivery of new ideas,
susceptible to only minor stylistic or design revisions.
When a new print journal is launched, we're more likely to
ask what it's about than what it looks - let alone feels -
like. With digital media, we're much more prone to fixate
on form, as many of the lexia of this editorial statement
do. Perhaps it seems that scant attention has been paid to
content in this process, but, as we've done the work to
launch Vectors, we've undertaken a thorough rethinking of
the dynamic relationship of form to content, situating the
terms in sustained feedback loops that also understands
the importance of context.
```

Please type in a keyword to begin your search:       i

[          ] submit

map tools

```
                                    dynamic
                                      text
                                       interface
                                        composites
                                         interactivity
                        form            annotation
                                         display
                                        senses
                                       emotion
                                      creativity
```

**W1.3** The Editorial Statement after the reader has submitted the word *form*. This query returned a lexia for the word, one of the organizing ideas for the piece. *Form* is associated with an array of secondary terms, including *dynamic, text, composites,* and *emotion.* Mousing over these terms reveals the code generating that action. Clicking one of these secondary terms reveals a series of associated terms.

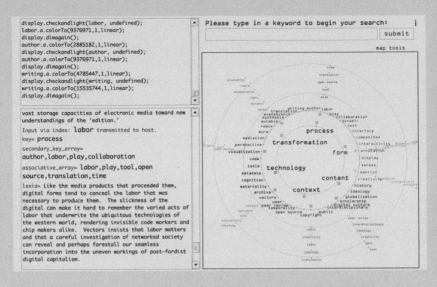

**W1.4** As the Editorial Statement is engaged by the persistent reader, the various terms that Steve and I framed as central to the journal's mission are slowly revealed. Our explication of each term appears in the box on the lower left. The form of the piece and the attention it requires serve to educate the reader about the modes of attention demanded by the journal's experimental aesthetics.

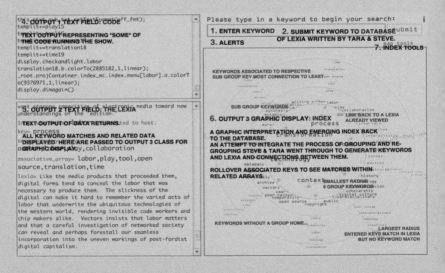

**W1.5** The small "i" in the upper right corner provided the reader with an overview of the Editorial Statement's function and design.

were not necessarily privileged over Raegan's programming or the output generated by the computer. The three output windows thus reflect the parallel "thought" processes of writer, designer, and processor. Finally, the system requires user collaboration in the form of keyword input and selection, patience, curiosity and a willingness to assemble meaning from diverse forms of human- and computer-generated lexia. We believe it is in this interplay of thinly veneered binary arrays that some of the most suggestive potentials of allographic composition may be found.
(Figs. W1.2 / W1.3 / W1.4 /W1.5)

# CHAPTER 2

# Assembling Scholarship: From *Vectors* to Scalar

------------------------------------------------

## On Process

In the late 1990s, soon after arriving at the University of Southern California, I was a faculty fellow at USC's Institute for Multimedia Literacy (IML), a space deeply engaged in fostering multimedia expression in pedagogical practice. Faculty who taught in the program attended a short digital boot camp in the summer and then worked closely with teaching assistants from USC's School of Cinematic Arts to implement multimedia projects in the classroom. Importantly, the classes were subject-based offerings that integrated multimodal expression, not classes focused on simply learning tools or digital authoring programs. Eventually, IML launched a multimedia honors program and then, over the course of a decade, evolved into the cinema school's present-day Media Arts + Practice (MAP) Division. Explorations in digital production were deeply integrated into scholarly content and context. IML and now MAP work with classrooms and students from across the curriculum, so it is not strictly a "humanities" endeavor. IML's vision was at once broader (welcoming all of campus) and more specific (with a focus on the expressive capacities of digital media, which was appropriate to its film school setting.) Also, in the late 1990s, I worked side by side with Marsha Kinder, Alison Trope, and others on the Interactive Frictions conference and exhibit, a wide-ranging event that sought to bring digital production, the arts, and media theory into deep dialogue.[1] In the program copy we observed: "Interactive narrative did not begin in cyberspace. It has deep, tangled roots in an array of earlier forms. But the new electronic media provoke us to reconceptualize these two concepts—narrative and interactivity—their distinctive functions and pleasures, and their complex relations with history and subjectivity. These are the starting premises of this conference, which we hope will generate new, productive frictions in theory and practice across a wide range of cultural forms." Across these two experiences and in the subsequent Race in Digital Space events I co-organized at MIT and USC, I was afforded an opening to think about theory and practice together across pedagogy, scholarship, and artistic practice. In a discussion with Dean Elizabeth Daley around 2002, I lamented that the types of

Featured Speaker Sandy
Stone

Featured Speaker Marcos
Novak

Round Table with Katherine
Hayles

**2.1 / 2.2**
Website
documentation
of the Interactive
Frictions
Conference and
Exhibition.

**2.3**
The Labyrinth
Project,
directed by
Marsha Kinder,
offered an early
collaborative
model for the
productions
of database
narratives.

experiments emerging across these spaces were not easy to "locate" within the academy, particularly within the humanities. We decided to build such a space at USC, drawing inspiration both from the IML and from Marsha Kinder's groundbreaking Labyrinth Project, an endeavor that brought together designers and well-known artists like Pat O'Neill, John Rechy, and Nina Menkes to produce a series of imaginative "database documentaries" and "city symphonies."[2] Teaching at the IML and working on the conferences also led me to Steve Anderson, first as my teaching assistant and then as a close collaborator and friend as he became a postdoc and then a faculty colleague at USC. (Figs. 2.1 / 2.2 / 2.3)

Steve and I began planning for what would become the Vectors Lab in the fall of 2002 and in June 2003 hosted a gathering of scholars to help us in our thinking. The participants included Anne Balsamo, Stephanie Barish, Nick Gessler, David Theo Goldberg, Herman Gray, John Hartley, Peter Lyman, Hideo Mabuchi, Toby Miller, Viet Nguyen, Simon Penny, Barrie Thorne, Jeffrey Schnapp, Vibeke Sorenson, Sharon Traweek, Holly Willis, and Kathy Woodward. The conversation was wide-ranging but also generative (see the box titled "Excerpts from the *Vectors* Planning Session") and helped shape the directions our project would take. The first work of the lab would be on the journal *Vectors*.

- - - - - - - - - - - - - - - - - - - - - - - - - - - - - - - - - - - - - - - - - -

Excerpts from the *Vectors* Planning Session

From Tara McPherson's opening remarks:
Some of these examples suggest models for encouraging response, or online community; others use multiple media forms, as well as nonlinear branching structures, structures

that will help us rethink the linearity of (particularly humanities-based) scholarship and research. They also hint at the power of simulation, of processing, of visualization to take us in different directions. They suggest models for reworking the concept of the "issue," the space-time of the journal, and what databases might mean in relation to research and humanities that take us beyond the online journal as a series of text-centric pages. They also mediate between theory and practice in interesting ways, blurring the distinction between the two in productive and provocative dimensions. Such examples encourage us to get scholars and technologists working together and to really focus on process.

There are interesting questions to ask here: What does "tactility" mean for scholarship? How might "gesture" influence digital scholarship? What does "immersion" mean in these spaces? What does modeling do for the audience's experience of knowledge, and how do you interact with such knowledge? What does "interactivity" mean in the context of scholarly work? I'm not sure most scholars are ready for interactivity in their research outcomes. What does it mean to build interactivity into our scholarly modes and outputs? Finally, is it possible to forecast five, ten, fifty, or a hundred years into the future of electronic publishing, especially recognizing the brief moment in time the web now represents?

Selected participant comments:

Sharon Traweek: Some of us, looking at the history of making knowledge and the sciences over the last fifty years, think that, yes, there's very much something new in the world going on, new ways of making knowledge.

Toby Miller: One of the things that I'd like the journal to consider is "cybertarianism", not something I like very much, a kind of libertarianism that says that with new forms of technology will emerge new freedoms.

Herman Gray: Information technologies must be seen in the wake of various kinds of global developments. It's important that one of the social implications of the journal is to produce a kind of counternarrative to terror and surveillance, a way of defining the use of new technologies and new information, particularly given that so much of the globe's populations are subjected to Western surveillance and regulation.

Nick Gessler: I wonder about the definition of "literacy," and what people have in mind. . . . There's another dimension of understanding when someone can look at a finished product and say, "I know how that's put together."

Anne Balsamo: I would want it to be a kind of "journal of inspiration." . . . I would want it to be someplace where you would go each time to see something unusual, so that it would resist formula at every turn, and that it would be provocative.

David Theo Goldberg: I think a journal like this would be interesting in providing a forum, a space, a stage, a performance, a set of possibilities, to bring together, under one roof, cutting-edge kind of work. Our goal should be to encourage experimentation at the interface of those areas. One of the possibilities that multimedia technologies provide is to identify or to enable the identification of new and different relationalities between things, layerings of things, connectivities that you don't find in text-based or text-driven kinds of consideration.

Toby Miller: It seems to me one of the really important things about knowledge is to acknowledge that it's embedded it's embedded in a place, embedded in a time. This is a moment when we're interested in links between art, technology, social science, and science in ways that haven't been so true for about a century or so.

Kathy Woodward: Some of the subjects I would want to see addressed would be things like theories of emergence and substantiations of emergence. . . . Really, what it seems that we're talking about is a series of some kind. It's a series.

Jeffrey Schnapp: I think that some kind of model of "located knowledge" or "embodied knowledge" needs to be inserted into the discussion. . . . I think one of the answers has to do with models of collaboration and teamwork.

— — — — — — — — — — — — — — — — — — — — — — — — — — — — — — — — — — — — —

From the beginning, *Vectors* was conceived as a space for collaborative aesthetic experimentation coupled with a strong allegiance to open-access publishing. At the outset we were thinking less in terms of the archival and TEI work being undertaken at existing "technology and humanities" centers like CHNM or MITH and more in terms of screen languages and the expressive capacities of media and interface design. Our commitment was to moving beyond the "text with pictures" format of much of the online publishing that existed at the time while also challenging certain tenets of "transparent" web design that were emerging from corporate spaces. (Figs. 2.4 / 2.5) We wanted to create scholarship that could not exist in print and located our research at the intersections of the humanities and the arts, even as we worked with technological systems. We were operating in tracks parallel to those of much work being done in the "computational" humanities, although these tracks would increasingly converge over the next decade. Our initial process of production was quite different from that of journals that receive largely "finished" articles ready for review. Although this has very recently begun to shift, at the time few humanities scholars were able to produce multimodal work on

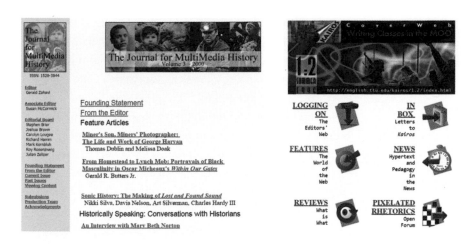

their own. Joining the models of IML and Labyrinth in a new mix, we developed a fellowship model in order to build a rich space for collaboration. (Even in the early days of *Vectors,* we did accept submissions outside our fellowship model, works that were peer-reviewed in a more traditional fashion, and also aggregated such work from the existing web, in an early model of journal-by-curation.) Applications were invited on the themes of "Evidence" and "Mobility." Noting that we were interested in fellows who valued collaboration and who were producing original scholarship within their fields, the call for applications included the following:

> We are seeking project proposals that creatively address issues related to the first two themes of Evidence and Mobility. While the format of the journal is meant to explore innovative forms of multimedia scholarship, we are not necessarily looking for projects that are *about* new media. Rather, we are interested in the various ways that new media suggest a transformation of scholarship, art and communication practices and their relevance to everyday

2.4 The *Journal of MultiMedia History,* launched in 1998, was an early attempt at an open-access journal that featured images and clips alongside text.

2.5 *Kairos,* a journal in the fields of composition and rhetoric, was a very early effort to explore the possibilities of HTML for online publishing. It was launched in 1996.

life in an unevenly mediated world.

Applicants are encouraged to think beyond the computer screen to consider possibilities created by the proliferation of wireless technology, handheld devices, alternative exhibition venues, etc. . . . Projects may translate existing scholarly work or be entirely conceived for new media. We are particularly interested in work that re-imagines the role of the user and seeks to reach broader publics while creatively exploring the value of collaboration and interactivity.

Scholars were also asked to detail *why* digital media was important for the project they envisioned, even if they had no clear idea of how this might be realized. We hosted our first group of fellows in the summer of 2004 for what soon became known as *Vectors* camp, an event we continued over the next three summers, before expanding into a monthlong institute by means of NEH funding for three additional summers. In that first summer, we were lucky enough to have hired our co-creative directors, Erik Loyer and Raegan Kelly. Finding such talented artists to join our tiny team was no small feat. Their capacity for intellectual generosity and creative collaboration set the stage for all the work that followed. The weeklong workshop was exhilarating and exhausting all at once. We asked a good deal of the fellows, particularly in that first summer, when the outcome of our shared labor was still a projection on a horizon not yet reached. During the workshop each fellow had an intensive design meeting with one designer (Raegan or Erik) and one editor (Steve or me). Those first meetings proved to be an important part of our work process and helped create a shared language to scaffold the collaborations that would later unfold. Over time, we refined a set of questions for use in these meetings (and in our call for applications) that helped guide and shape a necessarily free-flowing conversation.

---

Early Guidelines Used by the Editors and Designers in *Vectors* Design Meetings with Fellows

Basic parameters/components of the individual design meetings:

- conceptual issues: scholarship (translated from print or born digital, key arguments)
- design concepts (overall look and feel; experience desired; possible models)
- how do conceptual and design concepts interrelate
- metadata: also keywords for the Vector Space
- interactive and multimodal elements: how they function and integrate in the project
- modes of authorship + reception: key functions of project: archival, experiential, argumentative, explorational, immersive, spatial
- existing resources (images, clips, articles, etc.)
- logistical issues: rough production schedule, workflow, modes of collaboration, and team delegation
- technical issues: software-hardware, database needs, hosting location, formats and compatibility, development resources
- really force issue of *Vectors*-specific outcome: what will be published?

---

Once the workshop ended, scholars, designers, and editors would work together long-distance by means of phone and screen (before the days of Skype), orchestrating deep collaborations that typically lasted three to six months, squeezed in around the scholars' day-to-day lives. The editors were usually involved most heavily first early in the process, helping build productive alliances between the fellow and his or her design partner and translating between the languages of theory and of practice, and then near the completion of each piece as we moved to publication. These partnerships pushed back against the siloed knowledges of the university, building a space for shared practice across very different skill sets. (One might understand the contemporary university to be partitioned into isolated departments in a manner that mimics the modularity of the database; this structure makes meaningful "joins" across different methodologies quite difficult.) Hence, we were building assemblages that were more than simply "interdisciplinary"; we were interested in putting diverse ways of seeing and knowing in productive tension, placing the production of theoretically inflected scholarship into new modes of alliance, generating intersections across and among differences and in relation to computation. In distinction to the "More Hack, Less Yack" motto emerging from DH, Erik Loyer once described our process as "Start Wordy. End Nerdy." This process valued theory and critique, but we found that it was helpful for our workflow to begin generatively, withholding intensive critique early in the collaborations. Initial design meetings began with a process of show and tell, in which scholars described their nascent project ideas and shared a variety of materials, including images, video, maps, and the like, that might serve as evidence within their work or as inspiration for the design process. As scholar, editor, designer, and technology specialist formed working relations and productive entanglements, we aimed to generate a field of possibility before turning to critique. Certainly, critique became essential as the process moved along, but it was rarely the best place to start. Jane Bennett has argued that, faced with the challenges of contemporary life, we will "require not only a vigilant critique… but also positive, even utopian alternatives" (xv). One route toward such alternatives can occur in shared spaces of making and collaboration, where diverse skill sets can be brought into productive play. The process of collaborative making is, of course, not inherently utopian, but it can engage registers of knowing and being that are different from those activated by critique, especially when undertaken in a carefully calibrated environment. Our *Vectors* fellows came to find their relationships to their research materials and their writing reconfigured through the collaborative design process, engaging in a form of Puar's tactile knowledge.

# The Look + Feel of *Vectors*

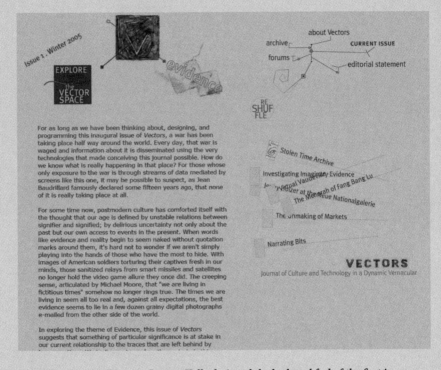

Issue 1 · Winter 2005

EXPLORE the VECTOR SPACE

evidence

For as long as we have been thinking about, designing, and programming this inaugural issue of *Vectors*, a war has been taking place half way around the world. Every day, that war is waged and information about it is disseminated using the very technologies that made conceiving this journal possible. How do we know what is really happening in that place? For those whose only exposure to the war is through streams of data mediated by screens like this one, it may be possible to suspect, as Jean Baudrillard famously declared some fifteen years ago, that none of it is really taking place at all.

For some time now, postmodern culture has comforted itself with the thought that our age is defined by unstable relations between signifier and signified; by delirious uncertainty not only about the past but our own access to events in the present. When words like evidence and reality begin to seem naked without quotation marks around them, it's hard not to wonder if we aren't simply playing into the hands of those who have the most to hide. With images of American soldiers torturing their captives fresh in our minds, those sanitized relays from smart missiles and satellites no longer hold the video game allure they once did. The creeping sense, articulated by Michael Moore, that "we are living in fictitious times" somehow no longer rings true. The times we are living in seem all too real and, against all expectations, the best evidence seems to lie in a few dozen grainy digital photographs e-mailed from the other side of the world.

In exploring the theme of Evidence, this issue of *Vectors* suggests that something of particular significance is at stake in our current relationship to the traces that are left behind by

about Vectors

archive
forums

CURRENT ISSUE

editorial statement

RE SHUF FLE

Stolen Time Archive

Investigating Imaginary Evidence

Joy... Welzer at th... wah of Fang Bang Lu

The Wie Neue Nationalgalerie

The unmaking of Markets

Narrating Bits

**VECTORS**
Journal of Culture and Technology in a Dynamic Vernacular

**W2.1** Co-Creative Director Raegan Kelly designed the look and feel of the first issue on the theme of "Evidence." The design deliberately referred to the work of the hand and the hand-drawn, particularly in the "V" logo, to counter a certain gridded slickness in commercial web design at the time. The table of contents for the issue is a jumble of titles in orange along the right of the image, recalling pickup sticks. Mousing over the small rectangles highlighted the project title, and hitting the Reshuffle button rearranged the titles in a new flow. The random structure of the table of contents was meant to underscore the fact that the linear ordering of a print journal's contents was no longer necessary in the digital realm.

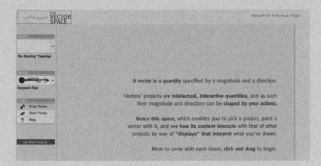

W2.2  Early issues of *Vectors* also featured the Vector Space, designed by Erik Loyer. The Vector Space was a playful way to interact with various metadata associated with each project.

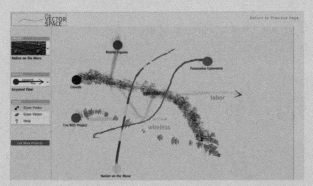

W2.3  The Vector Space allowed users to explore keywords or "textracts" associated with various projects and to note intersections between projects within or across issues. Authors could customize the look and feel of the vector representing their project. This space represented a very early way in which we were thinking through the possibility of intersectional cuts. Though the Vector Space felt innovative in 2005, long before the ubiquity of tag clouds, it later came to feel less relevant and was discontinued with the "Memory" issue in 2012.

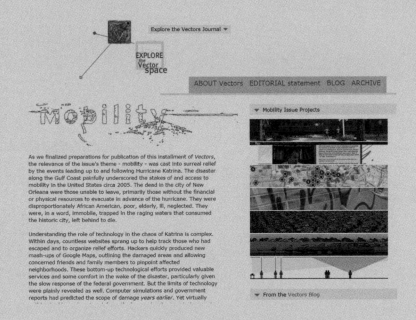

W2.4  Issue 2, on "Mobility," introduced a slightly more streamlined design for the journal, including a more blocklike table of contents. Here each project is represented by an image; mousing over an image reveals the project's title and author. Highlighting images from each project in this way served to underscore the visual and multimodal nature of the journal. Each time the issue page is loaded, the table of contents rearranges, so there is still no set order to the projects.

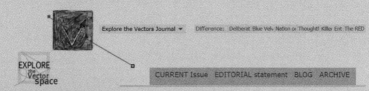

EXPLORE
the
Vector
space

CURRENT Issue   EDITORIAL statement   BLOG   ARCHIVE

**Programmed Visions**
By Wendy Hui Kyong Chun
Design by Raegan Kelly

Editor's Introduction

The opening screen of "Programmed Visions" promises its users an archive, and an archive it delivers. But this archive will most likely defy and resist any predetermined notion of the archive you bring with you to the project. The digitization initiatives that drive so much of contemporary online culture -- from Google Books to our local universities -- envision the virtual archive as a kind of seamless information machine bringing the riches of the world to a screen near you with a quick tap of the finger. Such archives privilege transparency, accessibility, standardization, interoperability, and ease of use, lofty goals all, and quite useful when confronted with reams of data. But Wendy Chun and Reagan Kelly want us to think the archive differently. As with several other projects in this issue of *Vectors*, the piece urges you to shift your line of vision and to think about the larger stakes our frenzy of digitization might likely conceal.

The piece begins by locating race as an archive and also as a potential origin for all archives, "as justifying the desire for an order and an origin." As the user begins to navigate, traditional expectations of the cursor's effect are frustrated and denied. Text shifts and emerges via an internal logic that confounds our epistemophilic desires. Historical texts, scientific treatises, legal documents, excerpts of theory, and snippets of fiction all collide. Quotes are cut off, sources are unclear, everything's a bit opaque and chaotic: all in all an archivist's nightmare. Clicking the blue triangle reveals a map of sorts, but there is no easy transit from this overlay to the

**Editor's Introduction**
**Author's Statement**
**Designer's Statement**
**View Peer Response + Discuss**
**Project Credits**

**VIEW PROJECT**

**Project Technologies**
Technical Feedback
Report technical issues to developers. Please include platform and browser version.

Plug-in(s) you will need to view this project:

Flash 9 Plug-in  Browser application providing fluid vector-based graphics and interface

Development and data handling applications:

CSS  2  CSS is short for Cascading Style Sheets, the standard markup for changing the layout, colors, and other visible characteristics of a Web page.

MySQL 5.0  Open-source relational database

PHP 5.0.4  PHP Hypertext Preprocessor

XML  Extensible Markup Language

**VECTORS**
Journal of Culture and Technology in a Dynamic Vernacular

**W2.5**  Each project has its own landing page that includes an editorial introduction, author's and designer's statements, a public peer response, and readers' comments. Later issues also included an interactive index that later served as an early prototype for visualizations in Scalar.

Despite this evocation of play, the process was not without its frictions. When our work on the first issue got under way following the 2004 summer camp, we came to realize that several of the projects and the journal itself would require more back-end support than we had initially realized. After a difficult search, we hired Craig Dietrich, who worked for us long-distance through the production of the first issue late in the fall of 2004. We first met him in person when we launched the inaugural issue of *Vectors* at Los Angeles' Museum of Contemporary Art in early 2005. As we settled into our working rhythms those first few years, we noticed that many scholars would sometimes experience the process of collaboration as a deskilling, if only at particular moments. Traditional scholarly talents for humanists—the crafting of long-form prose, a solitary formulation of ideas, the privileging of text—were no longer the sole terrain of working. This discomfort would typically surface most palpably when we asked scholars to begin working directly with our database software. I'll return to this software shortly, but, after the first issue, this middleware, built by Dietrich, created a shared infrastructure for the journal that meant each project need not be entirely crafted as a one-off. This back-end software allowed the data structures for each project to be generated more quickly while still permitting custom work on the front end. As the design process unfolded, scholars were asked to start working with the software before the outputs of their labor could be seen at the front end. For the front end to be generated, the scholars had to begin to populate the database. This often meant "chunking" their writing in a manner that felt quite odd for humanities scholars used to producing long-form scholarship. They were encountering the modular logic of the database, and this often produced unease.[3] One of our commitments was to having scholars use this software themselves, as a way of entering into a

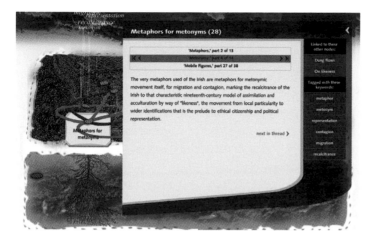

conversation with computational devices as well as the human interlocutors on our design and editorial team. We were building projects not *for* scholars but *with* scholars. This produced long-term gains but short-term tensions. The postcolonial and Irish studies scholar David Lloyd collaborated with Erik Loyer on the piece "Mobile Figures," a rhizomatic exploration of the figure of the Irish during the years of the famine of 1845–1851. Lloyd was working transmedially, as he was converting a long essay into a digital interactive project, producing a form of what we might now call transmedia scholarship.[4] Confronted by the modular demands of the database, he initially balked. He felt its chunked form was destroying the careful subordination of his prose and weakening his well-wrought linear chain of argument. For such an accomplished and beautiful writer, to be asked to think in a new form was disconcerting and was initially experienced as a loss. Lloyd pushed though this discomfort, however, and soon adapted to the database, even as Craig Dietrich and Erik Loyer used this experience to begin to rethink our database software. (Fig. 2.6)

Though *Vectors* projects were initially conceived as

2.6 David Lloyd's "Mobile Figures," designed by Erik Loyer.

experiments at the surface of the screen, at the level of interface they soon led us toward building tools and thinking about infrastructures. Following the experience with Lloyd and other fellows, we began to grapple with the database as an object to think with and to think against. Many of the scholars we worked with came to us with their own collections of evidence and objects that they wanted to animate and engage in new ways. We found that the constraints of much relational database software were not particularly well suited to the ways in which our fellows thought and worked, even as the database could also open up new possibilities. Humanities scholars involved in computation have debated the possibilities and limits of databases for both quantitative and qualitative scholarship for many years. For instance, William Thomas has traced the debates over relational database design for the field of computational history. He notes that the widespread availability and adoption of commercial database platforms in a "third wave" of historical computing had serious implications for the analysis of the "fuzzy" or "incomplete" data often at play in historical research. Alan Liu comes to similar conclusions in an elegant passage in *Local Transcendence,* referring to himself in the third person: "*Yet, the more he learned about the workings of databases, the more he woke to the fact that the great, digitally sharp massifs of detail they rendered only set off by contrast all the presence not there—whatever could not be cut up and cut down to fit the granular structures of databases, whatever could appear only as a ghost limned in the ceaseless froth of redundant or contradictory entries, overlapping dates, null values, and other database noise attesting to the pressure of the unstructured and unknown*" (240; emphasis in original). If Hayles has argued that relational databases cannot deal with the indeterminacy of narratives, neither were such databases designed to accommodate the ambiguity at play in much humanities scholarship. The database is not a neutral object. As Ken Price notes, "Argument is always there from the beginning in how those constructing a database choose to categorize information—the initial understanding of the materials governs how more fine-grained views will appear because of the way the objects of attention are shaped by divisions and subdivisions within the database." In this way, the database is similar to the archive, functioning in fundamental ways to shape what can be seen or enunciated. If for Jacques Derrida "effective democratization can always be measured by... the participation in and access to the archive, its constitution, and its interpretation" (4), the same might be said today of the database. If our attentions as humanities scholars have long been attuned to the archive, we must now also engage the database even with and because of its limits.

There is no natural fit between the logic of the relational database and the interpretative methodologies favored by many humanities scholars. Productive tensions emerge, however, when humanities scholars turn their attention to the database. As Stephen Ramsay reminds us, "A number of fascinating problems and intellectual opportunities lurk beneath" the seemingly practical issues of database design (177). I would argue that no one is now better poised to inform and shape technological development than scholars who have devoted years to analyzing text, to interpreting images, and to thinking through complex questions of the emotions, of embodiment, of representation, and of power. We might help technology better handle the complexity of our interpretative frameworks. We can participate in designing technological systems that better suit our needs and modes of analysis, joining critique and creative "carpentry." Along the way, we will come to understand better how our machines are also redesigning us.

Price's observation that an "argument is always there from the beginning" in database design points toward the difficulties our team encountered when working with relational databases. Once created, relational databases are not easy to adapt. They work best when a data model has been predetermined and then implemented in a particular database design. A relational database is composed of a group of tables, made up of columns and rows. Most relational databases have only one value per cell (where a column and row intersect); in this design pattern, one-to-one relationships within a table are privileged, although they are not the only possibility. Data structures are "normalized" to ensure data consistency and to reduce duplication, but this rigid, modular structuring also makes addressing ambiguity very difficult. When a database is queried through SQL (Structured Query Language), the tables are "joined," usually by means of criteria defined in the table relationship columns. I will not go deeply into the technical nature of relational databases here (Alan Liu does so very nicely in *Local Transcendence*), but, for our purpose, it is helpful to note that the data model is defined in advance through a strongly typed schema. This produces constraints to maintain "data integrity." A database is not an assemblage in a feminist materialist sense. It more closely (if not entirely) resembles a grid, that technology of modernism that Rosalind Krauss has called "a staircase to the universal" (52). For early *Vectors* projects, designers would work with the scholar and editor to determine a project plan, zeroing in on key concepts or themes that would drive the interface and interactivity, and then work with Dietrich to implement a database structure, but these structures were rarely adequate to the iterative research and design practice that followed. As the project took shape at the surface of the screen and in the iterative collaboration among designer, middleware tool, and scholar, the ini-

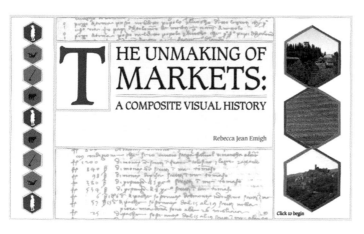

2.6a
The historian Rebecca Emigh commented on the *Vectors* design process with Eric Loyer in the Author's Statement to "The Unmaking of Markets," observing that "we worked on the design process in a completely iterative way: I had no idea what to write until I saw what Loyer had designed; he often needed to see my text to know what to design… In this process, Loyer's design has shaped the content and form of my argument just as much as my substantive argument informed the design decisions. Along the way, we delved into deep issues about evidence, method, style, and technology that became central to the piece itself."

tial categories or themes would often no longer suffice. We needed the database to behave more like a shifting and mutable assemblage open to wily partnerships with our scholars and designers. (Fig. 2.6a)

In response to this need, the *Vectors* team created the DBG (Database Backend Generator), a middleware tool built by Dietrich that allowed more flexibility in how scholars could iteratively work within our middleware, allowing them to modify the database and its tables more easily. The shape of the tool emerged from deep and close work with our fellows, and its construction began in summer 2005. In that process, Loyer and Kelly reflected on the iteration at the heart of their collaborations with scholars and articulated the need for a different kind of middleware. Loyer aimed to have the database work more like a sketchpad than a grid, noting in an early design document authored by our whole team that "a sketch is where visual ideas are worked out in concrete form; the light touch of its technique allows for flexibility, iteration and constructive revision. It is the 'reality check' for the artist, and a realm where visual ideas are refined until they are ready to be executed in more permanent forms. Similarly, an easy-to-use database authoring tool could function as a kind of intellectual sketch pad, allowing scholars to easily experiment with various ways of organizing their ideas until arriving at a structure that could serve as the foundation for future work." While the notion of the sketchpad is richer than the software we implemented, the DBG attempted to split the difference between off-the-shelf database packages and Loyer's vision of the sketchpad. (See below for a more technical description of the DBG.) The adjustments made to standard relational database middleware systems by the DBG were not revolutionary by any means, but, importantly, they emerged organically from our process and from our desires to nudge the normalizing structures of the database in new directions. They would also plant the seed for our future work on the authoring platform Scalar. We were after a database tool that could shift computational relations toward more intersectional forms, allowing iterative possibilities that would permit scholars to work with their materials in highly flexible ways. The DBG was our first pass at a technological platform that (to recall Braidotti) combined creative figuration with critique. Scholars could begin to build out a set of intersections between their research materials and their analyses, see those relations take shape at the level of interface design, and then shift and refine these relations in a more mutable manner than commercial database software typically allowed.

----

DBG version 3.3, circa 2006, combined four tables (the root table, a direct-relation table [top pull-down], a third-party table, and a relational table [bottom pull-down]) into one HTML output. Though the DBG helped make the

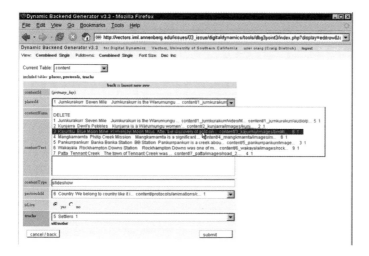

database more amenable to humanities scholarship, these figures also suggest that the middleware working environment was still perhaps a bit alien to most scholars. There were advantages to this type of engagement with the ma-

2.7 View 1: Table view.

2.8 View 2: Edit view (selected content from a second-party table).

chine by the scholar, but because working with the platform was difficult, a good deal of hand-holding was required. Our later work on Scalar would attempt to strike a different balance between working with databases and working with screen interfaces. (Figs. 2.7 / 2.8 / 2.9)

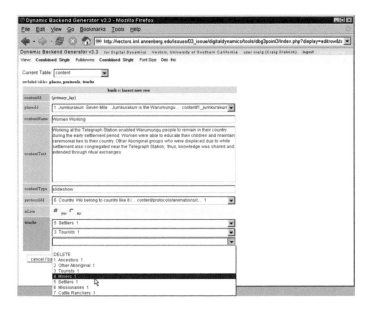

2.9  View 3:
Edit view
(selecting content
from a third-
party table).

# Making "Stolen Time"

The first *Vectors* project was "The Stolen Time Archive," a collaboration between the literary scholar Alice Gambrell and the designer Raegan Kelly. The Editors' Statement for the piece explains:

> As Alice Gambrell notes in her erudite "Author's Statement," *Stolen Time* is at once an archive and an argument, as it offers a powerful *argument* about the archive and exposes archival logics as always inherently ideological. Importantly, the piece *enacts* its argument, requiring its user to explore this virtual archive in order to access the argument constructed there via the user's own navigations. The argument is emergent, unfolding as the user becomes more and more immersed in the piece itself. It stands as a provocative and playful example of experiential argument, pushing scholarly practices such as research, annotation, and citation in lively new directions. This archive also encapsulates and preserves a history of labor practices, limning both the oppressive and the expressive potentials encapsulated in a variety of office work and office machines. As such, it offers evidence to the creativity of all manner of text workers. Such histories are vitally important in a moment such as our own when the forces of globalization seem to encourage our seamless incorporation into capital and the networks through which it flows. *Stolen Time* reminds us of resistance.
>
> While the piece bears a clear relationship to *Writing Is Work,* the book that Gambrell is now completing, *Stolen Time* is not simply a translation of that print project to the digital realm. It stands easily alone, obeying its own internal principles while radically reworking our understanding of form's relationship to content. The project's "design" or "form" is not separable from the "content" or "argument" it makes. Such an argument may seem self-evident in the tanta-

lizing realms of the digital, but *Stolen Time* also historicizes this relationship, underscoring that that form and content, or, put differently, the technical and the creative, have always existed in tight feedback loops. The construction of the project literalized these circuits of exchange as Gambrell and Kelly collaborated in an intense production process. While we've long been urged not to judge a book by its cover, *Stolen Time* powerfully insists that such an adage works to conceal the myriad traces of labor that congeal in any textual artifact. As such, the project offers another take on a claim that *Vectors* as a whole seeks to make: the long-standing scholarly distinction between tools and theories is profoundly destabilized by digital media, demanding a rethinking of long-held tenets of technological determinism.

Gambrell describes the collaboration, the content of, and the scholarly context for the piece in these excerpts from her Author's Statement:

Off and on throughout the second half of 2004, Raegan Kelly and I worked on *Stolen Time,* a collaborative experiment in the ordering, interpretation, and distribution of a particular kind of evidence. *Stolen Time* is constructed around a small group of ephemeral materials produced by, for, and about office workers in the twentieth-century United States.

On one hand, the archive includes didactic texts and objects (handbook entries, magazine advertisements, secretary gifts, industrial guides—most of them from the 1940s and 1950s) whose primary purpose was to maximize office-worker productivity. On the other, however, it also includes more resistant texts: primarily zines that were self-published on the fly by office workers themselves—cut and pasted, handmade, duplicated, and informally distributed—over the course of the last twenty-five or so years. Since elements in the first category provide much of the subject matter and motivation for elements in the second, the relationship between the two turns out to be intimate and combative in equal measures.

The *Stolen Time* project also situates itself at a point where several distinct scholarly conversations converge: a long-standing labor-history literature; a literature concerned with the sociology and anthropology of office work; and finally, a quite recent flowering of literary criticism that takes up the relationship between clerical work, medial technologies, and literary expression.

Kelly and Gambrell began working together in advance of our first summer camp so that we'd have at least an early prototype to share at the workshop with the incoming fellows. Included here are some snapshots of the design process as well as images of the final piece.

Early design meetings helped delineate the potential directions the piece might take and built common ground among Gambrell and Kelly and the editors. These notes, taken by Steve Anderson, are from a session well into this initial phase.

---

`"Stolen Time" Archive Meeting`

Alice Gambrell, Raegan Kelly, Steve Anderson, May 10, 2004

Collage vs. files

Transformation of ephemera into non-ephemera

C. Wright Mills White Collar

Socialist critique of office work metaphorizes office buildings as filing structure for workers technician (memo/technical) vs. intellectual/artist (letter/creative)

Timing function in project

create awareness of speed, elapsed time

Letter vs. Memo

Letter ⇒ authorship
letter of the alphabet
memo ⇒ memory; corporate/obfuscated authorship

Template for letter writing in background

Tool kit for moving through ephemera

Alice's writing can appear in response to selected ephemera
collage from pieces of images with annotation
first pass through copier reduces to B/W images, second includes Alice's
text; third includes histories, etc.
want to avoid impression of illustrated images
select an object, automatically added to letter
Ransom Note fonts; Courier for body text

Letter production space includes images, Alice's text in small splats
like Post-it notes

will text have life outside of objects?
will we be able to access text that has been read before? May be important for being able to cite and refer to text

How to solicit user's workplace tales

can track session time, then prompt user spontaneously to enter their
story
user enters story then it disappears
can we include other forms of reward?
importance of indexing and cross-referencing

Letter becomes an index; links created through user movement

Alice's scholarship is destroyed by user navigation?
project produces residue

3 Categories of materials:

    Didactics: guides, fetishistic histories
    Toys: commercial ads, posters
    Revisionist texts: (e.g., Processed World)

Overlays as a strategy for accessing different parts of the index

opening up new connections
possibilities of digression; medium specificity
collections as nodes within networks of fanatical collectors

Alice will compose multiple annotations for each object
Raegan will work on system for filing and associating these texts

first index can have depth
collapse and expand menus
some associations can be ephemeral; while others persist

Alice is feeling responsibility for academic legitimacy of the journal

project will need old-fashioned bibliography

Settings for photocopier?

how much information to preserve?
object histories
work traces
degraded, photocopied B/W
bibliography as photocopier setting?

Need to find a way to warn users that their actions are monitored and recorded

Timeline:

> Alice: will try to have text composition in 2 weeks
> Raegan: needs to establish structural elements of
> interface

Evidence of considerable prior use

object histories
commentaries
bibliography
category list

---

Raegan Kelly shared an early design document a few weeks later, following additional meetings. A portion is reproduced here, illustrating the main interface elements. Though aspects of this design are evident in the final piece, several changes happened in the production process.

(Fig. W3.1)

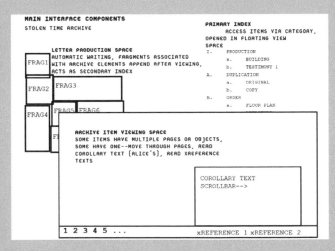

MAIN INTERFACE COMPONENTS
STOLEN TIME ARCHIVE

PRIMARY INDEX
ACCESS ITEMS VIA CATEGORY, OPENED IN FLOATING VIEW SPACE

LETTER PRODUCTION SPACE
AUTOMATIC WRITING, FRAGMENTS ASSOCIATED WITH ARCHIVE ELEMENTS APPEND AFTER VIEWING, ACTS AS SECONDARY INDEX

FRAG1
FRAG2  FRAG3
FRAG4  FRAG5 FRAG6
F

I.   PRODUCTION
     a.   BUILDING
     b.   TESTIMONY 1
A.   DUPLICATION
     a.   ORIGINAL
     b.   COPY
B.   ORDER
     a.   FLOOR PLAN

ARCHIVE ITEM VIEWING SPACE
SOME ITEMS HAVE MULTIPLE PAGES OR OBJECTS, SOME HAVE ONE--MOVE THROUGH PAGES, READ COROLLARY TEXT (ALICE'S), READ XREFERENCE TEXTS

COROLLARY TEXT
SCROLLBAR-->

1 2 3 4 5 . . .          xREFERENCE 1 xREFERENCE 2

W3.1

**W3.2**

Upon launching the finished project, the reader encounters snippets of text about "stolen time" at work. Later in the project, the reader will have a chance to enter her own story. As she explores the interface, she discovers that she can click on "practice." Soon she'll have an opportunity to practice her shorthand. (Fig. W3.2 / W3.3)

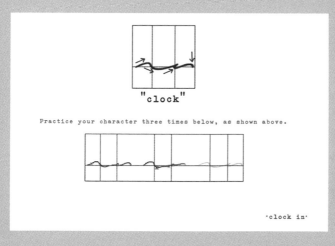

**W3.3**

143

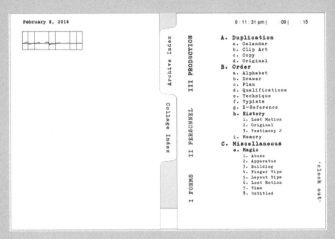

W3.4

Using a mouse or touchpad, the reader tries to trace the characters. Her errors are highlighted in orange. Once the reader clocks in, she'll find the project's main interface, a refinement of the design document referred to above. (Fig. W3.4)

At this point, the reader can explore the contents of the project, "opening up" the files to explore various artifacts and read Gambrell's explications of them. (Fig. W3.5)

W3.5

As the reader interacts with the materials in the project, she begins to build a collage of her trajectory through the archive. (Fig. W3.6) Clicking on these image snippets will return the reader to the object. When she clocks out, the collage becomes a static black-and-white photocopy.

W3.6

## Reimagining Content and Form

Even as we were reconceptualizing database middleware, we were aiming to bend the database's modular logics to our desires, softening its rigid structure through interface design and minor hacking. When I presented *Vectors* to audiences, I was often asked why we didn't just develop a template for the journal, but we were resisting the templatization of design in order to explore the expressive capacities of the interface in more experimental registers. Of course, we were still working with computers in all their modularity, but we were also exploring how design might structure new relations of form to content. In these undertakings we were also committed to particular kinds of content, choosing to work with scholars who were engaging issues of gender, race, affect, memory, sexuality, nationhood, mediation, space, and social justice. These themes are at the heart of our research, and they deeply shape how we use and design technological systems. *Vectors* projects bear little resemblance to articles in typical print journals or to PDF-driven online journals, although we did use a rolling model of peer review, beginning with the review of fellowship applications and continuing throughout the development process. The work of our lab was motivated by specific research questions. We were interested in how multimodal scholarship might structure unique relationships of form to content and sought to explore the specific affordances of digital media for scholarly communication. We were interested in the expressive and emotive possibilities of scholarship. We asked how interactivity might change scholarship, structuring new possibilities for immersion and nonlinearity. We were drawing from popular vernaculars, including film and video games. We were operating at the intersection of design and the humanities much more than the quantitative endeavors that drive some other digital humanities research. Our early projects were speculative in the sense that Johanna Drucker describes, committed to pushing back against the cultural authority of rationalism in the digital humanities and in digital design. While they incorporate various modes of evidence, they are not data driven in a positivist sense. Our impulse was not to mine large data sets but to operate at the intersections of database and design.

*Vectors* projects practiced a defamiliarization at the level of aesthetic design for the reader and at the level of collaboration and construction for the author. If Braidotti sees the work of theory as still valuable to the extent that it pushes us beyond comfort zones and a belief in the transparency of language, *Vectors* projects engaged such a methodology in the visual field, moving us beyond the tyranny of corporate "lowest-common-denominator" design. Experiments in the realm of the aesthetic, the visual, and the informatic are as important as experiments within and through the theoretical and the philosophical. Following various work in the new materialisms, this book's first essay calls for the integration of theory and practice and for scholars to operate at levels besides critique. The Vectors Lab sought this integration in the collaborations we fostered and through the software that we built. Our process carefully calibrated the balance of theoretical inquiry and principled making. If we desire polyvocality and an ethics of the intersectional cut, we cannot segregate our critical projects solely within the linguistic. The visual and the digital are crucial terrains for scholarly practice, not simply as objects of study but as modes of expression and of entangled being.

Consider the piece "Public Secrets," by Sharon Daniel, designed by Erik Loyer. (Figs. 2.10 / 2.11 / 2.12 / 2.13) The piece opens with a voiceover narration by Daniel describing her regulated entry into a prison near Chowchilla, California, the site of the two largest women's prisons in the world. After the opening, the user encounters a fairly minimalist black, white, and gray design comprising a moving line that horizontally redraws and divides the screen. Hovering over a block of text launches sound. Click through, and the screen resolves into an

2.10 / 2.11 / 2.12 / 2.13
A series of screengrabs illustrates different ways in which the user can slice through Sharon Daniel's "Public Secrets" project. The first shows a screen from early in the project, following the audio introduction. The second two images move through the project by following the theme "Life Outside" and by attending to an audio transcript by Linda Candelaria. The project reveals that one might zero in on a precise object— say, an audio file—while also understanding that file's relation to larger themes and contexts.

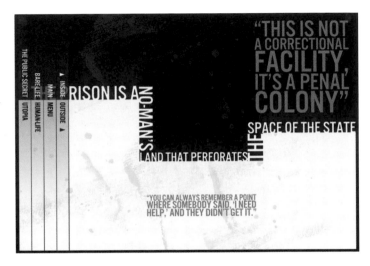

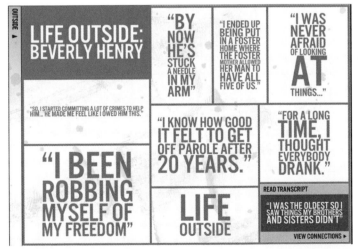

irregularly gridded tree map. The project includes many hours of audio footage, testimonies from imprisoned women that were collected by Daniel through her work with the activist organization Justice Now. The user can navigate the piece through a series of themes (inside-outside, bare life–human

The various files are contained in the structured cells of the project's database, but the design of the piece reconfigures that grid through both the morphing interface and the middleware used by the author and designer in its construction. The final image is from an earlier draft of "Public Secrets" that took a more didactic tone, asking readers a series of questions about their views on prisons. Daniel and Loyer moved away from this approach toward a more emergent and experiential form of argument, as Daniel wanted to explore "the doubleness of perception" at every level.

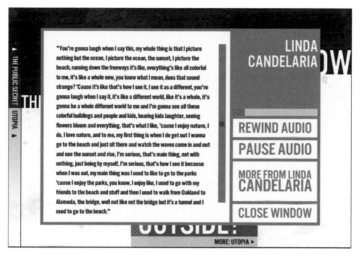

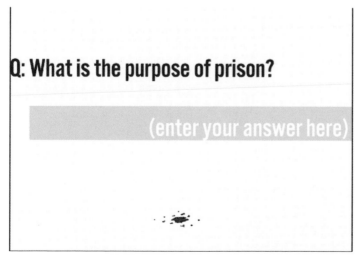

life, and public secret–utopia), through individual women's stories, or in a more random fashion (or through a combination of all these), creating an intersectional cut through the database to produce a temporary assemblage. In choosing to cut to one woman's story, the user turns the database toward a situated particularity, enacting a pathway that then intersects with other women's stories and with the larger argument of the work. The form recontextualizes the isolated cells of data with ethical intent. The aesthetic design and structure of the project reinforce its goals, calling our attention to the shifting borders between inside and outside, incarceration and freedom, oppression and resistance, despair and hope. Through navigating the piece, the fine lines demarcating such binaries will morph, shift, reconfigure, and grow fuzzy, unsettling any easy assumptions about "us" and "them" in the carceral state. Rather, inside and outside mutually determine and construct one another, sketching powerful vectors of relation between individual experiences and broader social systems as Daniel argues that we are all complicit with the prison-industrial complex. We experience the piece through eye, ear, and touch, opening scholarship to multiple sensory registers. A Webby honoree, the project also moves beyond the confines of the university, as it has been used by Justice Now in its work and has also been exhibited in museums and galleries worldwide. While the piece shares much with tenets of speculative design, it is also meant to be and to matter in the world.

A project like "Public Secrets" begins to imagine new possibilities for the archive as it mutates into the database. It is a database with a point of view: it very much relies on the database to structure its content (as well as on custom treemap and typographic algorithms designed by Loyer), but it also contextualizes the database, guiding the visitor's immersion in the piece, echoing the logic of the video game to unfold portions of the project at key moments. It plays with linearity but does not entirely abandon it. It encourages exploration more than mastery or completion. Its argument is affective and builds momentum in its temporal unfolding. If Manovich sees the database and narrative as "natural enemies," *Vectors* projects often insist on recoupling these modalities. In charting the emergence of the "anarchive" or the "dynarchive" (the archive as digital network), Wolfgang Ernst has written that narrative is being replaced by calculation (135). Technically, this may be true in the inner workings of the database and the algorithm, as the dynamic processes of digitization perpetually churn. But as humans we still engage with our machines through interfaces that offer rich possibilities for reimagining data narratives in and for the digital age.

For instance, the anthropologist Kim Christen and Chris Cooney worked with the *Vectors* team and our design collaborator Alessandro Ceglia to create "Digital Dynamics across Cultures," a project that draws on materials (including photographs and videos) collected during Christen's fieldwork to explore the knowledge protocols of the Warumungu aboriginal community in Australia. Rather than deploy these materials to illustrate some Western truth about the Warumungu, Christen envisioned a piece that would call into question our assumptions that the Internet should give us access to all that we desire. The piece is organized as a kind of speculative cartography that rejects Western spatial principles in favor of indigenous representations of place, particularly as place inflects memory, kinship, and mobility. As the user navigates the piece, she may come upon restricted areas to which she does not have access. Christen describes this further in an excerpt from her Author's Statement in *Vectors:*

> At the most basic level this system [of access to materials]
> operated within the logic of an "open"/"closed" binary.
> Some information is open, anyone has access. Other
> material is closed, only those with the proper knowledge
> have access. Yet the binary does not hold. Instead, there
> is a continuum between open and closed. Within this
> continuum various factors determine levels of access,
> gradations of control and multiple levels of engagement.
> These factors include (but are not limited to): gender, age,
> kin relations, country affiliations, and ritual knowledge.
> This is a dynamic system, then, that allows for the
> continual remaking and repackaging of Warumungu
> knowledge and tradition within various networks. And
> because Warumungu social networks include land
> ("country"), other-than-human relatives ("ancestors"),
> local kin groups ("mobs") as well as outsiders, the
> maintenance and creation of "proper"—but not static—
> traditional knowledge and cultural products involves
> constant negotiation.

"Digital Dynamics across Cultures" models these complex
cultural protocols involving access in its design, pushing
back against the libertarian logic that "all information wants
to be free." Here we see the necessity of understanding openness not as an inherent good but as a site for ethical practice.
(Figs. 2.14 / 2.15)

For indigenous peoples whose cultural production has
often been raided for colonial and capital gain, openness and
access are not inherently good. The design of this piece recognizes that opacity may be the best ethical choice. If Édouard
Glissant has theorized the value of opacity for oppressed peoples as both a counter-poetic and a strategy to resist surveillance, asserting that "we demand for all the right to opacity" to

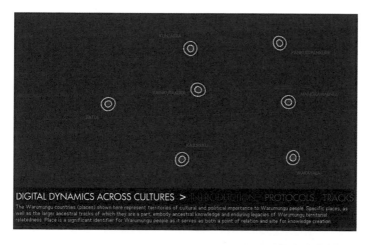

"protect the Diverse" (62), Christen, Cooney, and Ceglia explore opacity as a design strategy, insisting on the right to deny access and to refuse visibility as a powerful strategy for survival and being. Glissant writes of opacity in relation to the oppressed, but his poetics of relation and his call to mobilize opacity are tactics that should appeal to all of us in an era when our interactions on the web and our data are constantly being captured and processed by Google, Amazon, and others. While openness can certainly be a good thing (as is often the case with open-access publishing or open software), it also has

2.14
The opening screen of "Digital Dynamics across Cultures."

2.15 Access is not open to all in "Digital Dynamics across Cultures."

2.16 Protocols provide an alternative way of exploring "Digital Dynamics across Cultures." These types of thematic organization of content exist side by side with narrative analyses in many *Vectors* projects and influenced the design of Scalar.

2.17 Mukurtu is a content management system that accounts for non-Western cultural protocols in its very design and construction, underscoring the fact that our tools are never neutral.

strong ideological underpinnings that we would do well to attend to with care. (Fig. 2.16 / 2.17)

Following her work with the *Vectors* team, Christen has worked side by side with indigenous communities to create Mukurtu, a database platform and content management system that allows its users to control their own cultural heritage materials, resisting the colonial imperative that so often underwrote the archival impulse. Mukurtu seeks to add context, texture, and intentionality to the digital's dreams of ordered and open access. As the website notes, its technological practice endeavors to design systems that foster "relationships of respect and trust" rather than efficiency, commerce, or speed. Thus, the normalizing logic of databases might be remapped in their very use and implementation, melding, in Diana Taylor's terms, repertoire and archive. Cultural objects can be digitized and shared, but they carry other relationships with them on their virtual journeys, entangling various histories and building webs of context and meaning. They are not the randomly generated objects of an object-oriented ontology, sealed in on themselves. They exist in relation.

"Digital Dynamics" and others works in *Vectors,* including Judith Jackson Fossett's "Slavery's Ephemera" and David Theo Goldberg's "Blue Velvet" (both designed by Loyer), subtly draw on theories of the archive (while using the database and the interface) to underscore the politics of selection and interpretation always implicit in our technologies of memory and storage. "Blue Velvet" remakes a long-form print article that argues that Hurricane Katrina was as much a consequence of neoliberal neglect of infrastructure as it was a natural disaster. *Vectors'* implementation of this scholarship radically transforms it along affective and poetic registers. As Fox Harrell has commented, the piece *affects* the user along multiple sensory registers: "There is no way to stop this rapid descent [of words and images in the interface]—I want to stop it; I feel as if I have set a destructive event in motion" (315). The project reframes Goldberg's earlier writing, organizing it by means of a numbered sequence of argumentative themes that scroll across the top of the screen; when activated by a click of the mouse, a series of affiliated words rain down. For instance, clicking on "New Orleans" releases white words such at "delta," "city on edge," "racial 'purity,'" "gumbo ingredients," and "America's

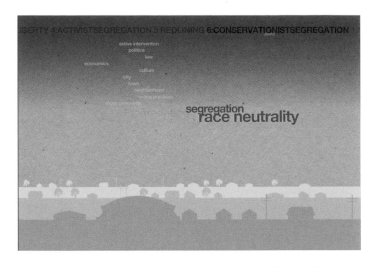

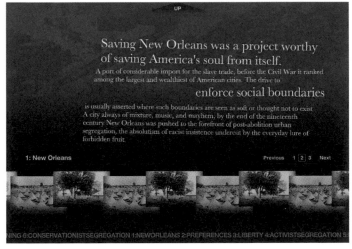

2.18 / 2.19
The "above water" and "below water" screens from "Blue Velvet," by David Theo Goldberg.

outlet," as well as larger, orange "related concepts" like "segregation" or "sociality." Upon clicking the orange words, the descent described by Harrell begins, as the user is submerged in the underworld of the flood and in an eclectic archive of text and visual evidence that helps the user explore various sup-

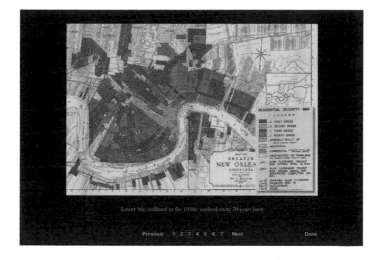

pressed pasts of New Orleans. As in much of Loyer's design work, sound is an important element of the experience, and the piece features commissioned music from Liu Sola that adds a level of sonic intensity to the underwater descent. Goldberg commented on the way in which writing for Loyer's interface design led him to rethink the structure of his prose, which prompted him to compose in a more aphoristic and poetic register. This form of composition best served the project's affective mode of argumentation; its central concepts accumulate for the viewer at many sensory levels, through eye, ear, brain, and hand. The Vectors Lab began by asking questions such as "How can we feel an argument?"; "Blue Velvet" provides one answer to that question. (Fig. 2.18 / 2.19 / 2.20 )

Stephen Best writes that the "visual archive of the slave past… is marked by the clash between the imperative to recover the past and the impossibility of doing so" (159). In exploring the failed infrastructures of New Orleans or the ghosts of Louisiana's plantation past at the intersection of data structure, visual evidence, and interface design, Gold-

2.20 David Theo Goldberg's "Blue Velvet" includes several historic maps that connect issues of redlining and segregation in New Orleans to the city's shape at the time of Katrina. These maps function in a register different from that of the often quantitative dreams promoted by many implementations of GIS.

157

berg and Fossett again remind us that our archives and our databases are neither transparent nor innocent.[5] (Fig. 2.21)

Many of the *Vectors* pieces are database-driven and database-dependent, but their impulse is to reanimate the archive through narrative and design—to bring a waning form to new life while blurring the line between form and content, repertoire and archive. They pay attention to specific things and experiences, resisting the decontextualizing logic of the database. They wield technology against its positivist self, foregrounding the work of the interface and refusing an easy transparency and corporate tenets of "good" design by means of the template. If Glissant tracks the tensions between opacity and transparency, the force of web design since the mid-1990s has certainly been to privilege a concept of ease and transparency that extends the programmer's mantra of "Keep It Simple, Stupid" into twenty-first-century visual culture. Lori Emerson has brilliantly tracked the ways in which a privileging of "ease of use" and transparency in digital design has actually had an inverse relationship to our capacity to use our computers in uniquely creative ways. Such seemingly transparent design can actually lock down and hermetically seal our devices, making them as hard to pry open as the black boxes of code. Resisting the "easy" interface can also encourage a different temporal engagement with digital projects, slowing down the rapid scroll and frenetic click. Lauren Berlant has lovingly described the advantages of taking pause: "Amidst the rise and fall of quotidian intensities a situation arises that provokes the need to think and adjust, to slow things down and to gather things up, to find things out and to wonder and ponder. What's going on?" (5). *Vectors* projects reward slow reading, requiring attention and care from the reader (much like any emerging discipline or new theo-

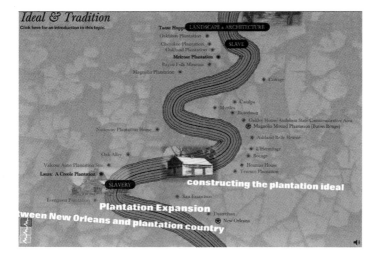

retical model). They ask us not only to stop and think but also to pause and feel. They most often complicate the database at the level of the screen, amping up the autocritique. They typically deploy the strategies we often associate with the avant-garde or experimental art in the service of scholarly argument.

Like an art or design studio, we were learning by doing, creating prototypes (if not always rapid ones), working by iteration. But as much as I love the work we do with *Vectors,* there are problems with it as well. At the level of the interface, the projects are mostly one-offs that are labor-intensive and demanding to create. Carefully integrating form and content for each piece requires hundreds of hours of design and programming time, even after the DBG streamlined the production process. In an ideal world, I still believe that each scholarly project should find the design and structure best suited to its unique evidence, argument, and purpose (and that format will sometimes be a print book!), but that world would be hard to fund and perhaps also

2.21 Judith Jackson Fossett's "Slavery's Ephemera," designed by Erik Loyer, maps touristic reconstructions of southern history as well as the phantasms that haunt that past.

harder to sustain and preserve, as each project would have its own capacities, needs, and quirks.[6] We are still building the infrastructure for that world and many forces work against it, from for-profit publishing to standardized software. We also need more collaborative work on making digital projects ADA-compliant, issues we have begun to address in our new work, but we still have far to go. Many of the early *Vectors* projects were done with the Adobe program Flash, so they are typically not accessible to those with audiovisual disabilities. They are also hard to preserve and do not necessarily play well with the wider world of linked data or with the proprietary world of the iPad, as Apple refuses to integrate Adobe products into its slick devices. Flash also "sealed off" our earliest projects from web crawlers (although today perhaps that might be seen as a good thing, as Google voraciously harvests the web). In many ways, these *Vectors* projects were anticipating apps, for they incorporated multiple senses, even touch, into beautifully designed packages that juxtaposed gesture, sound, image, and text.[7] Other *Vectors* projects, such as Eric Faden's self-produced video essay on silent cinema, "Tracking Theory," published early in 2007, not long after the arrival of YouTube, pointed the way toward the video-driven scholarship now thriving in journals like *[In] Transition,* a collaboration with MediaCommons. When we first launched *Vectors,* viewers were sometimes perplexed by the interfaces, although after several years of swiping across iPads, the interfaces seem decidedly less experimental today. Still, each project tended to call for a new reading practice, and such shifts in scholarly convention always pose challenges. (Fig. 2.22)

While we want to resist the web's call for simplicity and endless templates that shoehorn knowledge into small,

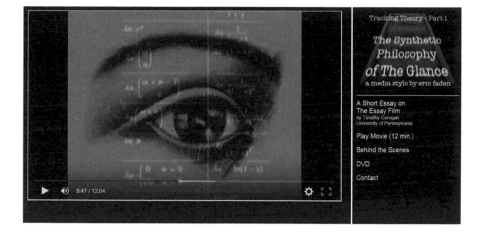

predesigned boxes, scholarship also often demands recognizable forms, even as this demand for recognition can stifle the creative experimentation that feminist materialism seems to strain toward. Earlier in the book, we explored these feminist calls for making and for new alliances but also noted that most of these calls were still circulating through print books sometimes published by for-profit presses. Scholars do not easily adapt to change. I sit here writing a print book about born-digital projects that are best experienced online. Issues regarding the evaluation of digital projects for tenure and promotion still remain a challenge, despite the hard work being down by scholarly societies such as the Modern Language Association (MLA), College Art Association (CAA), and the American Historical Association (AHA), along with countless individuals. (Brief guidelines for reviewing multimodal digital work appear as an appendix to this volume.) One motivation for our research in the lab was the realization that many of the ways that knowledge circulates within the academy (through black-boxed books in niche fields speaking largely

2.22 Eric Faden's video essay "Tracking Theory: The Synthetic Philosophy of the Glance."

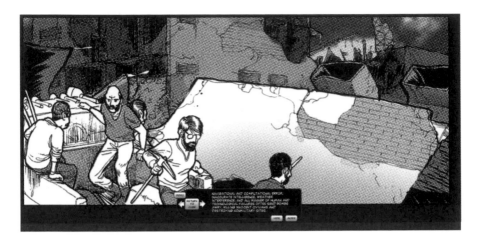

2.23 "Precision Targets" by Caren Kaplan, designed by Erik Loyer and illustrated by Ezra Claytan Daniels.

to the initiated few or behind locked-down corporate pay-walls) were themselves complicit with the modular logic of the database. But custom design is expensive work to do, particularly in a moment when universities seem intent on downsizing the humanities again and again. Increasingly our team realized that we needed to think about scaling our practices in new ways while exploring other parallel approaches for scholarly publishing that might be more easily sustained. The work on *Vectors* continues, but the intensive fellowship model that taught us so much has ended, as has much of the custom production, except in cases where scholars approach us with some funding of their own, as was the case with Caren Kaplan's "Precision Targets," funded by the American Council of Learned Societies, a follow-up to her earlier *Vectors* project "Dead Reckoning," created with Raegan Kelly for the Perception issue, and in Loyer's ongoing work with Sharon Daniel. But, happily, we have also arrived at a moment when many more scholars are capable of producing digital work without a design-and-programming team (or have found their own partners for this work). In 2017 *Vectors* was relaunched with ongoing publication of work submitted to the journal for review, along with specially curated issues. That first issue featured several projects created using Scalar's API, thus bringing our work full circle in many ways. (Fig. 2.23)

# Various *Vectors*

The projects published in *Vectors* take a wide variety of forms. To illustrate that range, this window features a sampling of projects drawn from several issues, including screen grabs and excerpts from Author's and Designer's Statements for each piece. I focus mainly on work not discussed in depth elsewhere in this book. (Figs. W4.1 / W4.2)

**W4.1 Jenny Holzer, Neue Nationalgalerie**

**W4.2 A 3-D animation captured the feel of the original Holzer exhibition.**

## From the Author's Statement by Ehren Fordyce

Why Jenny Holzer, why a retrospective at Berlin's Neue Nationalgalerie,

why an electronic journal, and why all three coming together in *Vectors'* inaugural issue devoted to "evidence"? Framing an answer brings to mind some phrases from Holzer's signature early work, *Truisms.*

First: "DESCRIPTION IS MORE VALUABLE THAN METAPHOR." Like all of Holzer's truisms, some rhetorical seduction and sleight-of-hand are at work here. The phrase sounds so authoritative; it seems to compel assent; it must be true. But what's the context? Is the statement really a self-evident absolute truth; or is it only true in specific instances? What is missing is *deixis,* the extralinguistic indication of evidence that would allow you, the addressee of the phrase, to figure out the reference, context, and truth-value of the supposed truism.

Seen from one perspective, I think this truism actually says a lot about how Gwen Allen and I, the organizers of this project, tried to proceed methodologically. In the website, we place a premium on pointing. We like the indexical gesture, the gesture that simply points at the evidence and says to the reader: here is what it is, now you need to contextualize it, to put your own signature on it. It also seems to us that multimedia documentation is particularly useful for making an indexical gesture. In lieu of having to use 1,000 words to describe a picture of the Holzer installation, we can present a photograph, animation, or video and then be able to say, "here, take a look."

But there is, ultimately, a limit to the usefulness of just pointing. Or, perhaps more precisely, there is a limit to the idea that one can simply point and do nothing else. Basically, pointing presupposes framing. Another way to say this is that description always implies metaphor, and metaphor always implies description. One cannot describe without selecting out certain things to describe. Description is always from a perspective. As a result, it is always comparative to other perspectives. Metaphor is comparison, and to the extent that any pointing and describing requires a comparative theory for selecting what to point at and describe, description entails metaphor. Pointing already entails interpretation. Evidence is not simply what is seen; evidence is what is pulled out of the whole field of the seen and shown to be

important. *Ex* + *videre* = out of + to see. Ironically, 1,000 words are sometimes more important than a single picture.

So... in designing the Holzer site, we had to deal with the question of how our pointing at and framing of evidence, i.e., our interface, implies an interpretation of that evidence. (Fig. W4.3)

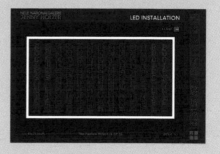

W4.3  Other portions of the project illustrated various LED techniques Holzer used in the exhibition.

## From the Designer's Statement by Alessandro Ceglia

My goal as designer/programmer was to build a site that served as a virtual record, an interactive documentary snapshot, of Holzer's installation at the Berlin Neue Nationalgalerie. The site features a clean, functional interface that is both easy to use and attuned to

Holzer's and Mies van der Rohe's modernist aesthetics. The site is also dynamically driven and therefore scalable; content can be modified, added, or removed with relative ease as new information or scholarly research becomes available. (Fig.W4.4)

**W4.4** Several layers of content provided context for the original exhibition and for the elements included in the *Vectors* piece.

**W4.5 Narrating Bits.**

## Author's Statement
## by N. Katherine Hayles

One of the frontiers of contemporary cultural and literary studies is multimedia criticism—that is, not criticism of multimedia works but rather criticism that itself uses the resources of multimedia to construct arguments, present evidence, and enact conclusions. This is still a very new field, and a period of experimentation is both necessary and inevitable. (Figs. W4.5 / W4.6)

For "Narrating Bits," I was delighted to work with Erik Loyer and the Stamen team, particularly Eric Rodenbeck, to conceptualize a design that would perform concepts crucial to the argument, especially the notion of a "possibility space" as a combinatorics that precedes both the storyworld and narration.

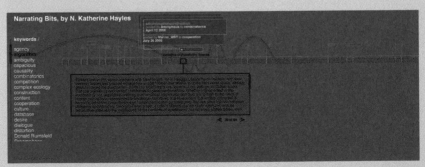

**W4.6** "Narrating Bits" is organized sequentially and thematically, which allows multiple modes of access for the reader. User commentary is also incorporated, although this aspect of the piece did not prove to be its most compelling.

166

While Erik Loyer, in collaboration with Stamen, spearheaded the production of the piece, we worked together on ideas that would let the experience become an interactive work of multimedia criticism.

An important part of the design concept was the creation of a dataspace where users can add their own comments and adaptations of my concepts as represented by keywords. In a sense, these activities represent the way that normal scholarly discourse operates, except that in print publication, the statements, modifications, and counter-statements take place over months and years, while the digital medium shrinks the time scale to hours or days. The difference amounts to a qualitative, not merely a quantitative, transformation. It makes scholarly discourse more like a conversation than a series of unpredictable and infrequent forays. When writing an article for a print journal, I am often painfully aware that my essay will appear years after I compose it, and that even more time will pass before someone responds (if anyone ever does), by which time I probably will have either forgotten or lost interest in the matter under discussion. Rather than lobbing ideas over a very high wall that I cannot see over and then waiting for months and years to see if whoever lurks on the other side is going to respond with a missile of her own, I now feel that I can actually *play* with others who may want to engage the topic.

I applaud the editors of *Vectors,* as well as Erik Loyer and the Stamen team, for this bold and visionary initiative. Even failures (if there are any such) become successes in this context, for they contribute to our growing understanding of how we can use multimedia criticism to create the scholarship of the present and the future. (Fig. W4.7)

W4.7 **Because they demanded new reading and interaction practices, many** *Vectors* **projects incorporated reading instructions in their design.**

## Designer's Statement by Erik Loyer

To design a videogame based on licensed intellectual property is a high-profile but often unenviable task. While most of us are free to construct our own vague topography of the storyworld implied by a particular IP, unencumbered by any strict need for rigor, the individual in this position must do so with machine-readable precision and in full public view. The resulting work is expected to embody the spirit of the license while simultaneously expanding it beyond the original conception of the author and translating it into a completely different medium than the one for which it was originally created. It's not surprising that many of these projects fail on multiple counts.

I bring up this point because it strikes me as the site where the arguments Hayles makes here about the interaction between fabula, sjuzhet, narrative, and database are currently being lived most publicly. The designer of a licensed videogame is constantly making decisions about which aspects of the storyworld to incarnate as static content, and which as combinatorics, while remaining constantly accountable to an increasingly savvy public ravenous for any detail of program design reported by the gaming press. The more beloved the property, the more fierce the design advocacy from fans; endless

ASCII has been spilled on the reasons why this or that game betrays either its namesake license or the sensibilities of hardcore gamers, and on what the game's designers should have done instead.

We have, under much happier and more supportive circumstances than these, undertaken to adapt Hayles's work into a possibility space whose central narrative is not only the article, but also the user's exploratory actions. The piece, designed in collaboration with Eric Rodenbeck, Tomas Apodaca, and Michal Migurski of the Stamen design studio in San Francisco, is built on the foundation of a database that allows us to tag each paragraph of Hayles's text thematically with keywords. These keywords can then be browsed for the trajectories they carve through the text, and the thread of a particular keyword traced to reveal a skeletal narrative that can be embellished with the comments of users. Our aim is an instantiation of a "collaborative complex ecology" between narrative and database of the type Hayles describes, and a forum where the fluidity of dialogue she seeks can be explored. Many thanks to Kate for her enthusiasm and willingness to open the text up in this way.

Erik Loyer in E-mail to Kate Hayles and Tara McPherson
during the Design of "Narrating Bits"

To put it another way: what I'd like to see is an interface where, if you took all the words off of it, the visual content would still convey a general impression of Kate's argument that the relationship between narrative and database can be complex and multilayered. Your actions within the interface should be an expression of that idea, not just functionally, but viscerally as well. That means coming up with a visual language that can signify "database" and "narrative" and provide visual analogies for how those things can intermingle.

### By Julian Bleecker
Design by Erik Loyer (Figs. W4.8 / W4.9)

**W4.8 WiFi. Bedouin.**

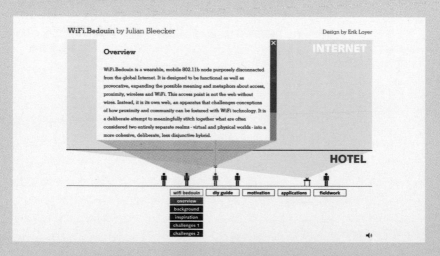

W4.9  This piece offered a playful exploration of the cultural, technical, and imaginative potentials of WiFi when WiFi was not yet ubiquitous. Part performance art, part do-it-yourself technical manual, part socio-materialist intervention, the project invited users to reflect on how WiFi networks would reconfigure sociality and the local. It also represents an interesting example of critical making.

169

## Author's Statement
by Julian Bleeker

WiFi.Bedouin is a wearable, mobile 802.11b node purposely disconnected from the global Internet. It is designed to be functional as well as provocative, expanding the possible meaning and metaphors about access, proximity, wireless, and WiFi. This access point is not the web without wires. Instead, it is its own web, an apparatus that forces one to reconsider and question notions of virtuality, materiality, displacement, proximity and community. It is a deliberate attempt to meaningfully stitch together what are often considered two entirely separate realms, "virtual and physical worlds," into a more cohesive, deliberate, less disjunctive hybrid.

WiFi.Bedouin is a thinking object, a designed and made technical instrument that helps work through the intellectual and material challenges of designing against convention. (Fig.W4.10)

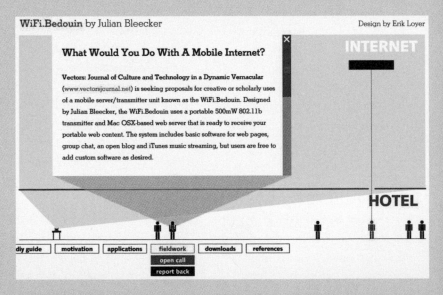

W4.10 For a limited time after the project was launched, readers were invited to apply to use the WiFi.Bedouin in their own projects.

## Designer's Statement
## by Erik Loyer

Let's say you're drawing a networking diagram. How would you draw a wired connection between two computers? Probably with a line. You'd draw the line, and you'd understand that it meant information could flow both ways between the two machines.

How would you draw a radio broadcast? Concentric circles or arcs, perhaps? We've seen it a thousand times, and we know that information only travels one way across those curves.

Now, how would you draw a call between wireless phones? You might have to stop and think for a second first. In keeping with the above-mentioned wireless tradition, you might find yourself using concentric circles again, drawing a satellite orbiting the earth as the source of a broadcast enveloping both handsets. But those ripples generally mean one-way communication only, and so they don't seem fully adequate to account for the interactive conversation taking place between the two mobile phone users. So, what else do we draw?

We run into the same conundrum when attempting to represent wireless Internet access. It's easy to diagram the broadcast area of a wireless hotspot with some concentric rings, but what about the activity taking place within that hotspot? What do we draw?

Julian Bleecker's WiFi.Bedouin complicates the issue further, by introducing the idea of a mobile WiFi hotspot that can, among other things, intercept and redirect the traffic of web surfers attempting to reach canonical websites. Intrigued by the way in which Julian's approach troubled our normal conceptions of wireless networks, I quickly became interested in the notion that we simply have not yet developed a popular visual vocabulary to adequately describe wireless connectivity—at least not in a way that would shed any light on people's behavior while using these networks. Working out such a vocabulary thus became the major focus of my work on this project, which is humbly offered as a step along the way.

It seemed important from the beginning to visualize wireless connectivity as a space where specific events could occur. WiFi access points thus became sources of this interactive space, and in my early sketches this was represented with cones of light, as if the wireless hotspot functioned like an overhead lamp whose illumination made useful activity possible in a darkened room. While this was a compelling metaphor, in the final analysis it carried too much physical baggage to be of much use. What proved more fruitful was inverting the cones of light, using them instead to carve out "airspace" above a physical location where network activity could take place. This is what you see in the final design.

There's significant terrain still to be explored in how we represent wireless connectivity visually, and thus how we describe to ourselves the methods we use to communicate and share information. One aspect that I noticed while putting this project together is how seeing the generic figures connecting to specific URLs immediately starts the narrative wheels turning in one's mind, speculating as to what this or that particular person is doing at this or that site. I found this to be a very visceral demonstration of just how much web addresses function for us as verbs, even as Julian's theoretical and technological innovations challenge us to reevaluate the potential meanings of those verbs.

**Cast-offs from the Golden Age**

W4.11 Cast-offs from the Golden Age.

## By Melanie Swalwell
Design by Erik Loyer (Fig.W4.11 / W4.12)

W4.12 "Cast-offs from the Golden Age" explores the history of video games in New Zealand through a design aesthetic that invites the user to become a researcher navigating the ephemeral evidence of that past.

## Author's Statement
## by Melanie Swalwell

In 2004, I was invited to undertake background research for a museum exhibition, "GamePLAY," on the history, art, and science of digital gaming in New Zealand. I was to focus on finding the New Zealand dimension and/or context for each of these areas, something that presented a challenge for me as an outsider: I didn't have my own experiences or knowledge gained from growing up with this history happening around me, in this place, and it was sometimes tricky to sort out the quite understandable desire to have a local focus from any inclination towards national exceptionalism. This stipulation, however, turned out to be something of a gift. Had I not been required to look into these New Zealand–specific questions, it is unlikely that I would have pursued the overlaps between the local and the nonlocal—issues such as the dates that particular international games systems arrived in New Zealand—to the extent that I did.

What I found was that there were significant differences between the accepted accounts of games history—typically told from US or Japanese perspectives—and the history of digital games in a place like New Zealand. Researching a history of a place distant from these "centres" offers the opportunity to realign some of the taken for granted "facts" or references in surprising, and sometimes quirky, ways. . . .

Setting out to search for material pertaining to the local situation, I quickly found that there was little standard textual material

on the subject, and even less in the way of material artifacts housed in New Zealand cultural institutions. This meant that I had to get creative and innovate as far as research methods were concerned. Ephemera collections quickly proved to be one of the best sources of information about games in New Zealand: the bits and pieces that many people wouldn't consider worthwhile, stuff like old advertising catalogues that is usually discarded, yielded a wealth of rich primary source material. . . .

"Cast-offs from the Golden Age" utilises samples of the ephemera I have sourced from both public and private collections, together with a range of other fragments to reconstruct and dramatise the research process for the user. The user is invited to step into the shoes of the researcher, seeking after information that will allow them to achieve their goals. Of course, research isn't only about completing goals: also part of the process and the experience are the moments of excitement at a serendipitous discovery, the frustration at dead ends or confusion at knock backs received, a wondering about where to turn next, or the sense that there are just too many avenues of inquiry to pursue. Finally, there is the interpretive work of piecing together fragments gleaned from a range of sources. To have been able to experiment with analogues between a researcher's process of conducting research and making sense of the resultant information and the experience of users of multimedia has been one of the great pleasures of this project. (Fig.W4.13)

## Designer's Statement
## by Erik Loyer

From the beginning, Melanie Swalwell was interested in making "Cast-offs from the Golden Age" an experience that would be eloquent of the ambiguities and loose ends of the research process. Ambiguity doesn't "just happen" in digital interactivity, however—it must be constructed out of well-defined structural elements which are fine enough in resolution to enable fluid recombination, yet coarse enough to signify recog-

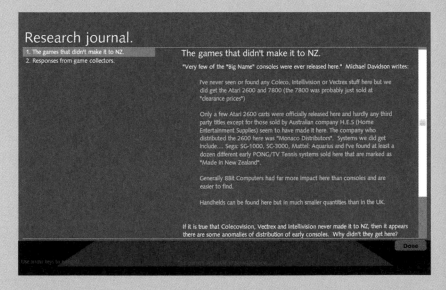

**W4.13** "Cast-offs from the Golden Age" explores the history of video games in New Zealand through a design aesthetic that invites the user to become a researcher navigating the ephemeral evidence of that past.

nizable ideas. The process, as a result, is thoroughly counterintuitive with respect to its objective.

A project like "Cast-offs" is heavily database-driven for a number of reasons, the most important of which is the organic quality which a dynamic content storage medium lends the entire process. We aim to create original works for *Vectors,* not adaptations, and as such the writing (and rewriting) process must happen concurrently with the design and programming—a tight feedback loop between the three is essential if the final piece is to be truly responsive to the demands of the medium.

The database, of course, must be designed, and it can be a challenging process—essentially the task is to create a rough (very rough) analogue to the concepts and ideas a scholar has been developing over the course of many years. Furthermore, since in this case the process was being applied not just to a conceptual framework Melanie had developed, but to her own lived experience as a researcher, she had all the justification in the world to reject the crude, rigid abstraction of life represented by the database design.

Fortunately, this proved not to be the case, and Melanie gamely threw herself into the formidable task of translating her experience and work into the rows, columns, and relations of the database, enabled by our excellent data entry tools engineered by Craig Dietrich, tools which adapt instantly to changes in the structure of the database and greatly enhance the fluidity of our development process.

One of the joys of a project like this is reaching the point at which all the analysis and categorization involved in the design process give way to the constructive and creative activities of experience building. At some point one's fluency both with the tools and with the emerging characteristics of the system being built become subconscious to the point where the rightness or wrongness of a particular element can be intuited. Many thanks to Melanie and to all the scholars we work with for being open enough to an unfamiliar process to allow those moments to occur.

**Unmarked Planes and Hidden Geographies**

W4.14 Unmarked Planes.

## By Trevor Paglen
Design by Craig Dietrich
and Raegan Kelly (Figs. W4.14 / W4.15)

## Author's Statement
## by Trevor Paglen

You can learn a lot about geography by tracking the movements of airplanes. Open up the in-flight magazine on any airplane and you'll see what I mean. Within the glossy pages of those magazines, you'll inevitably find maps of the world with lines connecting cit-

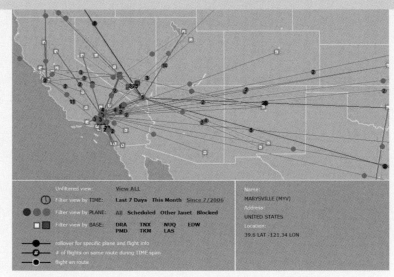

FLIGHT TRACKING : THE PLANES : THE BASES : UNUSUAL MOVEMENTS : FLIGHT PROCEDURES

**A Most Peculiar Airline**

The cell phone's alarm fills the dark hotel room with a plastic rendition of Edvard Grieg's "In the Hall of the Mountain King" – a tune befitting the obscenely early hour that we've chosen to rise. "No wonder they rule the world, they go to work at four in the morning," says my groggy friend Jenny, with whom I'm sharing an 18th floor room at the Tropicana's Island tower overlooking the Las Vegas airport. Jenny is in town working on a project about Vegas' booming real estate market. I'm attending a conference for retired CIA reconnaissance pilots and crews. In the mornings and evenings, we're using high-powered optics to observe and photograph the movements of one of Las Vegas' more obscure institutions: a small fleet of aircraft that call a cordoned-off terminal on the west side of the airport home. This terminal has a code name: "Gold Coast." The aircraft we're watching change their military call sign every month, but in civilian airspace they call themselves "Janets." Their raison d'être is to shuttle workers living in Las Vegas to and from a collection of secret military bases in the expansive Nellis Range to the north. These bases are part of a hidden military geography that is known in military and defense industry circles as the "black world." This morning, we've risen at an unholy hour in an attempt to glimpse the first flights of the day.

W4.15 For the first year following its publication, "Unmarked Planes and Hidden Geographies" included a live link to the Federal Aviation Administration's flight tracking information, which allowed the viewer to map the flight paths of obscure military aircraft nearly in real time.

ies to one another—these are of course routes flown by the airline whose plane you're sitting in. But they represent something more than that. Aircraft flights and routes help visualize a form of what geographers call "relational space": the often hidden ways in which noncontiguous spaces are in fact profoundly interwoven. London is intensely connected to New York to Los Angles to Tokyo—on the other hand, how many lines connect to Kinshasa? Ashgabat? Kabul? These absences represent a different kind of relational space.

But there are many, many kinds of aircraft besides the cramped, coach-class commercial planes that many of us are accustomed to. There are the private executive jets of the extremely rich; the light prop planes of recreational pilots; the cargo fleets of UPS, Federal Express, DHL, and the like; the helicopters and light planes of police departments; need I go on? Then there is, of course, the military. And within the military—which sometimes seems like a world unto itself—there are also scores of different aircraft types: cargo planes, fighters, bombers, trainers, transports, spy planes. Just as the movements of com-

mercial aircraft describe various kinds of relational space, so do the movements of military aircraft.

This project is about one very peculiar subset of military aircraft—a fleet of nondescript Boeing 737s and Beechcraft King Airs that use the call sign JANET when they're operating in civilian airspace. The JANETs are an airline operating in the service of the military whose purpose is to shuttle workers to and from a collection of secret military installations in the Southwest and to undertake support operations for some of the most obscure activities within the Military-Industrial Complex. The JANETs' movements represent a very peculiar kind of relational space indeed—a geography of secret projects, places, and people that military and defense-industry insiders refer to as the "black world."

To develop this project, we've taken advantage of an unlikely contradiction in the way that this fleet of aircraft is set up. Because the JANET fleet operates under the guise of a civilian (rather than military) organization, the fleet has to obey the conventions of civilian aviation. These conventions include filing plans with the

Federal Aviation Administration for each flight, and updating large files of maintenance records and registration histories with the FAA. For good reasons, these sorts of documents fall squarely in the public domain. Flight data from the JANETs, for example, are available in near real time.

To build this project, we've taken advantage of these public data sources in order to build an application that maps "in close to real time" the production and reproduction of the "black world's" secret geographies. (Fig.W4.16)

**FLIGHT TRACKING : THE PLANES : THE BASES : UNUSUAL MOVEMENTS : FLIGHT PROCEDURES**
THE 737S : THE BEECHCRAFTS

The regular Janet fleet is composed of six Boeing 737s and five Beechcraft King Air turboprops. The 737s are painted white with a red stripe down the center of the fuselage. The King Airs are also white, but painted with a blue strip down the plane. For the most part, the 737s perform about twenty scheduled flights between LAS, TNX, and Groom Lake daily. The King Airs typically fly workers to and from locations in southern California like Edwards AFB and Palmdale. The King Airs also seem to operate the bulk of unscheduled flights.

The airline is operated by the Special Projects division of EG&G (Edgerton, Germeshausen, and Grier, Inc.), whose headquarters is located in an office park south of Las Vegas' McCarren Airport. The red and white paint scheme on the 737s is probably a visual reference to EG&G's logo, which features a three-pronged red cross. From time to time, EG&G posts Las Vegas job openings for pilots and flight attendants, all of which require "Secret" security clearances or above.

W4.16 Trevor Paglen has a PhD in geography but is best known as an artist. His interest in capturing unseen worlds comes from both his critical and his creative training, and both are reflected in this piece. In the years since his Vectors Fellowship, Paglen has continued to explore themes of surveillance and military power in a wide variety of award-winning artworks and books. For more information, see his website, http://www.paglen.com/.

## Designers' Statement
## by Craig Dietrich and
## Raegan Kelly

The cornerstone of "Unmarked Planes and Hidden Geographies" is a dynamically generated map of the southwestern United States. Data collected are filtered according to predetermined fleets and each plane's flight activity from a fixed set of bases. The map engine, which started filtering data in July of 2006, has produced some interesting patterns—vector logs of JANETs operating in and out of some of the large and smaller regional public airports we use. The airborne "black world" is clearly not restricted to the confines of secret military facilities, and can be made visible to those who know where to look.

Early development research was inspired by "Trip Mapping with PHP" by David Sklar, author of *PHP Cookbook.* He outlines the necessary algorithms for converting longitude/latitude coordinates to pixels to write route lines on a map image. "Unmarked Planes and Hidden Geographies" expanded on these operations as we anticipated "black world" flight paths to North/South and East/West hemispheres, which are not supported in the original mathematical outlines. While pixels start at (0,0) in the lower left of an image and increase into infinity to the upper right, coordinates originate from 0 in the "middle," at Greenwich, England, and the equator, with corresponding plus and minus values. Each incoming coordinate is algorithmically converted to a plus-only pixel coordinate system and then written into the database.

Flight information originates from online route data based on queries formed from Trevor's research. Once logged, this database of stored information is written to the map using PHP's implementation of the GD graphics library. The data, represented by route lines on the map of the Southwest, build durationally to form a quick-glance overview of activity.

**W4.17 Digital Futures.**

**W4.18** The rich material contained in "Digital Futures" is not immediately available to the user; rather, it unfolds piece by piece, asking that the user undertake a principled engagement with representations of lived spaces and embodied histories in order to learn more. The viewer of the project does not travel through chronological time; he moves through the temporalities that the piece and its particular logic demand.

## Author's Statement by Elizabeth Povinelli

This project uses the life of Ruby Yarrowin to reflect on the building, managing, and celebration of indigenous digital archives in late liberalism. The project began as a conversation with Ruby about how to transfer the archive that I had accumulated over the last twenty-four years to her family who lived at Belyuen, a small indigenous community in northwestern Australia. (Figs.W4.17 / W4.18)

The project is inspired by recent attempts to embed alternative modes of social life in the operating systems of digital archives. These efforts operate in the shadow of Foucault's and Derrida's critical engagement with the Western state archive. They understand, as Ann Stoler noted, that archives are not sites of knowledge retrieval but of knowledge production; or, in the act of retrieving information from archives, the users of archives reproduce and conserve state power. Much of the focus of this work has been on how to encode alternative modes of circulation, access, and control of information into digital archives. Taking such critiques on board consciously or not, the authors of these digital archives assume—and foreground as part of the interaction protocol of the site—that the production and circulation of knowledge consolidates power—that power has a formation—is en-formed. And so they attempt to foreground and encode as protocols the competing organizations of knowledge and power in the very operation of a system of knowledge circulation and access.

This project also foregrounds the issue of power. But it asks what a postcolonial digital archive becomes if, instead of information, circulation, and access, we interrogate it from the perspective of socialities of obligation, responsibility, and attachment. What is not asked when we consider the archive from the perspective of knowledge production, circulation, and access? How are these problems imposed by the very ways that code and software depend on stranger sociality, whether that stranger is considered an individual or a set of cultural rules and protocols? Is it necessary to agree to this stranger sociality in order to play digitally? And if so, what forms of sociality are being extended even as we are allowed to provide different cultural rules and protocols? And, finally, how do the various interfaces of the archive—the code, software, and screen—interact in such a way that the user "feels" social difference without experiencing the transformations of the material sociology of knowledge occurring? (Fig. W4.19)

## Designer's Statement
## by Peter Cho

In December of last year, I huddled with Beth around her MacBook in a busy café in the West Village. She showed me the wealth of photographs, audio recordings, and other archival materials she has gathered over her decades-long work with aboriginal tribes in northern Australia. She showed me published accounts of "dreamings," tribal origin stories that tie people to the land. We played with Google Maps together and talked about the trope of "zooming in"—what it might mean to "get closer to a place" through a digital interface. We discussed the idea of using computer code to illustrate the gates of access that other postcolonial digital archives have used to try to replicate social structures of the cultures they represent.

W4.19 "Digital Futures" contains many videos collected by Elizabeth Povinelli in her fieldwork. They function as palimpsests, richly layered with details that activate multiples senses, destabilizing an easy belief in the indexical nature of images and inviting the user to rewind and replay them.

We talked about linking the archive content with statistics about aboriginal health, poverty, education to drive the argument that an archive can be a vehicle for social obligation and responsibility.

Over the course of several months the piece began slowly to take shape. Ruby Yarrowin became the main character, and her path through the region over the course of her life became an organizing framework. The contextual statistics about aboriginal health and welfare were woven together with video interviews, audio recordings, archival photographs, and other source material into short video narratives found at each place and time in the project's interface. Some ideas, such as including interactive genealogies or requiring the user to fill out surveys about their own economic and social status on entry, fell to the wayside as the project became a more focused narrative piece. This meant that Beth could focus on building her argument through the multi-layered video pieces that appear at each site, almost as a painter works: a few brushstrokes here and there, gradually filling in the canvas to create an overall image. As she created the videos and added them into the database, the map interface steadily took form, a complex picture of people, places, and social conditions.

My hope is that this project can begin to bridge the gap of physical distance, time, and bandwidth that separates the audience from the people and places introduced within. By following the threads and stories, visitors to the project can start to see the connections of personal relationships and responsibility around people Beth knows and cares about deeply.

W4.20 Totality for Kids.

## Author's Statement
## by McKenzie Wark

"Totality for Kids" turned out completely different from what I actually proposed. I had just done the "Gamer Theory" site with the Institute for the Future of the Book, and the *Vectors* people were interested in the participatory side of that. But things evolved. The *Vectors* team had a really nice way of creating a visual interface to an underlying database, so that seemed the place to start. (Figs. W4.20 / W4.21)

The idea was to present Kevin Pyle's art as something like a comic strip, but where the reader could dive down through two layers beneath it. One layer would be explanatory text, and the second would be documents. These could be a sort of Easter egg for anyone who spent some time with the site. I wanted the whole thing to use freely available noncopyright material, so I commissioned The Love Technology to perform a traditional French folk song relevant to the period. (France in the 50s had a folk revival not unlike the American one.) Likewise the art is all drawn from historical material but freely recast—*detourned* as the Situationists would say—so as to be available in the public domain again under the Creative Commons license. The text of the strip is also all detourned from the writings of Guy Debord and others. One aspect of the digital humanities that I think tends to get neglected is the aesthet-

W4.21 Created in collaboration with the designer Erik Loyer and the comic artist Kevin C. Pyle, McKenzie Wark's "Totality for Kids" brings together image, sound, and annotation in the style of an interactive comic to examine the work the Situationist International. The speech bubbles function as portals to further contextual material drawn from a wide variety of sources. The piece notes that "the struggle is to hold open the door of possibility that 1968 opened, even if only in memory."

ics of presenting research material, and what attracted me to *Vectors* is their exploratory attitude to this. (Fig. W4.22)

## Designer's Statement by Erik Loyer

Since its publication in 1993, interactive media designers have turned to Scott McCloud's *Understanding Comics* as a kind of bible for visual communication in the digital realm.

At first blush this may seem a bit odd, since the book doesn't make any great effort on its own to address digital technologies (unlike McCloud's later work *Reinventing Comics*). For me, however, and I think for many interactive media designers, the appeal lies in the way McCloud reveals that latent within comics is a ready-made, compact language for rich visual storytelling that, in its iconicity, lends itself to the symbolic languages of computers, not to mention low budgets.

W4.22 The interface for "Totality for Kids" features a rough, handmade aesthetic and makes use of maps in many of its panels. These maps have much more in common with the psychogeography favored by the Situationists than with the data-driven dreams of GIS.

Unlike in a AAA video game, compelling storytelling using the affordances of comics doesn't rely on photorealistic rendering, sophisticated artificial intelligence, legions of production artists, or other accoutrements typically out of reach of the individual designer. Instead, we find a set of simple, accessible, and powerful tropes for defining the shape of time, space, and perception.

The potentials that emerge when comics go digital have been a longtime fascination for me across multiple projects, and so when I learned that McKenzie Wark's project on the Situationist International involved a retelling of the history of the movement in comic book form, I immediately wanted to work on the project. Though our digital adaptation of the comic commissioned by Wark is more of a gesture toward these potentials than an in-depth exploration, I think the way the project makes digital objects of comic book visual-language fundamentals, like panels and dialogue bubbles, linking them to further explications of their content, hints at fruitful future directions. What happens when the content and characteristics of a panel in a digital comic become truly data-driven and responsive?

W4.23 *shi jian*: time.

## Excerpts from the Author's Statement by Mark Hansen

My proximate interest in developing this project for *Vectors* has been to provide a platform for exploring the multiplicity and hybridity of temporality as it is lived in China today. Without seeking to answer the theoretical questions raised by the problematic of a distinctly "Chinese" time (a task for which I am, to be sure, less than ideally qualified . . .), I hope to open up possibilities for discerning and indeed for experiencing the constitutive differences that may in fact still mark the Chinese experience of time, even at a historical point when all temporal experience is inescapably inflected by the common rhythms that undergird contemporary globalization and hypermodernization. (Fig. W4.23)

To do so, I have chosen to use my own time in China, across a full cycle of seasons from fall 2006 until summer 2007, as documented in the archive of photographs and short video clips that I accumulated over the course of this period, as the basis for a work that is meant to allow different potential temporalizations and retemporalizations of this time-specific documentary material. The organizational categories that structure the work and that differentiate the chronological time line (composed of the date-stamped images and videos) into divergent subsets of the documentary material include factors that are both intrinsic and extrinsic to the images themselves: place, type of light, point of view, type of time. Developed in collaboration with the artist-designer Raegan Kelly, these categories catalyze singular processes of retemporalization that, importantly for me, cut across the

phenomenology-cosmology divide introduced by the philosopher Paul Ricoeur in his analysis of time in *Time and Narrative.* In my own meditation on the Husserlian figure of the "temporal object," an object, e.g., a melody, that provides a surrogate for the otherwise ineffable flux of time through the brain, I have come to appreciate the significance of Ricoeur's argument that a phenomenology of time-consciousness is insufficient to address the "being of time" in its full scope. (Fig. W4.24)

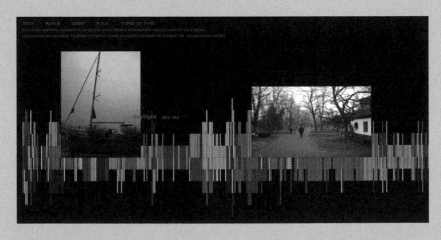

W4.24 Readers can explore Mark Hansen's large collection of photographs through a variety of lenses. This particular interface sorts the images by the quality of light they contain.

## Excerpts from the Editor's Statement by Tara McPherson

At its core, the piece consists of Hansen's personal media archive of several months spent living in Beijing—a database of over 1,200 images and 103 videos. The individual images are not wildly different from those populating Facebook or Flickr. They encapsulate familiar domestic and touristic scenes, the rituals of daily life and captured locales. Yet the interface design brings the data structure to form in precise and conceptually loaded ways, intent on shaking these images free from the conceit of the virtual album or tour.

Rather, it activates the archive across multiple axes, allowing the user to sort the collection by date, place, quality of light, point of view, and type of time. These methods of visualization—from a time line to a gorgeous color-coded interpretation of light sources—both organize and distance the photographs, ideally opening the user up to an experience of the heterogeneity of temporality. As such, Hansen's project seeks to wrench what might seem a personal archive of mediated memory toward a robust engagement with the very nature of time and transition, allowing for diverse retemporalizations. (Fig. W4.25)

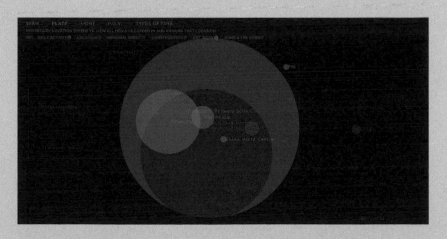

W4.25  Here the images are sorted by location. These various slices through the database of more than 1,300 media objects powerfully remind us that varied interfaces to a single collection can reveal different emotive and aesthetic aspects of the data.

## Scaling *Vectors*

Over the past several years, concurrent with the work on the journal, the *Vectors* team has also been expanding on the lessons learned through our ongoing research. With support from the Mellon Foundation and the National Endowment for the Humanities and in close collaboration with many colleagues (including especially Wendy Chun, Brian Goldfarb, Nicholas Mirzoeff, and Joan Saab, who were co–private investigators on the early work with Mellon, and Abby Smith Rumsey, who focused our efforts through the Scholarly Communication Institute), we have been forming a larger organization, the Alliance for Networking Visual Culture. Our goal is to formulate new ways of working with digitized archival materials within the humanities and to continue to push for new expressive modes of digital scholarly publishing. In the context of specific research questions in visual and media studies, the Alliance focuses on integrating the primary source materials available in online databases and archives more directly into born-digital scholarship, extending the work of the Vectors Lab in important new directions. Strategic partnerships with archives (including the Shoah Foundation, Critical Commons, the Hemispheric Institute's Digital Video Library, the Internet Archive, and the Getty Library), several university presses (MIT, California, Duke, Michigan, NYU, Oxford, and the Open Humanities Press), select humanities centers (at various points including University of California's Humanities Research Institute, the University of Washington, NYU, Duke, Notre Dame, Claremont, and Illinois, among others), and scholarly societies such as the CAA provide the testing ground for the investigation of new publishing platforms and protocols. Though Raegan Kelly has moved on from the team, our core of four has been enriched by several new members, espe-

## The Alliance for Networking Visual Culture

cially Phil Ethington, Alexei Taylor, Curtis Fletcher, micha cárdenas, Samantha Gorman, Michael Lynch, and Lucas Miller. (Fig. 2.24)

One particular area of research involves working with images, film, sound files, and video in livelier ways within our scholarly analyses, harking back to the days of the Eames Office. Obviously, as bandwidth has increased, moving images have exploded on the web. From popular video sites like YouTube to specialized archives like the Hemispheric Institute's Digital Video Library and the Shoah Foundation collection, a variety of moving-image media is now available for scholarly analysis. Indeed, YouTube claims that seventy-two hours of video are uploaded to its servers every minute. A key Scalar partner is Critical Commons, a user-generated video archive established by Steve Anderson of the Vectors Lab. On various websites he describes the resource as "a public media archive and fair use advocacy network that supports the transformative reuse of media in scholarly and creative contexts. . . . At the heart of Critical Commons is an online platform for viewing, tagging, sharing, annotating, curating, and spreading media." In the context of Scalar, Critical Commons becomes a safe harbor for scholars to post commercial media—from video to sound to images—for use in their Scalar projects. This serves at least three key functions. First, it helps enrich the archive available at Critical Commons, a valuable resource for teaching and research. Second, it strengthens the fair-use claim scholars have for using copyrighted media in transformative ways. Third, using Critical Commons provides a more stable location

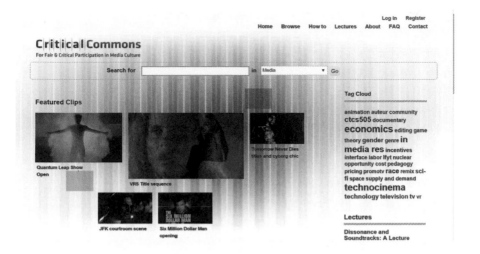

2.25 Critical
Commons enacts
key arguments
about fair use in
its design and its
communities
of use.

for project files than YouTube or other commercial platforms that may remove media at any time, particularly copyrighted media clips. (When Scalar authors "incorporate" media files into their projects, they are actually linking to that work; this practice both keeps the Scalar project smaller and nimbler and makes it easier to publish with a press, as the media file is only being cited, not technically published.) (Fig. 2.25)

These video and image materials are ripe for scholarly interpretation, particularly in a format that positions analysis side by side with archival material. Film scholars might now include clips alongside their interpretations, using annotations to facilitate more-detailed close readings and allowing their audience to test their claims with the media at hand. A scholar might work primarily in image, sound, and video, minimizing the role of text if that suits her aims. Emerging practices also point the way toward new time-based modes of argumentation and scholarship (like the previously mentioned video essays) and toward new engagements with archival materials.

There are lessons to be learned from our engagement with video about how scholarship itself might unfold temporally in response to a user's engagement with a digital archive. Though some projects might take the user along a scholar's carefully pruned and relatively fixed pathway or "cut" within such a collection, other projects can set the stage for the user to begin navigating her own pathways, adding new layers to the scholarly interpretation of a digital holding. Some of these interpretations could be vigorously peer-reviewed and warranted through relationships to established presses, libraries, or centers; others might encourage more open and bottom-up networks—new, livelier modes of collaboration and curation. Over time, we might begin to see how users respond to a variety of materials held within a collection and to produce analyses of how scholarly writing emerges within and across collections. Scholars might alternatively track the silences and absences of the archive within the space of the archive itself, haunting it with their own interpretations and poetics, foregrounding the impossibility of total knowledge or complete access. If libraries and museums have now carefully curated and digitized these troves of material, humanities scholars can and should engage these collections in ways that push beyond the linear book or article. How might we close the gap between archive and analysis?

Historically, the archive was officially meant to collect, preserve, and protect. Selection of, access to, and use of archival materials was rigorously regulated. The archive cultivated an ethos of the rare and the original. Careful order was imposed. The digitization of archives has upset this careful hierarchy. Digital archival materials might be circulated and shared more freely; the line between archive and library blurs. Amateur and expert might build archives together. We can begin to imagine the archive-as-database as a site of creation,

PANORAMA EPHEMERA

MANIFESTO
1. Why add to the population of orphaned artworks?
2. Don't presume that new work improves on old
3. Honor our ancestors by recycling their wisdom
4. The ideology of originality is arrogant and wasteful
5. Dregs are the sweetest drink
6. And leftovers were spared for a reason
7. Actors don't get a fair shake the first time around, let's give them another
8. The pleasure of recognition warms us on cold nights and cools us in hot summers
9. We reach the future only by roundabout means
10. As we wish to address the future, so the past desires to address us
11. Access to what's already happened is cheaper than access to what's happening now
12. Archives are justified by use
13. Make a quilt not an advertisement

FOUR STAGES OF AN ARCHIVISTS' CAREER
1. Each film is precious and unconditionally loved.

ECOMETAPHORIC FLOW
Plants to food to compost to soil to plants to food.

change, and emergence. In the past, humanities scholars have raided archives to capture those treasures for their books and articles. This relationship has often been unidirectional and vampiric, giving little back to the archive. In an era of connected data, our interpretations might live within the digital archive, curating pathways of analysis through its data sets or framing the archive through multiple points of view. (Fig. 2.26)

The Alliance for Networking Visual Culture is building both human and technological infrastructure in support of these goals, including the authoring and publishing platform Scalar, which was released in open beta in spring 2013 (receiving a *PC Magazine*'s Editors' Choice award) and given a substantial design revision in summer 2015. As of spring 2016, the platform had over 15,000 users. Scalar allows scholars to author with relative ease long-form multimedia projects that

**2.26**
Rick Prelinger's "Panorama Ephemera" from *Vectors*' "Ephemera" issue insists that "archives are justified by use." Design by Raegan Kelly.

incorporate a variety of digital materials while also connecting to digital collections, using built-in visualizations, exploring nonlinearity, supporting customization, and more. It draws from the lessons learned working on *Vectors* projects but allows scholars to produce digital scholarship without a design and programming team. It doesn't demand that scholars have mapped a rigid data structure in advance of authoring, which allows for flexibility in the relation between different components of a project. For instance, the visual culture scholar Nicholas Mirzoeff used Scalar to create an extension of his print book *The Right to Look.* In *"We Are All Children of Algeria": Visuality and Countervisuality, 1954–2011,* Mirzoeff not only incorporates a rich set of multimedia examples, but also structures his piece along multiple intersecting pathways in a manner that serves to reinforce his larger ideas about the value of the demonstration as a theoretical model. Form and content merge in very compelling ways. Though Mirzoeff and several others scholars have used Scalar to produce digital companions to print books, Scalar has also been used to create interactive exhibit reviews, born-digital scholarly articles for journals like *TDR (The Drama Review)* and *American Literature,* interactive textbooks, custom media experiences, entire born-digital books (sometimes multilingual), classroom assignments, electronic fiction, and many other projects. In many ways, it is already functioning as the sketchpad it was partially conceived to be.

# The Scalar Feature Set and Showcase

A free online authoring platform, Scalar is designed to allow scholars to author born-digital scholarship of a variety of lengths and formats. Well-suited for essay- or book-sized projects, Scalar can also be used to build media galleries or photo essays, author collaborative projects, collect and organize research, solicit reader feedback, create experimental projects or narrative games, and more. The second version of Scalar, with a newly designed look and feel, went live in summer 2015.

Some of Scalar's capacities are noted here. Our website and User's Guide provide even more details. (http://scalar.usc.edu/scalar/features/)

## Archival Partnerships

(Fig. W5.1)

The Scalar team has negotiated partnerships with a number of archives, including the Internet Archive, Critical Commons, and the Shoah Foundation. When a scholar uses Scalar's import feature to link to materials from these partners, the metadata affiliated with these objects are imported into Scalar, helping to keep the context of the material intact. Using trusted archives also helps ensure that a link will stay more robust, but, should the link not persist, the context for that file is still in the Scalar project. Cultivating archival partnerships is a key project of the Alliance for Networking Visual Culture, Scalar's home. Eventually, we hope that analyses created in Scalar might "roundtrip" back to the archive using emerging open linked data paradigms. We are currently developing a middleware system, Tensor, to explore these possibilities under the leadership of Craig Dietrich.

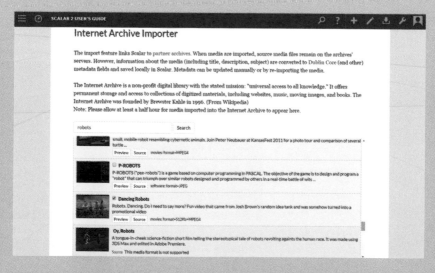

W5.1  Scalar's import feature, showing a search done on the holdings of the Internet Archive from within Scalar.

## Media Annotations
(Fig. W5.2)

Scalar enables scholars to work closely with visual and audio evidence (and even source code), providing tools that allow fine-grained, time-based annotations. These annotations become pages in their own right within the Scalar database, which allows a great deal of flexibility in how annotations might be used or reused in a project. A scholar might annotate source code with sound files or a film clip with still images. For the reader, Scalar currently incorporates the Hypothes.is annotation tools, allowing public or private markup of a Scalar project, although we are also working on other annotation tools as well.

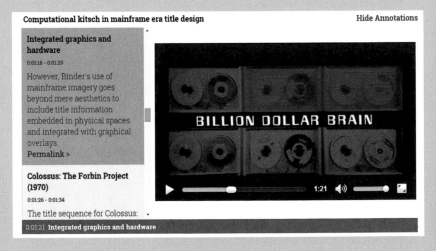

W5.2 Steve Anderson used extensive media annotations in his "Chaos and Control," a Scalar article published in the journal *American Literature*.

## Flexible Structure

(Fig. W5.3)

Scalar can do much more than simply create linear pages of text with embedded images (although it does that very well). The semantic elements in Scalar allow you to model conceptual structures in a variety of ways, exploring the full capacity for various sequences and groupings. For instance, you might investigate an idea through a series of linear paths (i.e., sets of sequential pages) but also through categorical groupings using tags or a gallery view. Paths can easily contain subpaths when appropriate; for instance, a subpath might be used to provide additional explanation of important concepts or to explore related material.

Tags can refer to other tags to create linked groupings. Some authors have used Scalar to create branched narratives for experimental fiction and gamelike projects.

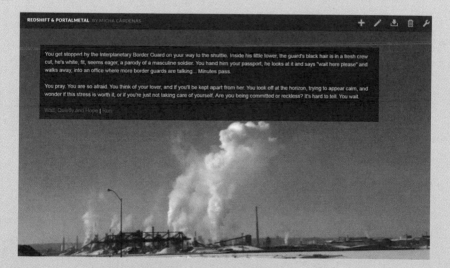

**W5.3** micha cárdenas's "Redshift and PortalMetal" used the flexibility of Scalar to create a branched-narrative interactive game.

## Open API and Customization

(Fig. W5.4)

Scalar projects can be uniquely customized using the platform's open application programming interface, or API. An API is s a set of routines, protocols, and tools for building software applications. Scalar's API allows an author to power a custom front end, combine Scalar with other data sources, or create new visualizations. All the content from an author's project is available either directly through URL-based requests in RDF-XML and JSON formats, or through a free JavaScript library that creates a unified model of downloaded Scalar data. This feature means that Scalar can support projects quite similar to *Vectors* projects.

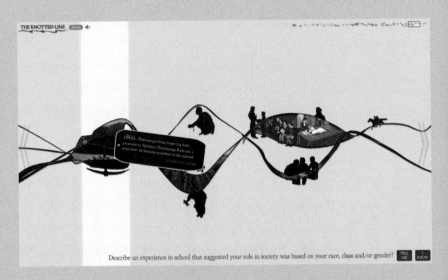

W5.4 "The Knotted Line," by Evan Bissell and Erik Loyer, uses Scalar's API to create a custom front end for a rich tactile, visual, and sonic experience.

## Visualizations

(Figs. W5.5 / W5.6)

Scalar includes a suite of visualizations that can quickly reveal a project's structure and relationships. These visualizations are automatically generated as an author creates a project and are available to both author and reader. Visualizations can also become part of a project's argument. For instance, a performance studies project might tag a series of media clips with various emotion tags. The tag visualization would then group those media automatically, allowing an alternative interface to the project that might then itself be incorporated into a narrative pathway.

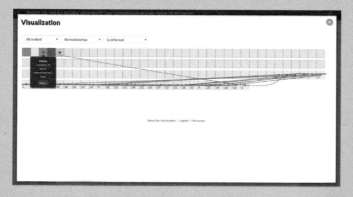

W5.5 / W5.6 These two images are different visualizations from the same project, Jentery Sayers's "Making the Perfect Record," published in *American Literature*. The top image is a grid view showing all the project content and relationships among the content; the second is a path or branched view showing the project's overall structure.

# Sample Scalar Projects
# Companions to Print Books

(Fig. W5.7)

W5.7 Jason Mittell's *Complex TV* was created as a digital companion to the print book of the same name. It features the television clips discussed in the book, housing the clips in the fair-use archive Critical Commons. The project includes pages that correspond to the book's chapters as well as a video gallery of all the media that uses Scalar's gallery feature. Other book companion projects in Scalar include Nicholas Mirzoeff's *"We Are All Children of Algeria": Visuality and Countervisuality, 1954–2011* (the print version of which is titled *The Right to Look*), which takes advantage of Scalar's flexible structure to illustrate his notion of the demonstration, and Matt Delmont's *The Nicest Kids in Town,* a media-rich extension of his print book of the same name.

## "Pathfinders" by Dene Grigar and Stuart Moulthrop

(Fig. W5.8)

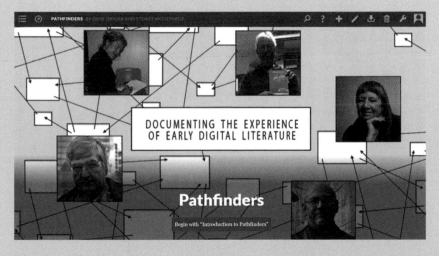

W5.8 "Pathfinders" is an ongoing collaborative research project that documents early digital literature. Making rich use of video, the authors document various readings of early electronic projects on their original computer platforms.

# The Civic Media Project

(Figs. W5.9 / W5.10)

W5.9  Spearheaded by Eric Gordon and Paul Mihailidis, the Civic Media Project functions as a research hub for a large-scale initiative documenting case studies of civic engagement and activism. Their work will include print books as well.

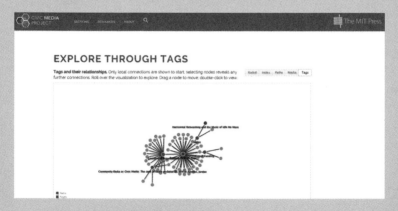

W5.10  The Civic Media Project makes use of Scalar's tagging feature to provide alternative groupings of the site's content.

# "Hearing the Music of the Hemispheres" by Erin Mee

(Fig. W5.11)

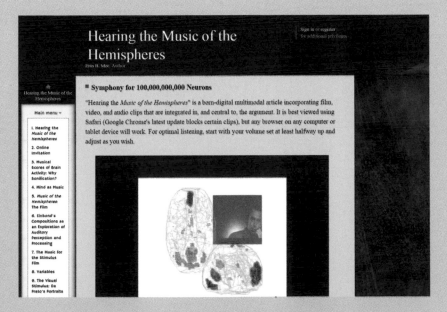

W5.11 Published as a multimodal essay in *TDR* (*The Drama Review*), Erin Mee's piece makes vivid use of sound. Scalar makes particular sense as a platform for scholars working with audiovisual materials.

## "Exhibitions Close Up— *Bernini: Sculpting in Clay*" by Sheryl Reiss

(Fig. W5.12)

W5.12 The journal *caa.reviews* used Scalar to create a layered and multimodal exhibition review, recalling an earlier *Vectors* project on Jenny Holzer.

*What Is Performance Studies?*
edited by Diana Taylor and
Marcos Steuernagel
(Fig. W5.13)

W5.13 The Scalar team has worked closely with the Hemispheric Institute and Duke University Press on a number of publications, including the interview-driven *What Is Performance Studies?* In addition to its strong social justice focus, the Hemispheric Institute also works in multiple languages, and both these elements have enriched our collaborations.

## "FemTechNet Critical Race and Ethnic Studies Pedagogy Workbook" by the Critical Race and Ethnic Studies (CRES) Committee

(Fig. W5.14)

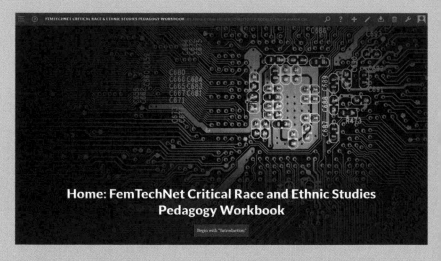

W5.14 The FemTechNet CRES Committee has been using Scalar to build a workbook of resources for teaching race and ethnic studies. Their interest in intersectionality (among other topics) dovetails with Scalar's own intersectional design, and the committee's collaborative and ongoing structure makes good use of Scalar's potential for multi-authored research. We have seen Scalar used extensively for pedagogical projects and are now enhancing the platform for that purpose. As of fall 2015, the CRES committee included Anne Cong-Huyen, Genevieve Carpio, Sharm Das, George Hoagland, Michael Mirer, Veronica Paredes, Amanda Phillips, and Christofer Rodelo.

# Digital dissertations

(Figs. W5.15 / W5.16)

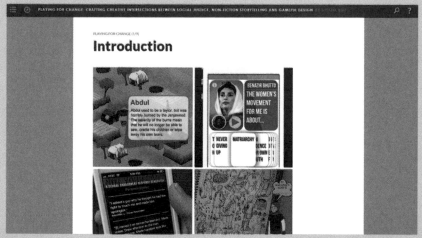

**W5.15 / W5.16** Scalar has now been used to create a number of digital dissertation projects, including Susana Ruiz's "Playing for Change" and Dwayne Dixon's "Endless Question."

Many of the scholars we have collaborated with are interested in allowing the users or readers of their research to engage with their primary evidence while also exploring the scholars' own interpretations of that evidence. Working in Scalar, scholars are pulling sets of visual materials from digitized collections into Scalar projects or "books"; this encourages a project's reader to examine these materials in their own right while also engaging with a scholar's analysis of the materials through careful annotation and juxtaposition. A good example is a project now under way by the media theorist Kara Keeling and the filmmaker Thenmozhi Soundararajan. Soundararajan previously founded a nonprofit, Third World Majority, focused on digital storytelling with global youth. Along with their Scalar collaborator micha cárdenas, she and Keeling have posted materials related to the organization on the Internet Archive, one of the Alliance's partners. These materials encompass hundreds of videos and still images, as well as text documents of various kinds. Keeling and Soundararajan have incorporated this work into a Scalar "book" and have invited several collaborators to author pathways through this material. When completed, a reader will be able to explore the collection of primary materials in a fairly open way, but she will also be able to follow one of several pathways through the materials that are authored by filmmakers, nonprofit workers, and several scholars of digital storytelling, media history, and global cinema. Such a project is neither solely a book nor solely an archive, neither simply database nor narrative, but rather a hybrid space between those binaries that blends an edited collection of essays with an abundant cache of primary materials. Using Scalar's built-in commenting features, the reader of the project can then add her own commentary, providing more context for the collection of primary materials or responses to the scholarly interpretations of the collection. In its role in the

Third World Majority project, Scalar begins to resemble a robust assemblage for generative making that might also be aligned with Keeling's own theoretical work on digital media. In her essay "I = Another," she mobilizes that title's equation to articulate "a renewed interest in forging dynamic models of commonality and belonging that exceed the prior logics of identity politics while remaining invested in the workings of difference that some versions of those politics made into politically salient sensibilities and strategies" (56). In effect, Keeling and Soundararajan are bringing together a set of geographically distributed contributors—academics, artists, activists—to engage a shared body of evidence but also to collaborate across difference through the platform itself. The authors will cut through the archive with ethical intent, exploring the fuzzy edges through which "I = Another" might begin to "gesture toward the radical potential it harbors." Several models of collaboration collide here: the original collaborative practices of Third World Majority come alive again within digital spaces, creative thinkers engage the material through the desires of the present, audiences are invited to join the process in possible futures, and authors and readers encounter the agency of the machine. (Fig. 2.27 )

2.27
An early design for the Third World Majority's Scalar project drew on the nonprofit's own graphic identity and color scheme.

A similar project spearheaded by Jacqueline Wernimont took a more pedagogical approach, incorporating students and scholars in a summer research intensive that explored the early twentieth-century photographs of Edward
Curtis. Aggregating over 2,500 image, sound, and document
files from several museum and library collections, "Performing Archive: Curtis and 'The Vanishing Race'" investigates
the photographer's oeuvre through multiple lenses, staging a
variety of intersectional cuts through this large collection
that reframe the controversial images through scholarly
analysis, historical context, and imaginative regroupings. As
the project authors note, their work is meant to operate on
many levels:

> Our narrative content provides one approach to moving
> through a small subset of the collections gathered
> here. We also wanted to provide users with ways to
> approach the material that were both more traditional
> and disruptive. The most traditional of these is the
> Book Structure Path.... Other more disruptive paths
> are designed to cut across The North American Indian
> collection and include material items that Curtis collected
> during his life.... Some of these paths group people or
> kinds of items together, for example the Tribe paths.
> Other paths are more interpretive, like the Keyword paths,
> which explore thematic groupings like gender, work, and
> costume. These are designed to stimulate questions and
> aid in exploration. (Figs. 2.28 / 2.29)

This type of connected and shared research and writing
space has emerged as a key area of interest for Alliance partners, who recognize the capacity of such practices to foster
new collaborations, to reach new audiences (certain paths

Media Gallery

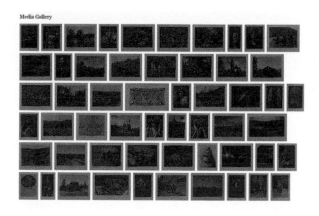

Ken Gonzales-Day, Scripps College

Curtis visited the Hopi on multiple occasions and went as early as 1900, went back in 1902, 1904, 1906, 1911, 1912, and 1919, so dating which images where shot when can pose something of a challenge, but he does note that the traditional squash blossom hairdo was discontinued by the second decade of the twentieth century. In these early images, ☒ "Watching the Dancers" and ☒ "The Hopi Maiden," Curtis captured young unwed women at a time when they still wore their hair in the traditional style. So one can understand that such images confirmed his, and other's views, that traditional ways of life where passing, and for Curtis, it confirmed the popular view, which his images helped to cement in the popular imagination —that Native Americans were a "vanishing race." His biographer, Tomas Egan writes:

*When he started in 1896, Indians were at their low ebb, with a total population that had dwindled to less than 250,000. Many scholars thought they would disappear within a generation's time. Curtis set out to document lifestyle, creation myths and language. He recorded more than 10,000 songs on a primitive wax cylinder, and wrote down vocabularies and pronunciation guides for 75 languages.*

"Watching the Dancers", 1906, volume 12, portfolio plate 405, photogravure, 46 x 31 cm., Special Collection, Honnold Library, Claremont. Source: Critical Cartesians

being more relevant to certain types of readers), and to facilitate close analysis and multiple forms of expression. Within a single project, we glimpse research operating across scales, as scholars are able to move from the micro level of a project (perhaps a single image or video annotation) to the structure of the entire project and its integrated media. The researcher can create careful close readings within a project of many components that can also be instantly represented as a whole collection, thus moving beyond the artificial binary of

2.28 / 2.29
Two screengrabs from "Performing Archive," the first in gallery view, the second a narrative pathway, from "The Literariness of the Curtis Photographs," by Cheryl Walker.

"distant" versus "close" reading that so often surfaces in conversations about the digital humanities, instead privileging the scaled reading that the classics and DH scholar Martin Mueller has called for. The result richly combines narrative interpretation with visualizations that are automatically generated by the semantic elements of the platform. These visualizations allow an author or reader to see the larger structure of a project that may have been built up more organically piece by piece, while also allowing iterative refinement to this structure. Visualizations can also allow a user to access and explore specific elements of a project, including tags, media files, and narrative pathways. Thus, the visualizations are not merely illustrative; they are also powerful interpretations that present a project's structure, evidence, and arguments in new ways. Scalar projects bring narrative analysis and external archives together with the database, potentially enriching each. This method of researching and

writing across scales now predominantly unfolds within a given Scalar project, but the possibility for integrating these modes of analysis back into our archival partners' larger holdings represents a key area for future research. (Figs. 2.30 / 2.31 / 2.32 / 2.33 / 2.34)

The software that underpins Scalar was born of the frustrations our scholars often experienced working with traditional database tools as well as with our own DBG. *Vectors* engaged intersectional, political, and feminist work at the level of content (what the projects were about) but also integrated form and content so that the theoretical implications of the work were manifest in the aesthetic and information design. Scalar is now seeking to integrate this methodology at the level of software design, infecting the database with feminist intent. Scalar takes our early experiments at deforming the database for *Vectors* projects to a very different level by wrapping a relational database in a very particular seman-

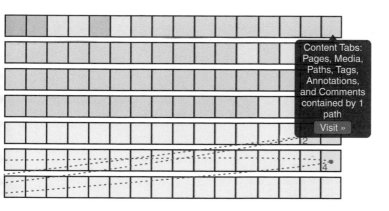

Content Tabs: Pages, Media, Paths, Tags, Annotations, and Comments contained by 1 path
Visit »

2.30 / 2.31 / 2.32 / 2.33 / 2.34 These five images from the Scalar *User's Guide* illustrate some of the visualizations that Scalar automatically creates for each project. From first to last: a grid view, a radial view, a path view, a media view, and a tag view.

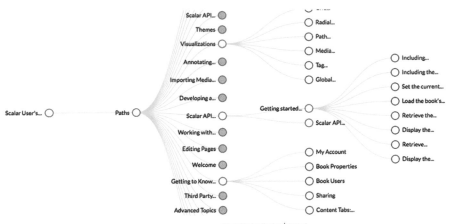

About this visualization | Legend

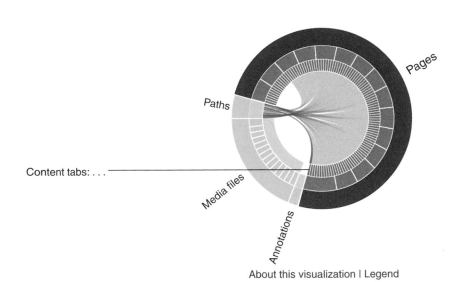

About this visualization | Legend

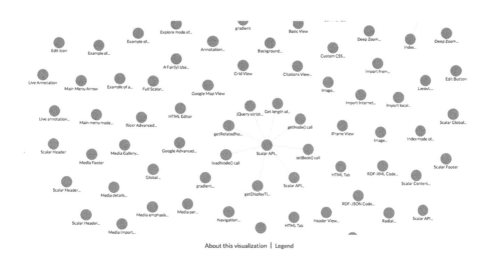

About this visualization | Legend

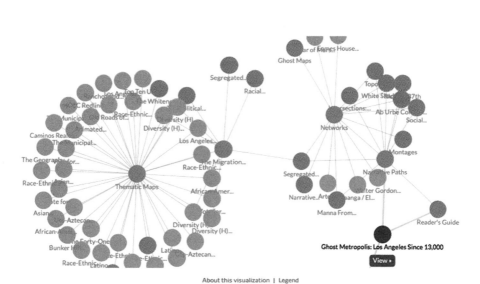

About this visualization | Legend

2.35 / 2.36
Our process has always been to actively prototype our ideas with scholars in ways that suit their needs. An important step between the DBG and Scalar was our work with the media scholar Alexandra Juhasz on *Learning from YouTube,* a born-digital book about YouTube that makes its argument in a form that both mimics and pushes back against YouTube's structure and information design. Video is integral to the piece, working not as simple illustration but as a key part of the argument. Craig Dietrich worked closely with Alex on the project. Her use of "tours" (shown in the second

tic layer, a process spearheaded by Craig Dietrich and Erik Loyer. (Figs. 2.35 / 2.36)

In effect, we wanted to build a system that respected the research methodologies of the scholars with whom we work. Scalar resists the modularity and compartmentalized logics of dominant computation design by flattening out the hierarchal structures of platforms such as WordPress. While easy to use, it also moves beyond the template structures that frequently categorize the web, allowing a high degree of customization and experiential front ends through its API. A project might be quite simple, looking much like contemporary web pages, or it might use the API to create a more *Vectors*-like experience. In his collaborations with the activist and artist Evan Bissell, Erik Loyer has used Scalar to design two richly interactive projects, "The Knotted Line" and "Freedom's Ring." Each of these projects begins with a custom interface designed by Loyer that "opens" to a set of contextual materials that look more conventional. These projects are "powered" by Scalar even as they look and feel quite different from each other and from other Scalar pieces. Thus, projects created in Scalar can mediate a whole set of binaries: between close and distant reading, user and author, interface and back end, micro and macro, theory and practice, archive and interpretation, text and image, database and narrative, and human and machine. It respects both the system and the node, or, Mirzoeff told me, "You can explore an issue and then develop its intersections with other issues" in a very dynamic way. Mirzoeff has described working with the platform as a kind of horizontal writing; I think we might also point to its associative, relational, and intersectional possibilities as well as to its capacity to model an in-between (of interface to code, of archive to scholarship, of author to audience, of object to context). (Figs. 2.37 / 2.38 / 2.39 / 2.40)

At the level of the individual page, authoring in Scalar in many ways feels similar to authoring in WordPress. In our early design explorations, we debated adapting WordPress for our platform, but Dietrich found its structure confining. Its origins as blogging software shape its features in particular ways, and adapting these structures is very challenging for the typical scholar, although those with more advanced programming skills can often bend WordPress to their will. As the DBG evolved, the team debated its affordances, imagining how it might be extended as the kind of sketchpad Loyer had earlier envisioned. Kelly wrote in one collaborative design document

image) helped shape the ways in which our team would develop paths in Scalar. Our collaboration with Alex was important both for the lessons learned in working with a press (MIT) on a born-digital book and for thinking about the directions Scalar might take. Alex was a fellow in our first NEH Vectors Summer Institute (partnered with the UC Humanities Research Institute) and has written extensively about her experiences teaching about YouTube and the process of making her "book" with us on her blog, Media Praxis (https://aljean.wordpress.com/) and elsewhere.

2.37 / 2.38 / 2.39 / 2.40 These two pairs of images are from two projects by Evan Bissell and Erik Loyer (top: "The Knotted Line"; bottom: "Freedom's Ring"). Both projects use Scalar's API to create a custom interface to a project built in Scalar. The first images in each pair are the initial interfaces to the projects; tapping certain sections opens or unfolds the project to additional layers of historical and contextual information. "The Knotted Line" explores the tensions between

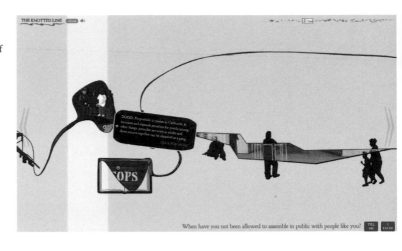

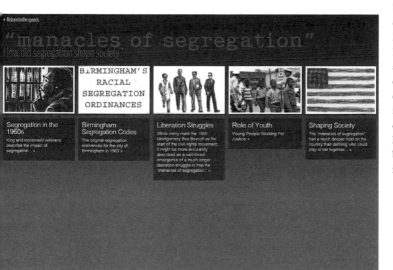

freedom and incarceration in US history through a nonchronological time line and a rich collection of supplemental material. It has been used extensively in after-school programs. The audio-rich "Freedom's Ring" was commissioned by the King Center at Stanford University to contextualize Martin Luther King Jr.'s famous speech. The piece challenges a certain sanitized image of King, connecting his activism to broader struggles for change.

that we wanted to avoid "*organizational dynamics* from a top down perspective." She continued, noting that "the structure [should] EMERGE FROM an engagement with the content and between the... collaborators. Yes, ultimately the process of working with the DBG imposes structural integrity (hopefully : ) ) but only after hearing the author/designer out." Loyer responded at length:

> I agree that emergence is one of the main points of difference here. One thing that pains me sometimes in the Vectors process is when I realize that my class definitions have squashed a scholar's concept that I didn't fully understand, but the realization comes too late in the process to do anything about it, and the scholar has to work around the issue. My process usually ends up being about making a best guess about structure after a brief immersion in the scholar's work, hopefully allowing enough freedom for evolution and change, but not so much that the piece becomes a zero-gravity of structure. One of the things we are proposing, however, is that with the proper tools, scholars should actually be able to do a better job conceptualizing their work as objects than we can. Not that the perspective of the designer/outsider/implementer wouldn't still bring something interesting to bear on the scholar's work, but that that process could happen on a more level playing field.

Though we began the design process imagining a system that would guide a scholar through the initial setup of her data structure using some sort of enhanced Eliza-like Q + A, Scalar instead generates that structure for scholars as they link to archival materials, create pages, sculpt pathways, and use tags. This structure is highly flexible, allowing a scholar to move things around and build new relations with relative ease. We imagined a platform that would privilege emergence over rigidity, flexibility over top-down structure.

We did not say, "Let's build an assemblage!" We were not reading the feminist theorist Liz Grosz in our planning sessions (although some of us were reading her at home). But we were prototyping Scalar on the basis of an assemblage we had already pulled together, one that involved work with well over a hundred scholars; with an evolving platform; with forms of critical thinking that privileged affect, emotion, embodiment, and difference; with emerging and experimental aesthetic registers; and with extended collaboration. Feminist and materialist thinking is in there—in Scalar—from the context of our practice. We could of course describe Scalar without reference to feminist or other theories of difference (certainly our grant applications often did). But Scalar emerged from the context of over a decade of work with scholars seeking to mobilize theories of difference and modes of activism to reimagine the relationship of technology to scholarship. The space from which it took shape encouraged an ongoing process of making, iteration, and remaking in which theory, human, and machine continually reshaped each other. We need to build more spaces for such reenactments to unfold. If Miriam Posner has written about DH needing to value people over things or projects, we might tweak this formulation to understand DH as needing to put people, technology, and projects in productive and generative relations. Jane Bennett's discussion of modification is interesting in this regard. She writes, "The process of modification is not under the control of any one mode—no mode is an agent in the hierarchal sense. Neither is the process without tension, for each mode vies with and against the (changing) affections of (a changing set of) other modes, all the while being subject to the element of chance or contingency intrinsic to any encounter" (22). (Figs. 2.41 / 2.42)

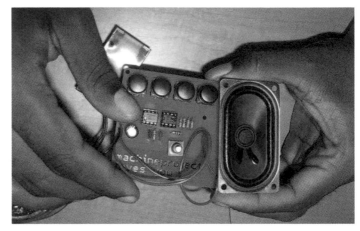

2.41 / 2.42 Most of our Scalar summer institutes involved computational activities beyond the keyboard, including workshops led by Machine Project and Garnet Hertz that allowed scholars to solder together simple synthesizers and to circuit-bend toys. Such workshops helped underscore the material nature of electronic devices. The first image is of a completed synthesizer; the second shows Marcela Fuentes, Craig Dietrich, and Brian Goldfarb hacking toys at a 2010 institute workshop led by Hertz.

Scalar differs from more hierarchical platforms like WordPress in its core technical structure. Consider the diagram from the WordPress site. It maps the database for WordPress 3.8. In a conversation about this image, Dietrich noted that the limits of WordPress for our purposes "can be summed up by just looking at the image: there are a bunch of differently sized shapes connected by rigid lines that looks more like an engine diagram than a digital ecosystem." I would observe that it also looks rather like the exploded-view diagrams of Bogost's *Alien Phenomenology*. He adds, "If one were to make a similar diagram for Scalar, it would be 'Page' table in the middle, with looping circles through each of the relationship types (path, tag, etc.), back to the original Page table. That would look much more like an ecosystem." It also recalls Anne Balsamo's diagram of the relations between culture and technology. (Fig. 2.43)

If WordPress privileges hierarchy, Scalar prefers immanence. Scalar might be thought of as a speculative remapping of rigidly logical structures toward more conceptual ones, creating possibilities for many-to-many relations of diverse and varied kinds, both human and machinic. If the Latourian litany is a flat list, a string of separate, self-contained things, the flatness of Scalar operates differently through its insistence on context and on relation. Scalar can give an object its due, but it also pursues that object's intersections with other objects and ideas. It is not a platform as a series of concentric boxes, but instead a platform for imagining relation. It is not simply speculative fiction, a utopian fantasy, a game that will never be played, however; it is an immanent reality, existing in both conceptual and technological registers. This materiality, this realness, this functionality, matters in every sense of the word, even if only for the moment. Of course, none of this means that WordPress cannot be used for good or Scalar for evil. WordPress certainly has a much larger user base and hence a better chance of long-term survival. It's a fellow traveler, if one that has arranged its bits quite differently. As we push for new forms of digital scholarship, the more the merrier.

Scalar is relational but more in the modes of the feminist

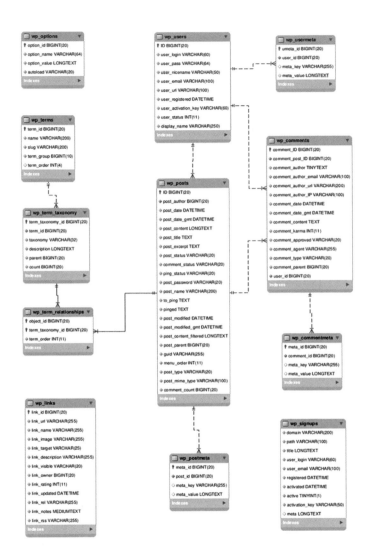

2.43

---------------------------------------------------------------

Craig Dietrich on the Technical Implementation of Scalar

Comparing Scalar to WordPress

In WordPress, there is a "one–to–many" relationship
(one parent, many children). They set it up like this, I
presume, because what on earth would the front end do with
pages that had multiple parents? This is of course a rhetorical question, because we know what a front end would do.
(In Scalar a page is contained by multiple paths.)

WordPress in this case is just thinking inside the box:
a parent has children. With Scalar we thought outside the
box (children can have many parents), but it took some effort to figure out how to make this work in the front–end
experience.

It's also difficult to express many–to–many relationships outside the database structure. XML is hierarchical so
actually can't express many–to–many relationships (many parents, many children), only one–to–many relationships (parent
node, many children nodes), unless one incorporates other
means like ID numbers.

We're fortunate to have come across RDF [Resource Description Framework] at just the right time in Scalar's development, since it can express many–to–many . . . but,
technically speaking, it uses ID numbers to accomplish this
(it just calls ID numbers "URIs" [Uniform Resource Identifi-
ers]), but RDF is more robust than XML in general.

Scalar definitely uses relational database features and
joins,
Pages table join > scalar_db_annotations join > Pages table
But, since we're joining pages recursively with other
pages (in this case through the annotations table), it's

circular, which to me is nonhierarchical and closer to what the RDF—semantic web is trying to accomplish than WordPress's database. I wish I had a better example, but what I usually like to say is that:

Wordpress tells you what its content is; Scalar suggests what its content is

— — — — — — — — — — — — — — — — — — — — — — — — — — — — — — — — — — — — — — —

Craig Dietrich on Scalar and Relational Databases

Technically speaking, we're using the relational database (DB) exactly for what it was designed for. We have a DB table called "pages" (there's a separate versions table that is linked to the pages table for multiple versions per page), then a set of tables that link pages to other pages:
Pages table -> relationship table -> Pages table
So, if a page is a path that contains other pages, the system looks at "scalar_db_contains"; for annotations it looks at "scalar_db_annotations," and so forth. Inside these relationship tables are keys for the source page and the destination page. This is a classic many—to—many relational setup.
I think where we successfully hacked convention, however, is in how we express the many—to—many relationships in the front end. Like the original database generator (DBG) — where we output a spreadsheet, then underneath each row had "sub-spreadsheets" of the connecting material from other tables — Scalar expresses the many—to—many relationships overtly in its front—end interface by allowing one or more pages to be linked to one or more pages (a video game might do this, e.g., by having a bunch of characters and a bunch of weapons and you can add weapons to characters and vice versa) and isn't something seen too often in content management sys-

tems. For example, Magento is an e-commerce platform used by small companies, and its flow is

Root category > subcategory > Products

Products can be grouped together, but this is where it gets really messy. Product groups are expressed on Product pages, so you can navigate along groupings or categories; this gets confusing! For Magento to be like Scalar, it would need to be work like this:

Products > groups/categories > Products

Then it would have to let the user define what a grouping is, whether it acts like a category, subcategory, grouping, or whatever. By trying to define things top-down, Magento limits the usefulness of categories and groupings or, more practically, limits what front-end designers can do with data originating in Magento.

--------------------------------------------------------

Craig Dietrich on Scalar, RDF, and "Flatness"

I'm usually hesitant to say that RDF makes Scalar flat, since ARC (appmosphere RDF classes) is only part of the overall database (which also includes many-to-many tables), and prefer to say that "an RDF philosophy" makes Scalar flat. However, because we output all Scalar data in RDF format through the application program interface (API) (Scalar takes material from our hybrid DB, crunches it into RDF, and outputs it), because much of Scalar's front end uses this API to get its data, and because outside systems (like "The Knotted Line") have pulled the same RDF data to drive their interfaces, I think this is more than enough evidence that RDF is what drives Scalar's flattened data hierarchy.

```
Scalar has an RDF installed (ARC) that is "flat," in that
when we save a page there are certain core fields that are
required (title, content, URL), but then, through the API,
we can send any other fields through: dcterms:subject, ip-
tc:SubjectReference, and so on. When the system encounters
these fields it simply dumps them into the ARC database;
when the page is asked for later, it pulls these back up.
On the one hand, these fields aren't useful to the inter-
face (they're metadata), but they're of course very useful
for people using the interface (such as archivists).
Going back to the Magento example: to install a new field
for Product (e.g., to add "Thread size" as a field in the
Product form), takes a bunch of steps. In Scalar, a new
field would just save into ARC without any context other
than the page it is attached to.
```

- - - - - - - - - - - - - - - - - - - - - - - - - - - - - - - - - - - - - - - -

materialists than on the terms of the relational database. Even while Scalar deploys an RDB as its core, it mitigates the relentless force of encapsulation that is at the heart of so much of object-oriented programming. It is contextual and friendly (to anthropomorphize). Take the media files an author might point to when working within Scalar. If an author is using an archive with good metadata practices, she can pull that metadata into Scalar, keeping the context for that information intact. At each moment of media addition, Scalar gently prompts the user to add more metadata, using existing standards while also allowing the user to adjust and tweak these standards, adding wily metadata of her own. The object, the media file, is not "really" there in Scalar (it stays safe in its archival home, a choice made to enable easier publishing in our rights-contentious times), but Scalar still treats the object with care and respect, attending to it meticulously, getting to know it (or its digital surrogate, itself an object in its own right) while also retaining relation and context. Drawing from lessons learned in *Vectors* projects by Daniel, Christen, and others, Scalar attends to context and to intersectional relation. Wendy Chun and the literary scholar Matthew Kirschenbaum remind us that the web is durable even as it feels ephemeral. Our traces there endure, susceptible to forensics. And yet our experience of the web is often one of loss. We visit a Pinterest board and find the perfect shade of paint for a remodel, only to have the trail to its name or manufacturer dead-end our desires. Link rot thwarts our ambitions. When I save an image from the web to my desktop to use in a PowerPoint presentation, I cut it free from its context in a way that's hard to resurrect for a casual user. Our technical systems might better value webs of relation. This desire to connect to archives and to treat (digital) objects more carefully emerged from the planning processes of the Alliance for Networking Visual Culture and the concerns of scholars and archivists, but Craig Dietrich made it so technologically, riffing on the database form. Thus, Scalar mitigates encapsulation in two ways. It does this, first, through the care it gives its objects, allowing scholars to study them intimately, to attend to them, to annotate them, to locate them, while also making them anew through new metadata, new contexts, and new relations. Second, Scalar also makes the database more relational, in our embodied and theoretical sense, encouraging an easier entanglement and intra-action of and with data and evidence.

Scalar takes seriously feminist methodologies ranging from the cut to theories of alliance, intersectionality, and assemblage not only in support of scholars undertaking individual projects but also in our technological and design principles. As authors work with the platform, they enter into a flow of becoming through the creation of a database on the fly and through an engagement with the otherness of the machine. Scalar respects machinic agency but does not cede everything to it.

As Anne Balsamo reminds us, "Every intra-action that constitutes a technology offers an opportunity to do things differently" (35). Scalar offers a way to explore the rich intra-actions that link matter and discourse, to engage the alterity of technology, and to cut through plenitude with ethical, intersectional intent. Our goal is to build technology in order that we might better understand it and its entanglements with culture; we aim to bend the digital to our desires and to use it in our utopias, if only in the instant. In theories of difference and relation, we already find bountiful ways in which we might rewire these circuits. Feminists and scholars of difference have long brought together those who value hybrid practices: artist-theorists, activist scholars, theoretical archivists, queer failures, experimental filmmakers, mestiza cyborgs.

We now need also to extend our critical and creative practices to include at least passing familiarity with code languages, operating systems, algorithmic thinking, and systems design. We have to shake ourselves out of our small field-based boxes and take seriously the possibility that our own knowledge practices are "normalized," "modular," and "black boxed" in much the same way as the code we might study or use in our work. That is, our very scholarly practices tend to undervalue broad contexts, meaningful relation, and promiscuous border crossing. Many of us "identify" as interdisciplinary, but very few of us extend that border crossing very far (theorists tune out the technical, the technologists are impatient of theoretical meandering, scholars of race mock the digital humanities). I am suggesting that the intense narrowing of our academic specialties over the past fifty years can actually be seen as an effect of or as complicit with the logics of modularity and the relational database. Just as the relational database works by normalizing data—that is, by stripping it of meaningful context and the idiosyncratic, creating a system of interchangeable equivalencies—our own scholarly practices tend to exist in relatively hermetically sealed boxes or nodes. Critical theory and poststructuralism have been powerful operating systems that have served us well; they were as hard to learn as the complex structures of C++, and we have dutifully learned them. They are also software systems in desperate need of updating and patching. They are lovely, and they are not enough. They cannot be all we do, but that is not to say that are not of any value.

In universities that simply shut down "old-school" departments—such as, at my university, German and geography; in the UK, Middlesex's philosophy program; in Arizona, perhaps all of ethnic studies; in Wisconsin, anything they can, including tenure—we scholars must engage the vernacular digital forms that make us nervous, authoring in them to better understand them and to re-create in technological spaces the possibility of doing the work that moves us. We need new practices and new modes of collaboration; we need to take seriously the casualization of labor in the university; we need to be literate in emerging scientific and technological methodologies but also in theories of race, globalization, materialism, and gender. We'll gain that literacy at least partially through an intellectual generosity or curiosity toward those whose practices are not our own. We need to privilege systemic modes of thinking that can understand relation and honor complexity, even while valuing precision and specificity. We need nimbler ways of linking the network and the node, operation and unit, and digital form and content, and we need to understand that categories like race and gender profoundly shape both form and content. In short, we need a good deal more exchange between the materialists and the digital makers of many kinds so that we might develop some shared languages and goals.

We must remember that computers are themselves encoders of culture. If, in the 1960s and 1970s, UNIX hardwired an emerging system of covert racism into our mainframes and our minds, then computation responds to culture as much as it controls it. Code and race are deeply intertwined, even as the structures of code labor to disavow these very connections. Politically committed academics with humanities skill sets must engage technology and its production, not simply as an object of our scorn, critique, or fascination, but as a productive and generative space that is always emergent and never fully determined.

# Outro: Scholarship in the Wild

Failure can become a potent form of critique, a repudiation of capitalism and profit margins, a refusal of the norm, an indifference to assimilation and a route to other ways of being in the world. —J. Halberstam (Fig. 3.1)

Due to technological obsolescence and other factors, a number of *Vectors Journal* projects have become unavailable since their original publication.

**In the News** unfortunately falls into this category, but an archival site is available.

Our apologies for the inconvenience. If you have questions about this project, please contact *Vectors* staff at usc.vectors@gmail.com.

3.1 Placeholder for a 2005 *Vectors* project that is no longer active.

This book has covered in some detail the kind of projects the Vectors Lab has produced and collaborated on, situating those in a broader history, but I have not much touched on the infrastructures for academic publishing. The Alliance for Networking Visual Culture has worked with different presses on various projects undertaken in Scalar, including Alex Juhasz's lively born-digital free book, *Learning from YouTube,* published by MIT Press in 2011, several collaborations between Duke University Press and the Hemispheric Institute, and Phil Ethington's expansive *Ghost Metropolis,* which will be published for sale by the University of California Press in both born-digital and print versions. We have worked with several other scholars on press-affiliated projects as well, including digital companion projects and special journal issues. The Andrew W. Mellon Foundation has helped us pursue this work, and it is continuing to seed small pockets of change among university presses, including recent grants to Stanford University Press and the University of Minnesota Press in partnership with Matt Gold of CUNY, among others. These small shifts are important, as they help university presses try out new platforms and new genres of digital scholarship while continuing their bread-and-butter business. Some of these

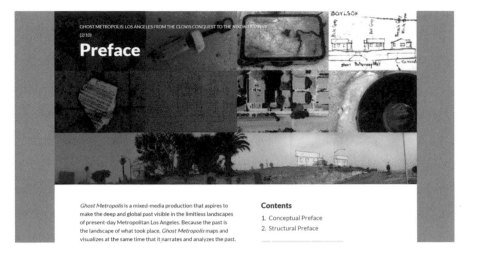

GHOST METROPOLIS: LOS ANGELES FROM THE CLOVIS CONQUEST TO THE NIXON TYRANNY
(2/10)

**Preface**

BOYLSON

*Ghost Metropolis* is a mixed-media production that aspires to make the deep and global past visible in the limitless landscapes of present-day Metropolitan Los Angeles. Because the past is the landscape of what took place, *Ghost Metropolis* maps and visualizes at the same time that it narrates and analyzes the past.

**Contents**

1. Conceptual Preface
2. Structural Preface

presses, including Stanford, are working in more experimental modes, imagining new relationships of form to content that draw on the capacities of the digital to model knowledge differently, not unlike works published in *Vectors*. Others, such as University of California, are rethinking the infrastructure for publishing electronic books and journals. (Fig. 3.2)

Nonetheless, from university libraries to scholarly societies to foundation offices, the need for new models for scholarly publishing is sorely felt and broadly acknowledged. Kathleen Fitzpatrick has carefully mapped this terrain in her book *Planned Obsolescence,* and she argues that "scholarly publishing as an enterprise is going to be difficult to make self-sustaining, but that doesn't mean that we can simply allow it to die; if scholars are to publish, their institutions must accept responsibility for—and fully support—the platforms that make such publishing possible" (186). In her move to serve as director of scholarly communication at the Modern Language Association, she is working hard to help build toward this sea

3.2 Phil Ethington's *Ghost Metropolis,* forthcoming from the University of California Press in both digital and print formats.

236

change, but there too the going is slow. Others have decided to sidestep the market and its slow changes and move quickly toward open-access publishing in a variety of forms. Within the sciences, whole communities have created their own infrastructures for publishing, breaking the stranglehold on their subfields of for-profit presses like Elsevier and Springer that continue to harvest academic labor while reaping exceptional profits that are not returned to the scholarly ecosystem.[1] The Association of Research Libraries (ARL), the umbrella organization for the top U.S. and Canadian university research libraries, has convened committees to support digital scholarship and to push back against the distorting effect of companies like Elsevier on their budgets.

In the humanities and social sciences we are also seeing changes. The Open Journal System (OJS) of the Public Knowledge Project was founded in 1998 by John Willinsky to build sustainable infrastructure for open-access scholarly publishing. It has steadily grown, adding software for open conferences and open monographs. Encompassing a wide range of disciplines, OJS is used by over six thousand journals in more than thirty languages, providing important publishing infrastructure, particularly in countries that lack access to publishing venues. Their software has been fairly text-centric to date, but they are working to change this. The Open Humanities Press has been championing open access since its founding in 2006 by Gary Hall, Sigi Jottkandt, and David Ottina. Hall has been a clarion voice for changing publishing since the late 1990s, when the open-access journal *Culture Machine* was launched. With Joanna Zylinska and Clare Birchall, he also spearheads the Living Books about Life series, an experiment in open-access transdisciplinary book curation. Janneke Adema and he have recently argued that open access should explore its

❚ Living Books About Life

more radical potential. They write: "One of the advantages of conceptualizing open access as a process of struggle rather than as a model to be implemented would be that doing so would create more space for radically different, conflicting, even incommensurable positions within the larger movement, including those that are concerned with experimenting critically with the form of the book and the way our system of scholarly communication currently operates" (35). They call not only for increasing access but also for expanding our critical imaginaries about what a scholarly book is, whom it serves, and whether the very form of books need not be reconsidered. (Fig. 3.3)

And, yet, most humanities scholars have never heard of Open Humanities Press (OHP), nor would they consider publishing there, despite its impressive editorial board, especially for scholars whose research has a theoretical bent.

3.3 The Living Books about Life series aggregates new digital books from open-access materials available freely online.

It is time we listened to Hall. As our modes of writing and reading increasingly take shape across our various screens, we humanities scholars must ask ourselves why we continue to fetishize print books and even online text above all other forms within the academy. Because they count and can be counted? Because they are familiar? Because they serve our individual careers? Which audiences do we foreclose by holding on to business as usual? What different ways of seeing and knowing do we ignore? Might we think not only of books and publishing but also of new flows of knowledge, of scholarship at various scales? This is not to say (as you probably read these words printed on paper) that we shouldn't publish print books, particularly with university presses. We should. But we should not do so automatically, without evaluating our choices and without also working in other formats and collaborations at the same time when our scholarship demands it. If our research attends to moving-image media, why not publish in digital formats that include those media, allowing a closer attention to our objects of study while permitting our audience to better test our claims? If our scholarship pursues a spatial analysis across time, why not use interactive maps when we present our work? In particular, tenured full professors have little to lose and much to gain by circulating their work for free through venues like OHP, in print or online. They might experiment with form, exploring the multimodal dimensions of digital scholarship if such endeavors enrich their research. Professors should also continue to work with nonprofit (or barely-for-profit) university presses to find new ways of creating and sharing our research and our writing. (Fig. 3.4)

Ted Striphas has challenged academics to rethink the ways in which we publish our work, often with companies

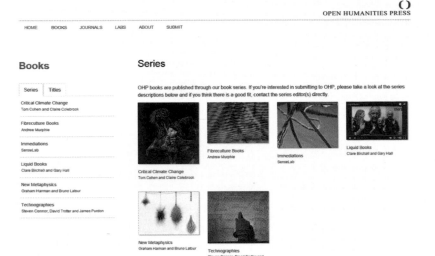

HOME    BOOKS    JOURNALS    LABS    ABOUT    SUBMIT

## Books

Series | Titles

Critical Climate Change
Tom Cohen and Claire Colebrook

Fibreculture Books
Andrew Murphie

Immediations
SenseLab

Liquid Books
Clare Birchall and Gary Hall

New Metaphysics
Graham Harman and Bruno Latour

Technographies
Steven Connor, David Trotter and James Purdon

## Series

OHP books are published through our book series. If you're interested in submitting to OHP, please take a look at the series descriptions below and if you think there is a good fit, contact the series editor(s) directly.

Critical Climate Change
Tom Cohen and Claire Colebrook

Fibreculture Books
Andrew Murphie

Immediations
SenseLab

Liquid Books
Clare Birchall and Gary Hall

New Metaphysics
Graham Harman and Bruno Latour

Technographies
Steven Connor, David Trotter and James Purdon

**3.4 The Open Humanities Press includes several series of free and print-on-demand monographs and journals.**

whose business practices are in direct contrast to the political goals we espouse in in our scholarship. (His example is Taylor and Francis and its parent corporation, Informa.) In commenting on the suicide of the open-access activist Aaron Swartz, Timothy Burke has argued that "the transformative impact of open access on inequality is already well-documented, and it's in keeping with the obligations and values that scholars allege to be central to their work." He observes that the "major thing that stands in the way… of this change [toward open access for scholarship] is the passivity of scholars themselves." Hall, Striphas, Burke, and a growing chorus of other voices urge us to take action. The ongoing work of the Vectors Lab is in solidarity with voices such as these, even as we understand the vulnerabilities inherent in our endeavors. (Fig. 3.5)

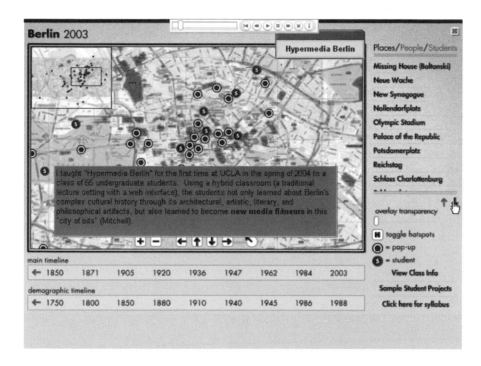

I am not especially naive. I know that Scalar is not a deep challenge to the workings of corporate and computational capital. I know that it is unlikely to persist decades into the future (although I believe we have designed it well enough that the content in Scalar projects can move forward). Our friend Todd Presner and his colleagues have written eloquently about the challenges of launching and sustaining *HyperCities*, yet their book in this series also attests to the enduring value of that project as a space for collaborative research into the insights and possibilities of thick mapping at an important juncture in time. Such scholarly software projects also help us better understand the limits and complexities of corporate platforms such as Google Maps. They shift our attention as scholars to an in-

3.5
Todd Presner previewed an early version of *HyperCities* in *Vectors* in 2006.

vestigation of process and to infrastructure. When we turn our attention to the infrastructures for scholarly publishing, we are also reminded that our current system of publication is itself relatively new, a historical process that is open to change and adjustment.

Our lab is in time likely to join the good company of many scholarly software, publishing, and design projects in what Bethany Nowviskie and Dot Porter have framed as "graceful degradation."[2] Our end may not even be graceful. The maintenance and funding of practice-based work in the humanities is extremely challenging. The total word count of the grant applications I have written or helped write is probably on par with that of my scholarship, though much less likely to receive professional credit. The meetings with presses, libraries, archives, humanities centers, and scholarly societies are ongoing. This work has taken and continues to take a great deal of time and has required me to learn new habits of thought and interaction and to develop the capacity to translate the language of communities that that do not often interact with one another. It is at once rewarding and frustrating, enlightening and maddening. Humanities scholars eager to produce digital scholarship feel stymied by an academic reward structures better suited to print monographs. Scholars working at the intersection of theory and practice do not fit neatly into existing departmental structures. Their practices often blur the boundaries of the traditional academic categories of service, teaching, and research, creating challenges for evaluation.

And yet … I would not take it back. The tedious parts of the labor that our team does to sustain what we have built have offered us a rare opportunity to collaborate, learn, and create together. Our work has joined that of others in maintaining practices in the digital humanities that move away from positivism toward design, ethical openness, contextual authoring, and progressive politics. We've built a shared space through which hundreds of scholars have passed, enabling many to rethink their relationship to the computational and to enter into a complex assemblage of aesthetics, technology, pedagogy, creativity, and new publics. We've built software that has engaged thousands of users. We have built both human and technological infrastructures and mined the intersection of the two. We have centered issues of race, gender, and difference within digital theory and digital practice in both the content and form of various projects. We've explored the materiality and design of technological platforms with feminist intent, pushing software into new shapes and new possibilities. If this is failure, sign me up.

# Guidelines for Evaluating Multimedia Scholarship

Excerpted from Steve Anderson and Tara McPherson, "Engaging Digital Scholarship: Thoughts on Evaluating Multimedia Scholarship," *Profession* (October 2011): 136–151.

## Respect Experimentation and Emerging Genres

While digital scholarship in its simplest form might simply mean publishing "traditional" work online, we should encourage a variety of approaches and nascent forms that better take advantage of the affordances of computation and allow us to ask new research questions. The experimental projects produced for *Vectors* have explored multiple emerging genres: the animated archive, the experiential argument, the interactive documentary, and the spatialized essay, as well as various forms of simulation or visualization. To these we might add new forms of curation, from digital scholarly editions to multilayered and heavily annotated archives. These distinctions are not fixed and fast; they can overlap in a single project that draws on the multiple capacities of digital media. In this inchoate period of multimedia scholarship, there are advantages to such mutability, and it is important to continue to test and experiment. At the same time, we need to evolve standardized structures and interfaces that will allow us to delineate stable genres and to scale digital scholarship.

## Understand Process

As noted in CAA guidelines, multimedia scholarship often involves a long research process. This length of time reflects the need to acquire expanded research methodologies but also reflects the labor involved in making new forms of research. At *Vectors,* we have come to realize that our process is what scholars find most transformative and intellectually compelling. It is time to shift our notions of humanities scholarship away from a fixation on product and even publication toward a new understanding of process. The affordances of digital media for process—for the understanding born of doing—are tremendous. The power of process resides less in end products themselves than in the very act of making. We will need more finely grained accounts of the processes involved in the production of multimedia scholarship in order to evaluate properly the labor required in such research.

## Appreciate Transdisciplinary and Collaborative Approaches

Multimedia scholarship is often produced through intense collaborations that extend across very different disciplinary traditions, including the humanities, the arts, computer science, and engineering. Projects produced by *Vectors* often pair scholars, designers, editors, and technologists in close, iterative collaborations that last many months. The creative directors Erik Loyer and Raegan Kelly and the information designer Craig Dietrich (and several others) were essential to the process precisely because they were trained in different disciplines. Each collaborator comes to a shared understanding of the research at hand that exceeds any one person's initial expertise or expectation. As one of our authors noted, "The designers, as well as the database architects, influenced my theoretical perspectives" (Christen). The humanities have not developed adequate measures for evaluating deep collaboration, particularly given the ongoing focus on single-author monographs. We need to design modes of evaluation that draw from other areas where collaborative work is taken seriously, including both the sciences and practices like architecture and film production, while also understanding that it is often impossible to quantify who did what in some ongoing collaborative projects.

246

## Adapt Current Models of Citation and Peer Review

From new modes of scientific publishing and data curation, like those evidenced in *arXiv* and *DataONE,* to the open peer review experiments in humanities publishing undertaken by the *Shakespeare Quarterly* and others, evidence is accruing that we need not sacrifice quality and rigor if we adapt current models of citation assessment and review for digital environments. Kathleen Fitzpatrick has convincingly argued for new models of review that depend on peer-to-peer review, open review, reputation economies, and community-based filtering. Jon Ippolito and his coauthors argue for a more expansive understanding of citation, particularly given the inadequacy of traditional citation models for work in new or interdisciplinary fields. The traditional impulse of many tenure and promotion committees to seek reviewers from Ivy League universities will likely fail to produce reviewers well versed in experimental design practices or the methodologies and practices of the digital humanities. At *Vectors,* we found that multiple models of peer review were required. Projects produced outside our collaborative production process (about a third of the pieces we published) underwent traditional peer review; in-house projects were reviewed at the proposal stage, during the development process, and near completion. An adequate review process often necessitated one aspect of review (or one reviewer) focused on content and another focused on design.

## Remain Flexible

As is no doubt already evident from this list, meaningful evaluation of multimedia scholarship requires a flexible approach that situates the work within its broader context.

Now is not the time for rigid or highly quantified standards.
To draw an example from the MLA wiki checklist, some projects might rightly be evaluated by how they "link to other
projects," but linking itself should not be an inflexible standard
for how multimedia scholarship gets evaluated. Likewise,
while "open and well documented standards" are extremely
important for much digital scholarship, multimedia scholarship may also draw upon proprietary standards and platforms,
as in the *Flash*-based projects published in *Vectors*. If authors
or teams do choose a proprietary tool or platform, they should
be able to provide a strong rationale for the choice they have
made and articulate its advantages and shortcomings.

## Reward Openness and Appropriate Contribution to a Public Commons

Part of the power of digital scholarship resides precisely in its
potential to support and facilitate an extensible mode of scholarly production, a mode that anticipates and values revision,
debate, and community engagement. Although contrary to the
logic of traditional assumptions about copyright, intellectual
property, and sole authorship, digital scholarship is uniquely
positioned to support modes of public intellectual discourse
that benefit from open access and the contributions of others.
Academia has much to learn from the success of open source
software development—a nonhierarchical, communal programming that has resulted in some of the most powerful and
efficient software development of the past quarter century. As
the logic of open source continues to permeate other spheres
of artistic, scholarly, and technical endeavors, humanists
would do well to embrace an ethos of peer-to-peer information sharing and nonproprietary authoring. The increasingly

common deployment of Creative Commons licensing for academic publications, for example, has greatly hastened the distribution of ideas and broadened arenas of debate beyond that allowed by static, proprietary publishing models. It should not come as a surprise if younger generations of scholars begin to regard static, all-rights-reserved academic publishing with suspicion, as an outmoded artifact of an older model that can hinder the production and dissemination of knowledge. We allow *Vectors* authors to choose a Creative Commons license for their pieces. *Vectors* is open access and free, and we are affiliated with the Open Humanities Press.

## Value Tools and Infrastructure

In 2009, Johanna Drucker issued the following call to action for humanists invested in shaping the future of their disciplines: "If we are interested in creating in our work with digital technologies the subjective, inflected, and annotated processes central to humanistic inquiry, we must be committed to designing the digital systems and tools for our future work. Nothing less than the way we understand knowledge and our tasks as scholars are at stake. Software and hardware only put into effect the models structured into their design." Occasioned by the tensions related to physical versus electronic infrastructures currently being experienced by many academic institutions, Drucker's article proceeds to make an impassioned plea on behalf of a genuinely transformative, ground-up approach to shaping the rapidly approaching future of the digital humanities. But how can we take seriously Drucker's challenge to design digital tools that are specific to the needs of humanists? One answer is to reframe our understanding of tool design to align it with other scholarly endeavors—that is, to regard the development of tools as itself a scholarly endeavor deserving of recognition by the academic establishment. Drucker emphasizes the need for scholars to be directly engaged in every level of this process instead of turning the technical development over to IT specialists. *Vectors* has utilized such an approach: we always root our technological design within the needs and methodologies of the interpretative humanities, building tools in context.

Such a vision of the future of the humanities will require new kinds of workers and new models of production. The MLA wiki makes a useful argument about the need to evaluate tools, noting that "tools… instantiate hermeneutical positions about what questions are important," and recommends that we take tool development seriously. . . . We might extend this observation to the very infrastructures that enable scholarship in the digital humanities. While we typically see the creation of infrastructure—new journals, new centers (virtual or physical), new task forces and scholarly organizations, new technological platforms—as a type of administrative service, the creation of tools and other human and technological infrastructure for the digital humanities is better understood as a form of research practice, structuring the very grounds of possibility for digital scholarship. The tools and infrastructure are not only the preconditions for the work; at their best, they are also part and parcel of the work, deeply integrated into its methods and outcomes. Our tools and infrastructures are rich objects to think with. Any *Vectors* piece might be evaluated for its scholarly merit and design, but all the pieces we produced depend on a flexible database platform created to support the type of work undertaken by interpretative humanities scholars. The creation of this platform in turn depended on a rigorous and collaborative research process, and it is the basis of our ongoing work to scale the lessons learned from *Vectors*.

Our practices at *Vectors* approximate the work of a studio or lab, extending far beyond the traditional scope of a scholarly journal. There are many challenges facing the field of the digital humanities (and, indeed, the humanities at large), but a central and pressing challenge will be the development of meaningful and fair methods of evaluation for the largely misunderstood or miscategorized work undertaken at the level of infrastructure and tool. . . .

From emerging genres such as curation to broader collaborative processes to building infrastructure and tools, the research outcomes of multimedia scholarship (and the digital humanities in general) are a challenge to review, whether before publication or in promotion and tenure decisions. Some responsibility for a successful evaluation no doubt resides with the author or project creator. Care should be taken by the scholar to explain the unique contributions of a work, its relationship to existing fields, the labor involved in its creation, and the most useful ways of assessing influence and quality. Our departments, universities, and professional societies must also assume responsibility for adapting existing mechanisms of evaluation to ensure that this work is fairly reviewed.

But is the academic establishment—and are we as individual scholars—really ready to embrace and reward collaboration across disciplines and the creation of new platforms for knowledge? For centuries academia has operated successfully according to the logics of scarcity, individual expertise, and restricted access. It should come as no surprise that our institutions take a dim view of emerging genres when considering questions of tenure and promotion. Yet we resist such change at our peril. In a moment when universities and governments in the United States and abroad seem intent on shrinking the humanities and on interrogating their value, digital media offer an avenue to reinvigorate our scholarship and to communicate it in compelling new ways. This capacity of the digital to present work to a broader audience means that our work can circulate in multiple forms, in different affective registers, and in richer dialogues. At the same time, digital tools can inject new rigor into our scholarly practices by bringing our interpretative acts more closely in line with our objects of analysis—by, for instance, embedding our interpretations in the digital archive itself.

Whether we are willing to admit it or not, all humanities scholarship is now digital. From our electronic resources at the library to the software systems that produce our paychecks, to our course management software, networked information flows are the terrain of the twenty-first-century university. If we choose not to engage in a deep and sustained manner with the digital infrastructures that shape our universities, our presses, the media, the health care system, and the very engines of late capitalism, if we persist with the business of the humanities in the old and familiar forms, we also cede the opportunity to work as agents of change in those networks.

# Endnotes

## Preface: Opening Vectors

1 The phrase *sunset ideology* is drawn from a blog post by Tom Scheinfeldt, later republished in **Matthew K. Gold**, ed., *Debates in the Digital Humanities*. Critical making has recently been explored within the digital humanities and also in related fields such as science and technology studies and arts-based research, although we might understand a good deal of feminist art practice to also be a form of critical making, particularly in the work of feminist filmmakers like Laura Mulvey.

## 1. Designing for Difference

1 This essay joins together, revises, and expands previously published pieces, including "Post-Archive: The Humanities, the Archive, and the Database," "Designing for Difference," and "Why Are the Digital Humanities So White?"

2 This panel was organized by Glenn Hendler and Bruce Burgett, both of whom have worked quite tirelessly to engage the ASA community in conversations about the digital humanities. In addition to the three of us, Randy Bass, Sharon Daniel, Deborah Kimmey, and Curtis Marez were also on the panel. Tim Powell had been on the original program but was unable to attend.

3 These tensions between "traditional" humanities scholars and computational humanists are, of course, not new, as I note later in this essay. For examples of these dynamics within early waves of humanities computing, see Thomas and Craig. As these authors observe from within the realms of authorship studies and historical studies, these tensions often played out over the differences between quantitative and qualitative analysis and by means of debates on the status and validity of various modes of interpretation.

4 There is much that I value in Ian Bogost's work, and, though he is here situated alongside a number of others who argue that code and culture exist in separate realms, I do not think he would concur with them. His position is typically more sophisticated. I very much agree with his statement elsewhere in the forum that "to really show how gender assumptions are baked into computer systems is such an enormous task, it's hard to know how to begin sometimes." But begin we must. **Katie King**'s ideas about reenactments are developed in her recent book, *Networked Reenactments: Stories Transdisciplinary Knowledges Tell*. There is much that separates their work, but Bogost and King share an interest in things and our relations to them, an interest on which this essay also turns. The Lambda the Ultimate blog forum on critical code studies can be found at http://lambda-the-ultimate.org/node/3944.

5 Other comments in the forum push back against these assumptions that code exists apart from culture, including:

> I'm strongly in favor of opening an area of study which attempts to address these issues and bring them into the light. We could certainly call it CCS [critical code studies], although this may not be what is currently meant by that term. I'm strongly in favor of this despite (or perhaps because of) the fact that so many programmers will undoubtedly have a strong negative reac-

tion to any discussion of these issues, and even deny the existence of any issues to discuss. Of course programs are both mathematical artifacts and social creations situated in a particular context. (Matt Hellige, May 15, 2010) But more to the point, whether CCS is going to be the way to tackle it, I think there are plenty of important questions to be asked from the standpoint of rhetoric, sociology, genre theory, and even some more down-to-earth critical theory. After all, if we are to take seriously one of our favorite aphorisms ("Programs must be written for people to read, and only incidentally for machines to execute.") then lots of questions which are both literary and social arise very quickly. (S. Clover, May 19, 2010)

6 UNIX developed with some rapidity at least in part because the parent company of Bell Labs, AT&T, was unable to enter the computer business owing to a 1958 consent decree. **Eric Raymond** notes that "Bell Labs was required to license its nontelephone technology to anyone who asked" (33). Thus, a kind of "counterculture" chic developed around UNIX. Raymond provides a narrative version of this history, including the eventual "UNIX wars," in his book *The Art of UNIX Programming*. His account, while thorough, tends to romanticize the collaborative culture around UNIX. For a more objective analysis of the imbrications of the counterculture and early computing cultures, see **Fred Turner**'s *From Counterculture to Cyberculture*. See also **Tom Streeter**, "The Romantic Self and the Politics of Internet Commercialization," for a consideration

of liberal individualism and computing cultures.

7 The research presented here is focused particularly on the US context of racial politics, as the United States was the primary site for the development of the UNIX operating system. Of course, the military and corporate structures in which computation is emerging had a decidedly global focus in the 1960s and 1970s, even as US racial politics begin to move from a more radical global focus toward a liberal version of identity politics and civil rights.

8 Some scholars have questioned the "neutral" status of digital structures such as databases. See, for instance, David Golumbia's observations on the limits of the database and semantic computing for humanities analysis, as well as work on culturally contextual databases and ontologies undertaken by Kimberly Christen and Ramesh Srinivasan.

9 The two Race in Digital Space conferences and exhibitions took place at MIT in 2001 and at USC and the Museum of Contemporary Art in Los Angeles in 2002. They were organized by Anna Everett, Christiane Robbins, Erika Muhammad, Henry Jenkins, and me, among others. The two events brought together an impressive group of scholars, artists, activists, and policy makers, including Isaac Julien, Rubén D. Ortiz Torres, Paul D. Miller (aka DJ Spooky), Wendy Chun, Chela Sandoval, Lisa Nakamura, Juan Devis, Erik Loyer, Art McGee, Kip Fulbeck, Daniel Martinez, Surina Khan, Greg Tate, Sue Ellen Case, Farai Chideya, Coco Fusco, Alondra Nelson, Jessie Daniels, Vivek Bald, Beth Coleman, the Electronic Disturbance Theater, Leah Gilliam, Art Jones, Ulysses Jenkins, Pamela Jennings, Philip

Mallory Jones, Amitav Kaul, George E. Lewis, Glenn Ligon, Mongrel, Keith and Mendī Obadike, Paul Pfeiffer, Keith Piper, Alex Rivera, Cauleen Smith, Susan Smith-Pinelo, and Pamela Z.

10 **Michael S. Mahoney**, ed., "The Unix Oral History Project," http://www.princeton.edu/~hos/Mahoney/expotape.htm.

11 This observation is from Kernighan in "The Creation of the UNIX Operating System" originally hosted on the Bell Labs website and now archived at https://web.archive.org/web/20001214172500/http://www.bell-labs.com/history/unix/.

12 For Gramsci, "common sense" is a multi-layered phenomenon that can serve both dominant groups and oppressed ones. For oppressed groups, "common sense" may allow a method of speaking back to power and of rejiggering what counts as sensible. Kara Keeling profitably explores this possibility in her work on the black femme. Computer programmers in the 1970s were interestingly situated. They were on the one hand a subculture (often overlapping with the counterculture), but they were also part of an increasingly managerial class that would help society transition to regimes of neoliberalism and governmentality. Their dreams of "libraries" of code might have been democratic in impulse, but they also increasingly supported postindustrial forms of labor.

13 Other aspects of UNIX also encode "chunking," including the concept of the file. For a discussion of files in UNIX, see *You Are Not a Gadget* by **Jaron Lanier**. This account of UNIX, argues, among other things, that code and culture exist in complex feedback loops.

14 See, for instance, **Patricia Sullivan**'s *Days of Hope* for an account of the coalition politics of the South in the 1930s and 1940s that briefly brought together antiracist activists, labor organizers, and members of the Communist Party. Such a broad alliance became increasingly difficult to sustain after the Red Scare. I would argue that a broad cultural turn to modularity and encapsulation was both a response to these earlier political alliances and a way to short-circuit their viability in the 1960s. My *Reconstructing Dixie* examines the ways in which a lenticular logic infects both identity politics and the politics of difference, making productive alliance and relationality hard to achieve in either paradigm.

15 CIGCIS is a subset of the Society for the History of Technology (SHOT) and is composed, according to its website, of historians interested in the history of information technology. The responses to my earlier essay on UNIX among the group included outrage that I was paid to do such work at all, a declaration that race does not even exist, and arguments similar to those on the "Postcolonial Digital Humanities" blog that insisted on technology's neutrality. More nuanced responses took issue with my inability to provide the smoking gun that proves a connection between covert racism and structures within UNIX such as pipes. To my knowledge, no such smoking gun exists, but I am still interested in what we might learn from exploring certain sets of relations and correspondences. Those among the listserv who saw some value in my approach tended to agree. For instance, Bernard Geoghegan wrote:

> In this regard, I think that sometimes adjacent fields—sociology, media stud-

ies, literary studies, philosophy, even literature—can in certain instances get closer to the messy interrelations that "make history" or "are history," even though they are not the stuff of "historiography" in its disciplinary, academic iteration.

It's damn hard. Folks on this list such as Light, Medina, and Ensmenger have helped us start mapping out those relations historiographically. And yet, so much there will forever escape rigorous historiographic method. Does that mean those relations cannot be considered? Or that they cannot be considered empirically? Not at all, it seems to me. It is probably helpful that some folks from English or media studies can investigate these interrelations without worrying about the models of causality that govern mainstream disciplinary approaches to History. That's why so many of the major historiographic innovations don't originate in academic history, but instead migrate from other fields.

The exchange (and subsequent conversations with others, including David Golumbia) clarified for me the ways in which modularity also infects our own disciplines and makes certain conversations difficult to have across disciplinary lines.

16  To be fair, Newfield also explores a more radical impulse in literary study in the period, evident in the likes of (surprisingly) both Harold Bloom and Raymond Williams. This impulse valued literature precisely in its ability to offer an "unmanaged exploration of experience" (152).

17  For a discussion of TEI practices regarding the sex value attribute, see http://sourceforge.net/p/tei/feature-requests/425/?page=3.

18  David Berry comments nicely on Bogost and these lists in a blog post on Stunlaw. He also helpfully produces an appendix of the litanies that appear in Bogost's book. See http://stunlaw.blogspot.com/2012/05/uses-of-object-oriented-ontology.html and http://stunlaw.blogspot.com/search?q=litany.

19  I have written about the additive form of the lenticular in *Reconstructing Dixie*. There I note that the lenticular (as a mode of managing racism and racial representation) typically works by means of one of two forms. First, a separatist mode divides differences and focuses on only one. Thus, a television series like *Friends* imagines New York City as a largely white world. Second, an additive form multiples differences but still keeps each difference (or unit) distinct, repressing the connections between them. A syllabus might include a week on race and one on gender but not integrate these frameworks into the larger themes of the course.

20  I choose to focus on Bogost's work here as an example of OOO largely because his writing is so directly connected to digital media studies, particularly his earlier books and his own creative practice. As I noted earlier in this section, OOO (and the larger speculative realism) are broad fields. Bogost's take is less relational than many of the others, something that may indeed devolve from his own immersion in digital media studies. Someone like Michael O'Rourke sculpts a very different version of OOO.

21  Also of interest in Moten's essay is the second section, in which he speaks to unprocessed ways in which blackness figures in

the thinking of white artists and intellectuals. He tells of an encounter between the painter Ad Reinhardt and the musician Cecil Taylor (and others) set up in 1967 by *Arts/Canada* with the cooperation of Bell Telephone Company and the Canadian Broadcast Company on the topic of "black as a special concept."

22 See **David Berry**, "The Uses of Object-Oriented Ontology," on his blog, Stunlaw; http://stunlaw.blogspot.com/2012/05/uses-of-object-oriented-ontology.html.

23 See in particular **Michael O'Rourke**'s essay "Girls Welcome!!! Speculative Realism, Object-Oriented Ontology, and Queer Theory" and **Tim Morton**'s engagement with **Karen Barad** in "Treating Objects Like Women: Feminist Ontology and the Question of Essence."

24 See "Borrowed Energy," a dialogue between **Rosi Braidotti** and **Timotheus Vermeulen**; http://www.frieze.com/article/borrowed-energy.

25 Ferguson's reformulation of intersectionality still works within circuits of the subject and of language. I am not sure he would remap the term toward theories of affect and assemblage, but I am grateful for his work in reclaiming the concept from the terrain of positivism and would align my usage also with that of Katie King. She calls on us to see intersectionality as a kind of boundary object that can work across scales, resisting the more positivist ways the term has been used.

26 This list could include many others, particularly those scholars working within the #DHPoco, #TransformDH, HASTAC Scholar, FemTechNet, and FemBot rubrics, as well as many feminist artists. Certainly they would not agree on theoretical models or technical processes. I list here primarily those with whom I've had some working connection.

## 2. Assembling Scholarship: From Vectors to Scalar

1 A fuller record of the conference is available in the anthology *Transmedia Frictions: The Digital, the Arts and the Humanities*. The conference and exhibit brought together many speakers now well known in digital media studies: Katherine Hayles, Lev Manovich, Wendy Chun, Yuri Tsivian, Edward Branigan, Mark Hansen, Margaret Morse, Anne-Marie Duguet, Pat Mellencamp, Henry Jenkins, Justine Cassell, Yasmin Kafai, John Caldwell, Cristina Venegas, Hamid Naficy, Lisa Parks, Anna Everett, Alison Trope, Vivian Sobchack, Janet Murray, George Landow, Ellen Seiter, Randal Packer, Eric Freedman, Ian Bogost, Steve Anderson, Holly Willis, Steve Mamber, Peter Lunenfeld, and Richard Weinberg. Other participants included international artists and industry leaders: Rebecca Allen, Mark Amerika, Cindy Bernard, Sawad Brooks, Nancy Buchanan, Rosemary Comella, Vilsoni Hereniko, Fran Ilich, Adriene Jenik, Isaac Julien, Glenn Kaino, Kristy Kang, Brenda Laurel, George Legrady, Erik Loyer, Laird Malamed, Pedro Meyer, Michael Nash, Pat O'Neill, Christine Panushka, Sara Roberts, Vibeke Sorensen, Beth Stryker, Bill Viola, Femke Wolting, Norman Yonemoto, Jody Zellen, and Eric Zimmerman, to name just a few. Others blurred the boundaries between such distinctions: Michele Citron, Allison DeFren, Mary Flanagan, Norman Klein, Marcos Novak, Sandy Stone, James Tobias, and Fabian Wagmister.

2   More information on the Labyrinth Project is available at https://dornsife.usc.edu/labyrinth/laby.html.

3   Julia Flanders discusses the "productive unease" of humanities computing, noting that "this unease registers for the humanities scholar as a sense of friction between familiar mental habits and the affordances of the tool, but it is ideally a provocative friction, an irritation that prompts further thought and engagement" (paragraph 12).

4   Several *Vectors* and Scalar projects might be understood as transmedia scholarship, for many seek to adapt an existing work for different media platforms. Such a strategy can help scholarship travel to new audiences and achieve different affective registers. For instance, compare David Theo Goldberg and Erik Loyer's piece for *Vectors* to an earlier print version of Goldberg's work. The difference between the two has been explored by Andrew Jakubowicz. Anne Balsamo, Katie King, and Suzanne Scott and Chris Hanson all explore the idea of transmedia scholarship in their work.

5   In an excellent essay in *American Literature,* **Lauren Klein** offers a different take on how we might visualize absence in the archive by bringing together visualization techniques favored within the digital humanities, with a careful attention to what data visualization may distort or deform. She aims "to expose the impossibilities of recognition—and of cognition—that remain essential to our understanding of the archive of slavery today" while engaging in practices such as datamining and visualization.

6   I recently had a lovely conversation with Ed Ayers about this dilemma. He too is eager to pursue "custom" projects that meticulously suit form to content in multimedia and interactive registers. He has called for more imaginative scholarly output in a short manifesto published in the Educause newsletter.

7   In an early interactive "index," the *Vectors* journal had the user draw vectors across a screen to reveal project keywords, and the original opening splash page featured a similar approach, encouraging a gestural engagement from the viewer and hinting at what was to come. A project like Amelie Hastie's edited collection "Objects of Media Studies" includes a sequence that encourages vigorous mouse activity.

8   We went through many possibilities when trying to name *Vectors*. "Catalyze" was the working title for quite some time, but I think it was Erik Loyer who finally settled us on *Vectors*. He definitely named Scalar, choosing the name as a mathematical in-joke, since a scalar is a force that multiplies vectors. In-house, Craig Dietrich has deemed the first two versions of Scalar "honeydew" and "cantaloupe," acknowledging both our Mellon funding and his own interests in urban gardening. A new research workbench that Craig is prototyping is now called Tensor.

9   For a showcase of projects created in Scalar, see http://scalar.usc.edu/showcase. Scalar is free online, and anyone can create an account and start building. The software is also available for download from GitHub and can be installed on a user's or institution's own servers. Thousands have now created Scalar accounts, and many projects exist that we are not even aware of.

10  This book has not directly engaged the important and growing body of literature on immaterial labor (from Maurizio Lazzara-

to to Trebor Scholz to Tiziana Terranova)
and alternative-academic practices within
the academy (including Miriam Posner
and others), but these conditions form
important contexts for the work of the
Vectors Lab.

### Outro: Scholarship in the Wild

1  *The Economist* reports that Elsevier had
   revenues of $3.2 billion in 2012; the firm's
   profit margin was 38 percent, roughly 10
   percent more than Wal-Mart's in the same
   period. Springer, the second-largest journal publisher, made 36 percent profit on
   sales of $1.1 billion in 2011. See "Free-for-
   All," *Economist,* May 4, 2013, http://www.
   economist.com/news/science-and-tech-
   nology/21577035-open-access-scientif-
   ic-publishing-gaining-ground-free-all
   Elsevier has also executed an end-run
   around open access, rescinding recently
   even the already hollow gestures they had
   made in that regard. See https://www.
   coar-repositories.org/activities/advoca-
   cy-leadership/petition-against-elsevi-
   ers-sharing-policy/
2  **Bethanie Nowviskie,** "Graceful Degradation," July 10, 2009, http://nowviskie.
   org/2009/graceful-degradation/.

# Bibliography

Adema, Janneke, and Gary Hall. "The Political Nature of the Book: On Artists' Books and Radical Open Access." *New Formations* 78, no. 1 (2013): 138–156.

Anderson, Steve, and Tara McPherson. "Engaging Digital Scholarship: Thoughts on Evaluating Multimedia Scholarship." *Profession* (October 2011): 136–151.

AT&T Tech Channel. "AT&T Archives: The UNIX Operating System." https://www.youtube.com/watch?t=752&v=tc4ROCJYbm0.

Ayers, Edward. "Does Digital Scholarship Have a Future?" *EDUCAUSE Review* 48, no. 4 (2013), http://er.educause.edu/articles/2013/8/does-digital-scholarship-have-a-future.

Baldwin, Carliss, and Kim Clark. *Design Rules*, vol. 1, *The Power of Modularity*. Cambridge: MIT Press, 2000.

Balsamo, Anne. *Designing Culture: The Technological Imagination at Work*. Durham: Duke University Press, 2011.

Barad, Karen. *Meeting the Universe Halfway: Quantum Physics and the Entanglement of Matter and Meaning*. Durham: Duke University Press, 2007.

———. "Posthuman Performativity: Toward an Understanding of How Matter Comes to Matter." *Signs: Journal of Women in Culture and Society* 28, no. 3 (2003): 801–831.

Beller, Jonathan. "Periodizing Cinematic Production." Post to IDC Listserv, September 2, 2009. https://lists.thing.net/pipermail/idc/2009-September/003851.html.

Bell Labs. "The Creation of the UNIX Operating System." https://web.archive.org/web/20041024080305/http://www.bell-labs.com/history/unix/.

Bennett, Jane. *Vibrant Matter: A Political Ecology of Things*. Durham: Duke University Press, 2010.

Berlant, Lauren. "Thinking about Feeling Historical." *Emotion, Space and Society* 1 (2008): 4–9.

Berry, David. "The Digital Humanities Stack." *Stunlaw: Critique, Politics, Art and Technology*, April 14, 2016. http://stunlaw.blogspot.co.uk/2016/04/the-digital-humanities-stack.html.

Best, Stephen. "Neither Lost nor Found: Slavery and the Visual Archive." *Representations* 113, no. 1 (2011): 150–163.

Bissell, Evan, and Erik Loyer. "Freedom's Ring." http://freedomsring.stanford.edu/.

———. "The Knotted Line." http://knottedline.com/.

Blanchette, J.-F. "A Material History of Bits." *Journal of the American Society for Information Science and Technology* 62, no. 6 (2011): 1024–1057.

Bogost, Ian. *Alien Phenomenology; or, What It's Like to Be a Thing*. Minneapolis: University of Minnesota Press, 2012.

———. *Unit Operations: An Approach to Video Game Criticism*. Cambridge: MIT Press, 2006.

**Bogost, Ian, and Nick Monfort**. *Racing the Beam: The Atari Video Game System*. Cambridge: MIT Press, 2009.

**Bolter, Jay, and Richard Grusin**. *Remediations: Understanding New Media*. Cambridge: MIT Press, 2000.

**Braidotti, Rosi**. *The Posthuman*. Malden, MA: Polity Press, 2013.

**Brown, Travis**. "Critical Code Studies." *Lambda the Ultimate* (blog), May 11, 2010. http://lambda-the-ultimate.org/node/3944.

**Burke, Timothy**. "Now." https://blogs.swarthmore.edu/burke/blog/2013/01/14/now/.

**Canaday, Rudd**. "Building Unix." March 16, 2014. http://ruddcanaday.com/tag/multics/.

**cárdenas, micha**. "Shifting Poetics: Trans of Color Movement in Digital Media." Ph.D. diss., University of Southern California, 2015.

**Castelle, Michael**. "Relational and Non-Relational Models in the Entextualization of Bureaucracy." *Computational Culture* 3 (2013). http://computationalculture.net/article/relational-and-non-relational-models-in-the-entextualization-of-bureaucracy.

**Cecire, Natalia**. "When Digital Humanities Was in Vogue." *Journal of the Digital Humanities* 1, no. 1 (2011). http://journalofdigitalhumanities.org/1-1/when-digital-humanities-was-in-vogue-by-natalia-cecire/.

**Chaudhary, Zahid**. "Subjects in Difference: Walter Benjamin, Frantz Fanon, and Postcolonial Theory." *Differences* 23, no. 1 (2012): 151–183.

**Chen, Mel Y**. *Animacies: Biopolitics, Racial Mattering, and Queer Affect*. Durham: Duke University Press, 2012.

**Christen, Kimberly, and Chris Cooney**. "Digital Dynamics across Cultures." *Vectors* 2 no. 1 (2006). http://vectors.usc.edu/projects/index.php?project=67.

**Chun, Wendy**. *Programmed Visions: Software and Memory*. Cambridge: MIT Press, 2013.

**Clough, Patricia**. *Autoaffection: Unconscious Thought in the Age of Technology*. Minneapolis: University of Minnesota Press, 2000.

**Coates, R. D**. "Covert Racism in the USA and Globally." *Sociology Compass* 2 (2008): 208–231.

**Codd, E. F**. "Further Normalization of the Database Relational Model." In *Data Base Systems: Courant Computer Science Symposia 6*, edited by Randall Rustin, 65–98. Englewood Cliffs, NJ: Prentice-Hall, 1972.

**Craig, Hugh**. "Stylistic Analysis and Authorship Studies." In *A Companion to Digital Humanities*, edited by Susan Schreibman, Ray Siemens, and John Unsworth, 273–288. Oxford: Blackwell, 2004. http://www.digitalhumanities.org/companion/.

**Daniel, Sharon**. "Public Secrets." *Vectors* 2, no. 2 (2007). http://vectors.usc.edu/projects/index.php?project=57.

**Daniels, Jessie**. *Cyber Racism: White Suprem-*

acy Online and the New Attack on Civil Rights. Lanham, MD: Rowman & Littlefield, 2009.

**Derrida, Jacques**. *Archive Fever: A Freudian Impression,* translated by Eric Prenowitz. Chicago: University of Chicago Press, 1995.

**Dourish, Paul**. "No SQL: The Shifting Materialities of Database Technology." *Computational Culture* 4 (2014). http://computationalculture.net/article/no-sql-the-shifting-materialities-of-database-technology.

**Drucker, Johanna**. "Blind Spots." *Chronicle of Higher Education* 55, no. 30 (2009): B6

———. *SpecLab: Digital Aesthetics and Speculative Computing.* Chicago: University of Chicago Press, 2009.

**Dudziak, Mary L**. *Cold War Civil Rights: Race and the Image of American Democracy.* Princeton: Princeton University Press, 2000.

**Dyson, Frances**. "And Then It Was Now." http://www.fondation-langlois.org/html/e/page.php?NumPage=2143.

**Earhart, Amy E**. "Can Information Be Unfettered? Race and the New Digital Humanities Canon." In *Debates in the Digital Humanities,* edited by Matthew K. Gold, 309–318. Minneapolis: University of Minnesota Press, 2012.

**Emerson, Lori**. *Reading Writing Interfaces: From the Digital to the Bookbound.* Minneapolis: University of Minneapolis Press, 2014.

**Ernst, Wolfgang**. *Digital Memory and the Archive.* Edited by Jussi Parikka. Minneapolis: University of Minnesota Press, 2013.

**Ethington, Philip**. *Ghost Metropolis.* Berkeley: University of California Press, forthcoming.

**Everett, Anna**. *Digital Diaspora: A Race for Cyberspace.* Albany: SUNY Press, 2009.

**Ferguson, Roderick**. "Reading Intersectionality." *Trans-Scripts* 2 (2012): 91–99.

**Fitzpatrick, Kathleen**. *Planned Obsolescence: Publishing, Technology, and the Future of the Academy.* New York: New York University Press, 2011.

**Flanders, Julia**. "The Productive Unease of 21st-Century Digital Scholarship." *Digital Humanities Quarterly* 3, no. 3 (2009).

**Freire, Paulo**. *Pedagogy of the Oppressed.* New York: Continuum, 1970.

**Fuller, Matthew**. "Evil Media: Making Good Use of Weights, Chains and Ranks." Presentation at the Animating Archives Conference, Brown University, December 4, 2009. https://itunes.apple.com/itunes-u/animating-archives-conference/id381080290?mt=10#ls=1.

**Galloway, Alex**. "The Poverty of Philosophy: Realism and Post-Fordism." *Critical Inquiry* 39 (Winter 2013): 347–366.

———. *Protocol: How Control Exists after Decentralization.* Cambridge: MIT Press, 2006.

**Glissant, Édouard**. *Poetics of Relation.* Translated by Betsy Wing. Ann Arbor: University of Michigan Press, 1997.

**Goffey, Anderew**. "Algorithm." In *Software Studies: A Lexicon,* edited by Matthew Fuller, 15–20. Cambridge: MIT Press, 2008.

Gold, Matthew K. *Debates in the Digital Humanities*. Minneapolis: University of Minnesota Press, 2012.

Goldberg, David Theo. "Deva-stating Disasters: Race in the Shadow(s) of New Orleans," *Du Bois Review* 3, no. 1 (2006): 83–95.

Golumbia, David. *The Cultural Logic of Computation*. Cambridge: Harvard University Press, 2009.

Graff, Gerald. *Professing Literature: An Institutional History*. Chicago: University of Chicago Press, 1989.

Gramsci, Antonio. *Selections from the Prison Notebooks*. Translated and edited by Q. Hoare and G. Nowell Smith. London: Lawrence and Wishart, 1971.

Halberstam, Judith. *The Queer Art of Failure*. Durham: Duke University Press, 2011.

Hall, Gary. "Toward a Postdigital Humanities: Cultural Analytic and the Computational Turn to Data-Driven Scholarship." *American Literature* 85, no. 4 (2013): 781–809.

Halpern, Orit. *Beautiful Data: A History of Vision and Reason since 1945*. Durham: Duke University Press, 2015.

Hansen, Mark B. N. *Embodying Technesis: Technology beyond Writing*. Ann Arbor: University of Michigan Press, 2000.

Haraway, Donna. *Simians, Cyborgs, and Women: The Reinvention of Nature*. New York: Routledge, 1990.

Harrell, Fox. *Phantasmal Media: An Approach to Imagination, Computation, and Expression*. Cambridge: MIT Press, 2013.

Hayles, N. Katherine. *How We Think: Digital Media and Contemporary Technogenesis*. Chicago: University of Chicago Press, 2012.

Ippolito, Jon, et al. "New Criteria for New Media." *Leonardo* 42, no.1 (2009): 71-75.

Jakubowicz, Andrew, and Theo van Leeuwen. "The Goldberg Variations 1: Assessing the Academic Quality of Multidimensional Linear Texts and Their Re-emergence in Multimedia Publications." *Discourse and Communication* 4, no 4 (2010): 361–378.

Juhasz, Alexandra. *Learning from YouTube*. Cambridge: MIT Press, 2011.

Karger, Paul A., and Roger R. Schell. "Thirty Years Later: Lessons from the Multics Security Evaluation." In *Proceedings of the 18th Annual Computer Security Applications Conference*, 119–126. Los Alamitos: IEEE Computer Society, 2002.

Keeling, Kara. "I = Another." In *Strange Affinities: The Gender and Sexual Politics of Comparative Racialization*, edited by Grace Kyungwon Hong and Roderick A. Ferguson, 53–75. Durham: Duke University Press, 2011.

———. *The Witch's Flight: The Cinematic, the Black Femme, and the Image of Common Sense*. Durham: Duke University Press, 2007.

Kember, Sarah, and Joanna Zylinska. *Life after New Media: Mediation as a Vital Process*. Cambridge: MIT Press, 2012.

Kernighan, Brian, and Rob Pike. *The Unix Programming Environment*. Englewood Cliffs, NJ: Prentice-Hall, 1984.

Kernighan, Brian, and P. J. Plauger. *Software Tools*. Reading, MA: Addison-Wesley, 1976.

———. "Software Tools." *ACM SIGSOFT Software Engineering Notes* 1, no. 1 (1976): 15–20.

Kernighan, Brian, and D. M. Ritchie. *The C Programming Language*. 2nd edition. Englewood Cliffs, NJ: Prentice-Hall, 1988.

Kinder, Marsha. "Hot Spots, Avatars, and Narrative Fields Forever: Buñuel's Legacy for New Digital Media and Interactive Database Narrative." *Film Quarterly* 55, no. 4 (2002): 2–15.

———. "Narrative Equivocations between Movies and Games." In *The New Media Book*, edited by Dan Harries. London: British Film Industry, 2002.

King, Katie. *Networked Reenactments: Stories Transdisciplinary Knowledges Tell*. Durham: Duke University Press, 2012.

Klein, Julie Thompson. *Interdisciplining Digital Humanities: Boundary Work in an Emerging Field*. Ann Arbor: University of Michigan Press, 2014. http://dx.doi.org/10.3998/dh.12869322.0001.001.

Klein, Lauren. "The Image of Absence: Archival Silence, Data Visualization, and James Hemings." *American Literature* (special issue on American Literature and New Media, edited by Wendy Chun, Patrick Jagoda, and Tara McPherson) 85, no. 4 (2013): 661–688.

Klüver, Billy. *9 Evenings: Theatre and Engineering: Pressbriefing: Remarks* (September 29, 1966). In Daniel Langlois Foundation for Art, Science, and Technology, *Collection of Documents Published by Experiments in Art and Technology*. E.A.T. C1-27.

Koh, Adeline, and Roopika Risam. "Open Thread: The Digital Humanities as a Historical 'Refuge' from Race/Class/Gender/Sexuality/Disability?" *Postcolonial Digital Humanities* 29 (blog). http://dhpoco.org/blog/2013/05/10/open-thread-the-digital-humanities-as-a-historical-refuge-from-raceclassgendersexualitydisability.

Kolko, Beth E., Lisa Nakamura, and Gilbert B. Rodman, eds. *Race in Cyberspace*. New York: Routledge, 2000.

Krauss, Rosalind. "Grids." *October* 9 (Summer 1979): 50–64.

Laclau, Ernesto, and Chantal Mouffe. *Hegemony and Socialist Strategy: Towards a Radical Democratic Politics*. New York: Verso, 1985.

Landow, George. *Hypertext: The Convergence of Contemporary Critical Theory and Technology*. Baltimore: Johns Hopkins University Press, 1991.

———. *Hypertext 2.0: The Convergence of Contemporary Critical Theory and Technology*. Baltimore: Johns Hopkins University Press, 1997.

Lanier, Jaron. *You Are Not a Gadget: A Manifesto*. New York: Knopf, 2010.

Latour, Bruno. "Why Has Critique Run Out of Steam? From Matters of Fact to Matters of

Concern." *Critical Inquiry* 30 (Winter 2004): 225–248.

Laughlin, Kathleen, et al. "Is It Time to Jump Ship? Historians Rethink the Waves Metaphor." *Feminist Formations* 22, no. 1 (2010): 76–135.

Lewis, Martin W., and Kären Wigen. "A Maritime Response to the Crisis in Area Studies." *Geographical Review* 89, no. 2 (1999): 161–168.

Light, Jennifer. *From Warfare to Welfare: Defense Intellectuals and Urban Problems in Cold War America.* Baltimore: Johns Hopkins University Press, 2004.

Liu, Alan. *Local Transcendence: Essays on Postmodern Historicism and the Database.* Chicago: University of Chicago Press, 2008.

———. "Where Is Cultural Criticism in the Digital Humanities?" In *Debates in the Digital Humanities,* edited by Matthew K. Gold, 490–509. Minneapolis: University of Minnesota Press, 2012.

Mackenzie, Adrian. "The Performativity of Code: Software and Cultures of Circulation." *Theory, Culture & Society* 22, no. 1 (2005): 71–92.

Mahoney, Michael, ed. "The UNIX Oral History Project." http://www.princeton.edu/~hos/Mahoney/expotape.htm.

Manovich, Lev. *The Language of New Media.* Cambridge: MIT Press, 2002.

———. "We Have Never Been Modular." Post to Nettime Listserv. November 28, 2005.

http://www.nettime.org/Lists-Archives/nettime-l-0511/msg00106.html.

Manovich, Lev, and Andreas Kratky. *Soft Cinema: Navigating the Database.* Cambridge: MIT Press, 2005.

McLuhan, Marshall. *Understanding Media: The Extensions of Man.* Cambridge: MIT Press, 1994.

McPherson, Tara. "Designing for Difference." *Differences* 25, no. 1 (2014): 177–188.

———. "Introduction: Media Studies and the Digital Humanities." *Cinema Journal* 48, no. 2 (2009): 119–123.

———. "Post-Archive: The Humanities, the Archive, and the Database." In *Between Humanities and the Digital,* edited by David Theo Goldberg and Patrik Svensson, 483–502. Cambridge: MIT Press, 2015.

———. *Reconstructing Dixie: Race, Gender, and Nostalgia in the Imagined South.* Durham: Duke University Press, 2003.

———. "Why Are the Digital Humanities So White? or Thinking the Histories of Race and Computation." In *Debates in the Digital Humanities,* edited by Matthew K. Gold, 139–160. Minneapolis: University of Minnesota Press, 2012.

McPherson, Tara, and Steve Anderson, eds. *Vectors: Journal of Culture and Technology in a Dynamic Vernacular.* http://vectorsjournal.org.

Mirzoeff, Nicholas. *The Right to Look: A Counterhistory of Visuality.* Durham: Duke University Press, 2011.

———. "We Are All Children of Algeria": Visuality and Countervisuality, 1954–2011. Durham: Duke University Press, 2012. http://scalar.usc.edu/nehvectors/mirzoeff/.

Monfort, Nick. "Combat in Context." Game Studies 6, no. 1 (2006). http://gamestudies.org/0601/articles/montfort.

Morton, Timothy. "Treating Objects Like Women: Feminist Ontology and the Question of Essence." In International Perspectives in Feminist Ecocriticism, ed. Greta Gaard, Simon Estok, and Serpil Opperman, 56–69. New York: Routledge, 2013.

Moten, Fred. "The Case of Blackness." Criticism 50, no. 2 (2008): 177–218.

Mouffe, Chantal. "Artistic Activisim and Agonistic Spaces." Art & Research 1, no. 2 (2007). http://www.artandresearch.org.uk/v1n2/mouffe.html.

Mulvey, Laura. "Visual Pleasure and Narrative Cinema." Screen 16, no. 3 (1975): 6–18.

Nakamura, Lisa. Cybertypes: Race, Ethnicity, and Identity on the Internet. New York: Routledge, 2002.

Newfield, Christopher. Ivy and Industry: Business and the Making of the American University, 1880–1980. Durham: Duke University Press, 2004.

Nichols, Stephen G. "The Anxiety of Irrelevance: Digital Humanities and Contemporary Literary Theory." September 2013. https://www.academia.edu/4441824/The_Anxiety_of_Irrelevance_Digital_Humanities_and_Contemporary_Literary_Theory.

Nowviskie, Bethany. "Don't Circle the Wagons." March 4, 2012. http://nowviskie.org/2012/dont-circle-the-wagons/.

Omi, Michael, and Howard Winant. Racial Formation in the United States: From the 1960s to the 1980s. New York: Routledge and Kegan Paul, 1986.

O'Rourke, Michael. "'Girls Welcome!!!': Speculative Realism, Object-Oriented Ontology, and Queer Theory." Speculations 2 (2011): 275–312.

Penley, Constance. "Feminism, Film Theory and the Bachelor Machine." m/f 10 (1985): 39–59.

Posner, Miriam. "Commit to DH People, Not DH Projects." Miriam Posner's Blog, March 18, 2014. http://miriamposner.com/blog/commit-to-dh-people-not-dh-projects/.

———. "Some Things to Think about before You Exhort Everyone to Code." Miriam Posner's Blog, February 29, 2012, http://miriamposner.com/blog/some-things-to-think-about-before-you-exhort-everyone-to-code/.

———. "What's Next: The Radical, Unrealized Potential of Digital Humanities." Miriam Posner's Blog, July 27, 2015. http://miriamposner.com/blog/whats-next-the-radical-unrealized-potential-of-digital-humanities/.

Presner, Todd, David Shepard, and Yoh Kawano. HyperCities: Thick Mapping in the Digital Humanities. Cambridge: Harvard University Press, 2014.

Price, Kenneth. "Edition, Project, Database, Archive, Thematic Research Collection: What's in a Name?" *DHQ: Digital Humanities Quarterly* 3, no. 3 (2009). http://www.digitalhumanities.org/dhq/vol/3/3/000053/000053.html.

**Puar, Jasbir.** *Terrorist Assemblages: Homonationalism in Queer Times.* Durham: Duke University Press, 2007.

**Ramsay, Stephen.** "Databases." In *A Companion to Digital Humanities,* edited by Susan Schreibman, Ray Siemens, and John Unsworth, 177–197. Oxford: Blackwell, 2004. http://www.digitalhumanities.org/companion/.

**Ramsay, Stephen, and Geoffrey Rockwell.** "Developing Things: Notes toward an Epistemology of Building in the Digital Humanities." In *Debates in the Digital Humanities,* edited by Matthew K. Gold, 75–84. Minneapolis: University of Minnesota Press, 2012.

**Ratto, Matt, and Megan Boler, eds.** *DIY Citizenship: Critical Making and Social Media.* Cambridge: MIT Press, 2014.

**Raymond, Eric.** *The Art of UNIX Programming.* Reading, MA: Addison-Wesley, 2004.

**Ritchie, Dennis.** "The Evolution of the Unix Time-Sharing System." *AT&T Bell Laboratories Technical Journal* 63, no. 6, pt. 2 (1984): 1577–1593..

**Ritchie, D. M., and K. Thompson.** "The UNIX Time-Sharing System." *Bell System Technical Journal* 57 no. 6, pt. 2 (1978): 1905–1929.

**Ross, Kristen.** *May '68 and Its Afterlives.* Chicago: University of Chicago Press, 2004.

**Rowe, John Carlos.** "Areas of Concern: Area Studies and the New American Studies." In

*Re-framing the Transnational Turn in American Studies,* edited by Winfried Fluck, Donald Pease, and John Carlos Rowe, 321–336. Hanover, NH: University Press of New England, 2011.

**Russell, Andrew.** "Modularity: An Interdisciplinary History of an Ordering Concept." *Information & Culture* 47, no. 3 (2012): 257–287.

**Salus, Peter H.** *A Quarter-Century of Unix.* Reading, MA: Addison-Wesley, 1994.

**Sandoval, Chela.** *Methodology of the Oppressed.* Minneapolis: University of Minnesota Press, 2000.

**Sayers, Jentery.** "Why Fabricate?" *Scholarly and Research Communication* 6, no. 3 (2015). http://src-online.ca/index.php/src/article/view/209/428.

**Schreibman, Susan, Ray Siemens, and John Unsworth, eds.** *A Companion to Digital Humanities.* Oxford: Blackwell, 2004. http://www.digitalhumanities.org/companion/.

**Scott, Suzanne, and Christopher Hanson.** "Conceptualizing Transmedia Scholarship." In *Database | Narrative | Archive.* Edited by Matt Soar and Monika Gagnon. 2013. http://dnaanthology.com.

**Smith, Martha Nell.** "The Human Touch, Software of the Highest Order: Revisiting Editing as Interpretation." *Textual Cultures: Texts, Contexts, Interpretation* 2, no. 1 (2007): 1–15.

**Spivak, Gayatri.** *In Other Worlds: Essays in Cultural Politics.* New York: Routledge, 1987.

Srinivasan, Ramesh. "Re-thinking the Cultural Codes of New Media: The Question Concerning Ontology." *New Media & Society* 15, no. 2 (2013): 203–223.

Streeter, Thomas. "The Romantic Self and the Politics of Internet Commercialization." *Cultural Studies* 17, no. 5 (2003): 648–668.

Striphas, Ted. "Acknowledged Goods: Cultural Studies and the Politics of Academic Journal Publishing." *Communication and Critical/Cultural Studies* 7, no 1 (2010): 3–25.

Sugrue, Thomas J. *The Origins of the Urban Crisis: Race and Inequality in Post-War Detroit.* Princeton: Princeton University Press, 1998.

Sullivan, Patricia. *Days of Hope: Race and Democracy in the New Deal Era.* Chapel Hill: University of North Carolina Press, 1996.

Tallbear, Kim. "An Indigenous Ontological Reading of Cryopreservation Practices and Ethics (and Why I'd Rather Think about Pipestone)." http://www.kimtallbear.com/homeblog/an-indigenous-ontological-reading-of-cryopreservation-practices-and-ethics-and-why-id-rather-think-about-pipestone.

Terry, Jennifer. Author's Statement, "Killer Entertainments." *Vectors* 3, no. 1 (2007). http://www.vectorsjournal.org/projects/index.php?project=86&thread=AuthorsStatement.

Taylor, Diana. *The Archive and the Repertoire: Performing Cultural Memory in the Americas.* Durham: Duke University Press, 2003.

Thomas, William G., II. "Computing and the Historical Imagination." In *A Companion to Digital Humanities.* Edited by Susan Schreibman, Ray Siemens, and John Unsworth, 57–68. Oxford: Blackwell, 2004. http://www.digitalhumanities.org/companion/.

Tu, Thuy, Alondra Nelson, and Alicia Hedlam Hines, eds. *Technicolor: Race, Technology, and Everyday Life.* New York: New York University Press, 2001.

Turkle, Sherry. *Life on the Screen: Identity in the Age of the Internet.* New York: Simon and Schuster, 1997.

Turner, Fred. *From Counterculture to Cyberculture: Stewart Brand, the Whole Earth Network, and the Rise of Digital Utopianism.* Chicago: University of Chicago Press, 2006.

Watt, David A. *Programming Language Concepts and Paradigms.* New York: Prentice Hall. 1990.

Weiner, Alan J. *Design Requirements for the Data and Systems Support Essential to an Urban Blight Systems Analysis* (Los Angeles: Los Angeles Community Analysis Bureau, 1970).

Winston, Brian. *Technologies of Seeing: Photography, Cinematography and Television.* London: British Film Institute, 1996.

# Acknowledgments

As I hope this book makes abundantly clear, the work discussed within its pages involved sustained collaborations that reached far beyond more traditional humanities research. The Vectors Lab has directly worked with hundreds of scholars, students, librarians, designers, publishers, and technologists over the last dozen years. I cannot acknowledge them all here, but I do want to thank many people who have shaped the activities of the lab in ways big and small.

First, my largest debt is to our original core team, Steve Anderson, Craig Dietrich, Raegan Kelly, and Erik Loyer. I have learned an enormous amount from their generosity, creativity, and intellectual fierceness and feel incredibly privileged to have worked alongside them. More recently, Phil Ethington, Curtis Fletcher, Lucas Miller, and Alexei Taylor have brought valuable new energy and talent to our group. Our time together in the Vectors Lab has certainly proven that collaboration across difference is both possible and fruitful, if also sometimes challenging. I hope that this book has captured some of the richness of our shared and ongoing practice, even if it cannot adequately express my gratitude.

Our larger group has waxed and waned throughout the years, and I am appreciative of others who have led workshops, tested systems, contributed to our design and development process, and wrangled both people and paperwork. These include John Bell, Heather Blackmore, micha cárdenas, Alessandro Ceglia, Ingrid DeCook, Marcela Fuentes, Charlie Furman, Samantha Gorman, Chris Hanson, Jeanne Jo, Annie Johnson, Vanessa Lee, Jason Lipshin, Adam Liszkiewicz, Michael Lynch, Scott Mahoy, Andy Myers, Jillian O'Connor, Veronica Paredes, Willy Paredes, Gabriel Peters-Lazaro, Elizabeth Ramsey, Jackson Stakeman, Carolyn Tanner, and Holly Willis. None of our work would have been possible without the support of Dean Elizabeth Daley of the USC School of Cinematic Arts as well as the contributions of several foundations and agencies. Thanks to Don Waters at the Andrew W. Mellon Foundation, Brett Bobley, Jason Rhody, and Jennifer Serventi at the Office of Digital Humanities at the National Endowment for the Humanities, and Connie Yowell at the John D. and Catherine T. MacArthur Foundation. Wendy Chun, Brian Goldfarb, Nicholas Mirzoeff, and Joan Saab helped shape our first Alliance grants and the earliest development of Scalar as we worked alongside the inimitable Abby Smith Rumsey. They are all excellent travel companions, both literally and figuratively, and I very much value the time I've spent with each of them in various ways. Finally, I am deeply grateful to all of our *Vectors* authors and for the participants in our many summer institutes and other workshops. The iterative design process of our lab greatly benefited from our many engagements with the scholars, students, university presses, museums, libraries, and scholarly societies willing to reimagine research within digital realms alongside our team. Their collective contributions and interests shaped both our process and our code.

Jeffrey Schnapp has been the most patient of editors. Many thanks to him, the two manuscript readers, and everyone who shepherded the project for Harvard University Press, especially Emily Arkin, Kate Brick, Michael Fisher, Daniele Ledda, and Ann Twombly.

Many other friends and colleagues have offered advice, sharpened my thinking, highlighted shortcomings, kept me company, invited me to speak, experimented with Scalar, and generally influenced the shape of the Vectors Lab, the direction of my scholarship, and the quality of my life. Thanks to Sarah Banet-Weiser, Evan Bissell, John Seely Brown, Susan Brown, Bruce Burgett, Vicky Callahan, Daniel Chamberlain, Anita Say Chan, Kim Christen, Dan Cohen, Rosemary Comella, Anne Cong-Huyen, Paul Courant, Brian Croxall, Sharon Daniel, Rachel Deblinger, Matt Delmont, Linda Downs, Ellen Faran, Scott Fisher, Kathleen Fitzpatrick, Julia Flanders, Neil Fraistat, Mary Francis, Kevin Franklin, Amanda French, the late Anne Friedberg, Bernie Frischer, Matthew Fuller, Alice Gambrell, David Theo Goldberg, David Golumbia, Amanda Starling Gould, Dene Grigar, Gary Hall, Kevin Hamilton, Dianne Harris, N. Katherine Hayles, Daniel Herwitz, Betty Leigh Hutcheson, Sharon Irish, Mimi Ito, Patrick Jagoda, Priya Jaikumar, Henry Jenkins, Caren Kaplan, David Kim, Shana Kimball, Marsha Kinder, Matthew Kirschenbaum, Julie Klein, Lauren Klein, Adeline Koh, Virginia Kuhn, Josh Kun, Tim Lenoir, Dan Leshem, Joan Lippincott, Alan Liu, Liz Losh, Alexis Lothian, Richard Lucier, Cliff Lynch, Curtis Marez, Mark Marino, Minoo Moallem, Michelle Moravec, Stuart Moulthrop, Natalie Myers, Angel Nieves, Bethany Nowviskie, Edward O'Neill, Lisa Parks, Amanda Phillips, Miriam Posner, Todd Presner, Jessica Pressman, Catherine Quinlan, Rita Raley, Carrie Rentschler, Roopika Risam, Geoffrey Rockwell, Robin Romans, John Carlos Rowe, Katherine Rowe, Mike Roy, Jentery Sayers, Ellen Seiter, Laura Isabel Serna, Doug Sery, Jeffrey Shandler, Kim Simon, Martha Nell Smith, Sidonie Smith, Nicole Starosielski, Jonathan Sterne, Patrik Svensson, Diana Taylor, Jennifer Terry, Karen Tongson, John Unsworth, Jacqueline Wernimont, Dan Whaley, Steve Wheatley, Mark Williams, Ken Wissoker, and Daria Yudacufski. Cathy Davidson and Kathy Woodward have been invaluable mentors and friends for many years; they continually inspire me with their generosity and smarts. Anne Balsamo, Wendy Chun, Amelie Hastie, Alex Juhasz, Kara Keeling, Lisa Nakamura, and Wendy West have again and again gone above and beyond as co-conspirators, sounding boards, and, most of all, good friends.

My parents and siblings and their families continue to remind me of things that matter beyond the relentless churn of work. They all live far away from Los Angeles, but I carry them along in all that I do. Finally, my engagements with technology—academic or otherwise—are continually shaped and reshaped by the digital literacies of my husband, Rob, and our son, Dexter. Rob understands computation better than pretty much anyone and is an excellent geek-out partner. Dex is equally at home engaging with technology and critiquing it, and I look forward to his future explorations at the intersection of theory and practice. Beyond realms technological, they also bring great joy, wisdom, and fun into my life, as do our cats, Buster and Maya, who will happily sleep on any keyboard they encounter.

# Credits

https://commons.wikimedia.org/wiki/
File:Racial_Divide_Detroit_MI.png#/
media/File:Racial_Divide_Detroit_
MI.png

1.19 Redrawn from original in Alan J.
Weiner, *Design Requirements for the
Data and Systems Support Essential to
an Urban Blight Systems Analysis* (Los
Angeles: Los Angeles Community
Analysis Bureau, 1970)

1.20 http://www.tutorialspoint.com/unix/
unix-getting-started.htm

1.21 http://www.troff.org/books.html

1.22 http://www.troff.org/books.html

1.23 http://www.troff.org/books.html

1.24 http://www.postalesinventadas.
com/2011/07/expo-67-montreal-
canada-habitat-67-dear.html

1.25 *Ebony*, April 1970, p. 77

1.26 Courtesy of the author

1.27 http://neo4j.com/developer/graph-db-
vs-rdbms/

1.28 http://neo4j.com/developer/graph-db-
vs-rdbms/

1.29 http://www.apple.com/watch/
(accessed May 2015)

1.30 Redrawn from original in Brad Cox,
*Object-Oriented Programming An
Evolutionary Approach* (Reading, MA
Addison-Wesley, 1987)

1.31 http://bogost.com/writing/blog/
latour_litanizer/

1.32 http://www.vectorsjournal.org/
projects/index.php?project=65

1.33 http://www.vectorsjournal.org/
projects/index.php?project=72

1.34 http://www.vectorsjournal.org/
projects/index.php?project=83

1.35 https://faculty.washington.edu/
michamc/autonets/

1.36 http://bogost.com/games/aslowyear/

1.37 http://femtechnet.org/publications/

signalnoise-collected-student-works-
from-a-feminist-docc/

## 2. Assembling Scholarship

2.1 https://dornsife.usc.edu/labyrinth/
interactive_frictions/scrapbook.html

2.2 https://dornsife.usc.edu/labyrinth/
interactive_frictions/interactive1.html

2.3 https://dornsife.usc.edu/labyrinth/laby.
html

2.4 http://www.albany.edu/jmmh/

2.5 http://kairos.technorhetoric.net/

2.6 http://www.vectorsjournal.org/
projects/index.php?project=54

2.6a http://www.vectorsjournal.org/
projects/index.php?project=5

2.7 Courtesy of the author

2.8 Courtesy of the author

2.9 Courtesy of the author

2.10 http://www.vectorsjournal.org/
projects/index.php?project=57

2.11 http://www.vectorsjournal.org/
projects/index.php?project=57

2.12 http://www.vectorsjournal.org/
projects/index.php?project=57

2.13 Loyer design document, author's
collection

2.14 http://www.vectorsjournal.org/
projects/index.php?project=67

2.15 http://www.vectorsjournal.org/
projects/index.php?project=67

2.16 http://www.vectorsjournal.org/
projects/index.php?project=67

2.17 http://mukurtu.org/

2.18 http://www.vectorsjournal.org/
projects/index.php?project=56

2.19 http://www.vectorsjournal.org/
projects/index.php?project=82

2.20 http://www.vectorsjournal.org/
projects/index.php?project=82

2.21 http://www.vectorsjournal.org/

W3.3   http://www.vectorsjournal.org/
projects/index.php?project=10

W3.4   http://www.vectorsjournal.org/
projects/index.php?project=10

W3.5   http://www.vectorsjournal.org/
projects/index.php?project=10

W3.6   http://www.vectorsjournal.org/
projects/index.php?project=10

## Window 4. Various *Vectors*

W4.1   http://www.vectorsjournal.org/
projects/index.php?project=4

W4.2   http://www.vectorsjournal.org/
projects/index.php?project=4

W4.3   http://www.vectorsjournal.org/
projects/index.php?project=4

W4 4   http://www.vectorsjournal.org/
projects/index.php?project=4

W4.5   http://www.vectorsjournal.org/
projects/index.php?project=6

W4.6   http://www.vectorsjournal.org/
projects/index.php?project=6

W4.7   http://www.vectorsjournal.org/
projects/index.php?project=6

W4.8   http://www.vectorsjournal.org/
projects/index.php?project=12

W4.9   http://www.vectorsjournal.org/
projects/index.php?project=12

W4.10   http://www.vectorsjournal.org/
projects/index.php?project=12

W4.11   http://www.vectorsjournal.org/
projects/index.php?project=66

W4.12   http://www.vectorsjournal.org/
projects/index.php?project=66

W4.13   http://www.vectorsjournal.org/
projects/index.php?project=66

W4.14   http://www.vectorsjournal.org/
projects/index.php?project=59

W4.15   http://www.vectorsjournal.org/
projects/index.php?project=59

W4.16   http://www.vectorsjournal.org/
projects/index.php?project=59

W4.17   http://www.vectorsjournal.org/
projects/index.php?project=90

W4.18   http://www.vectorsjournal.org/
projects/index.php?project=90

W4.19   http://www.vectorsjournal.org/
projects/index.php?project=90

W4.20   http://www.vectorsjournal.org/
projects/index.php?project=99

W4.21   http://www.vectorsjournal.org/
projects/index.php?project=99

W4.22   http://www.vectorsjournal.org/
projects/index.php?project=99

W4.23   http://www.vectorsjournal.org/
projects/index.php?project=91

W4.24   http://vectors.usc.edu/projects/index.
php?project=91

W4.25   http://www.vectorsjournal.org/
projects/index.php?project=91

## Window 5. Scalar Feature Set and Showcase

W5.1   http://scalar.usc.edu/works/guide2/
import/internet_archive

W5.2   http://scalar.usc.edu/anvc/
chaosandcontrol/index

W5.3   http://scalar.usc.edu/works/redshift-
and-portalmetal/your-planet

W5.4   http://knottedline.com/

W5.5   http://scalar.usc.edu/maker/record

W5.6   http://scalar.usc.edu/maker/record

W5.7a   http://scalar.usc.edu/works/complex-
television

W5.7b   http://scalar.usc.edu/nehvectors/
mirzoeff

W5.8   http://scalar.usc.edu/works/pathfinders

W5.9   http://civicmediaproject.org/

W5.10   http://civicmediaproject.org/

W5.11   http://scalar.usc.edu/anvc/music-of-the-hemispheres

W5.12  http://scalar.usc.edu/hc/caa.reviews-bernini

W5.13  http://scalar.usc.edu/nehvectors/wips

W5.14  http://scalar.usc.edu/works/ftn-ethnic-studies-pedagogy-workbook-/index

W5.15  http://scalar.usc.edu/anvc/playing-for-change

W5.16  http://scalar.usc.edu/students/endlessquestion